SRA
Read to Achieve

Comprehending
Content-Area Text

Content Reader

Nancy Marchand-Martella
Ronald Martella

McGraw Hill **SRA**

Columbus, OH

SRAonline.com
SRADirectInstruction.com

Copyright © 2010 by SRA/McGraw-Hill.

All rights reserved. No part of this publication may be
reproduced or distributed in any form or by any means,
or stored in a database or retrieval system, without the
prior written consent of The McGraw-Hill Companies, Inc.,
including, but not limited to, network storage or
transmission, or broadcast for distance learning.

Printed in the United States of America.

Send all inquiries to this address:
SRA/McGraw-Hill
4400 Easton Commons
Columbus, OH 43219

ISBN: 978-0-07-621989-6
MHID: 0-07-621989-5

5 6 7 8 9 COU 13 12 11 10

Contents

▸ Science

▸ Social Studies

Contents

▷ Science

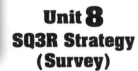

Contents

Contents

Contents

Tools for Reading

Content Reader

Comprehension Strategies

- *Make text connections.*
- *Identify text structure.*
- *Monitor comprehension.*
- *Take notes during class.*

- *Use information-gathering strategies before and as you read your text.*
- *Use information-gathering strategies for questions you still have.*

Vocabulary Strategies

- *Use word-learning strategies to help you figure out what words mean.*

- *Read difficult or unknown words.*

Fluency Strategies

- *Develop a better understanding of what you read.*

- *Develop reading speed and accuracy.*

2 Beyond the Book

Application of Skills

- *Improve your understanding of other informational text. Use strategies before you read, as you read, and after you read sources such as newspapers, magazines, Web sites, maps, and journals.*

3 Classroom Textbooks

Before You Read

- *Survey a section in your textbook.*

As You Read

- *Use strategies you've learned as you read a section in your textbook.*

After You Read

- *Use strategies you've learned after you read a section in your textbook.*

Program Objectives

In this program, students will learn to use the following strategies:

	Comprehension Strategies	Unit range
1	**Identify** lesson topics within theme-based units.	1–25
2	**Read** content-area text with a clearly established purpose.	1–25
3	**Use** background knowledge on specified topics.	1–25
4	**Use** text features to navigate textbooks and their contents.	1–25
5	**Examine** a variety of text structures, and explain their effect on text meaning.	2–25
6	**Use** descriptions and lists to identify the main idea and supporting details to determine meaning.	2–25
7	**Identify** the order and sequence of the text to determine meaning.	2–25
8	**Identify** cause-and-effect relationships to determine meaning.	2–25
9	**Compare** and contrast text to determine meaning.	2–25
10	**Use** pre-, during-, and post-reading strategies to improve text understanding.	8–25
11	**Use** graphic organizers to keep track of important information.	1–25
12	**Monitor** comprehension, including rereading and adjusting reading rate.	6–25
13	**Use** strategies such as SQ3R or QHL to organize information and to gain meaning from text.	8–25
14	**Write** detailed notes from text and lectures.	17–25

Vocabulary Strategies	Unit range
15 **Use** strategies to decode multipart words.	1–25
16 **Use** context clues to determine unfamiliar word meaning.	2–25
17 **Use** a glossary to determine unfamiliar word meaning.	6–25
18 **Use** a dictionary to determine unfamiliar word meaning.	7–25
19 **Use** a computer to determine unfamiliar word meaning.	8–25
20 **Use** graphic organizers to keep track of important information.	1–25

Higher-Order Thinking Skills	Unit range
21 **Answer** questions aligned with all levels of Bloom's Taxonomy.	1–25
22 **Answer** standardized-test questions.	1–25
23 **Use** graphic organizers to track important information.	1–25
24 **Use** metacognitive strategies to select strategies, and explain why you chose them.	1–25

Fluency Strategies	Unit range
25 **Read** content-area text fluently using repeated reading techniques.	1–25
26 **Use** various practice activities, such as oral, shared, and silent reading, to improve fluency and reading for meaning.	1–25

Unit 1
Science

Reading Skills and Strategies
- Make text connections.
- Decode multipart words.

Lesson 1

Studying Science

As YOU Read!

What You'll Learn
- What scientists do

Why It's Important
To study science, you must think like a scientist.

Key Terms
- science
- observing
- classifying
- inferring
- predicting
- making models

Skills Scientists Use

In all countries, people study nature to explain how or why something happens the way it does. The results of these studies help us understand the world around us. These studies also make us ask more questions. These questions lead to further study. This study of the natural world and the knowledge gained through that study is called **science.**

Have you ever thought about being a scientist? You might be surprised to learn that you already do many of the things scientists do. A scientist studies the natural world and tries to understand it. Perhaps you wonder why a glass of milk left out all night tastes sour in the morning. You are observing and trying to understand. Maybe you drop a big ball and a tiny ball at the same time. You observe that the balls hit the ground at the same time. You are noticing a scientific fact.

Every day you learn about the world you live in by using the same skills scientists use in their work. These skills include observing, classifying, inferring, predicting, and making models.

▶ Science is the study of the natural world. What might you learn by studying frogs?

Observing

Scientists spend a great deal of time **observing.** Like you, they use their five senses to make observations. A scientist studying life in a cave would take careful notes. The notes are a record of the animals the scientist sees, the sounds he or she hears, the feel of the stones underfoot, and the smells in the air. A scientist studying life in a rain forest would also take notes. These notes would tell what can be seen, heard, felt, tasted, and smelled. What observations do you think the scientist in this photograph is making?

◄ Scientists can observe many things in a rain forest.

Some observations can be expressed in numbers. The temperature of the air in a rain forest would be expressed in a number of degrees. Other observations are made by using descriptive words. A scientist might describe the color of a flower or the shape of a leaf. What kinds of observations do you think the scientist in the photograph is making? Would these observations likely be in numbers or in words?

No matter what kinds of observations scientists make, their observations must be accurate. Observations must also be recorded. They may be written in a notebook or on a computer. They may be recorded on a personal data assistant (PDA). Why is accuracy important to scientists?

Classifying

Classifying means putting together things that are alike. When you sort objects into categories, you classify them. You stack plates together in one place in the cupboard. You put cups in a different place. You put bowls in yet a different place. Scientists classify everything they learn about the natural world. Animals, plants, rocks, and stars are all classified in categories. How would you classify the animals in this picture?

► All objects and living things can be sorted into categories—including these animals.

Scientists classify things so they can talk and write about them more easily. Most scientists agree on the groupings. Can you imagine trying to describe every single animal in the world? Classification makes this process easier.

Inferring

Scientists are **inferring** when they observe something and then explain what they've observed. For example, the scientist in the rain forest finds tracks in the soil. An inference can be made that an animal has passed. By closely observing the tracks, the scientist can make an inference about the animal. You, too, make inferences every day. You pass a restaurant and smell something delicious. You infer the restaurant serves good food.

Scientists make inferences and later test them to see if the inferences are correct. If a scientist infers that large, deep tracks were made by a mountain lion, she can watch the area to see if a mountain lion appears. Then she can check to see if the tracks match the ones she saw before.

Predicting

Predicting means using experience to guess what will happen next. You can predict from experience that if you touch a hot burner on a stove, you are likely to be burned. Scientists use their knowledge and experience to make predictions about the weather, about the distance of a star from Earth, or about a good place to drill for oil.

Predictions and inferences are similar, but they're not the same. A prediction explains what *will* happen. An inference explains what *is* happening or what *has* happened. Which picture shows a prediction? Which picture shows an inference?

▶ A glass of milk before a spill . . .
. . . and after a spill.

Making Models

Scientists help their understanding by **making models.** A model can help a scientist understand a complex process. Models can be illustrations, charts, or maps. Models can also have three dimensions. Globes and physical structures are two more kinds of models.

Models allow scientists to show information they can't explain in words. For instance, suppose a scientist is studying the effect of waves on a beach. At times the waves rise far up the beach. At times the waves draw back and leave a wide beach for people to enjoy. The scientist's research shows that, over time, this back-and-forth movement of the waves has eroded the beach. She wants to record the results of her study in a way that's easy to understand. She makes a graph. The graph shows that many years ago, the beach was much wider than it is today. The scientist has made a model.

Here's a model of the water cycle.

Lesson Assessment

Review

1. **List** Write the five skills scientists use in their work.

2. **Define** Define each of the five skills scientists use in their work.

3. **Compare and Contrast** What is the difference between an inference and a prediction?

4. **Apply** Tell how a model could be used to show how much rain falls in a rain forest each month of the year. Tell what inferences and predictions you could make from this model.

Critical Thinking

Both birds and squirrels have been eating the seeds in your bird feeder. You put a different kind of seed in the feeder. The squirrels stop coming. What can you infer?

Writing in Science

Choose a familiar plant or animal in your environment. Write what you've learned about your subject by using your five senses.

◀ Water moves constantly from Earth's surface into the atmosphere, where it falls again as precipitation. What can you learn from this model?

Lesson 2
The Scientific Process

As YOU Read!

What You'll Learn
■ How scientists use scientific inquiry

Why It's Important
The process used in scientific inquiry is one of the best ways to find out if something is likely to be true.

Key Terms
■ scientific inquiry
■ hypothesis
■ variables
■ data

You're hungry for a snack. A peanut-butter sandwich sounds good. But when you reach into the bread bag, you notice something fuzzy and green on the bread. Mold! Where did it come from? What made it grow?

▶ Have you ever wondered why food sometimes turns green and fuzzy?

The Scientific Process

The process scientists use to study the natural world is called **scientific inquiry.** Scientific inquiry includes asking questions and making a hypothesis. It includes designing an experiment. It includes collecting and interpreting data. Finally, it includes drawing conclusions and communicating results. You can use scientific inquiry to find out what mold needs to grow.

Asking Questions

Have you ever observed something that sparked your curiosity? Did your observations lead you to ask a question about why or how it happened? A scientific question can be answered by observing and collecting information. You know that a plastic bag keeps bread from drying out. Does mold grow better in a moist or a dry environment?

Making a Hypothesis

A **hypothesis** is a prediction of what you expect to happen. "Mold needs a moist environment to grow" is a hypothesis you could test. The information you gather during an experiment can support or disprove your hypothesis. That is, the results show whether or not the hypothesis is likely to be true.

Designing an Experiment

To test a hypothesis, you must first design an experiment. When you design an experiment, you must identify the variables. **Variables** are the parts of an experiment that can change. You change only one variable, such as the environment in which the bread is kept. Other variables, such as the type and amount of bread, must be controlled, or kept the same. In this way, you can learn whether mold grows better in a moist or a dry environment.

◀ Scientists conduct experiments by identifying and controlling variables. What variables are present in this experiment?

Collecting and Interpreting Data and Drawing Conclusions

Data are the notes and measurements you collect as you do an experiment. Data are examined for patterns. Scientists use tables and graphs to organize their data. They write a summary, or conclusion, about whether the data support the hypothesis. You conclude that bread mold grows faster in a moist environment.

Communicating

The scientific process doesn't end when the experiment is finished. Scientists carefully describe their experiments so others can repeat them. They may communicate their ideas on the Internet. They may present papers at scientific meetings. They may publish articles in scientific journals.

Lesson Assessment

Review

1. **Describe** Describe the process scientists use in scientific inquiry.

2. **Define** What is a hypothesis? What are variables? What are data?

3. **Discuss** Why is it important for scientists to collect and interpret data and draw conclusions?

4. **Discuss** What scientific question are you wondering about? Explain why you are wondering about this.

Critical Thinking

- Why is it important to test a hypothesis?

- Suppose your boss has assigned you to perform a certain experiment. In what way will you communicate your findings? What details will you include?

Writing in Science

Write two lists. In one list, write three characteristics of scientific thinkers. In the other list, write three characteristics of unscientific thinkers.

Lesson 3 Technology

As YOU Read!

What You'll Learn
■ Different forms of technology

Why It's Important
Technology can improve the quality of life for millions of people.

Key Terms
■ prosthesis
■ technology
■ engineer
■ pollution

It takes talent and practice to excel in sports. How hard would it be to run a race with only one leg? One man born without his left leg has learned to run in competition. How? He has an artificial leg. An artificial body part is called a **prosthesis.** Thanks to technology, this man is realizing his dream to take part in sports.

▶ Scientific research has led to great inventions. Using an artificial leg, this man is able to compete.

Introduction

Artificial arms and legs are one form of technology. What do you think of when you hear the word *technology?* Digital cameras and cell phones? Video games and music players? Technology is more than medical devices and electronic gadgets. **Technology** is any way people change the world to meet their needs. The tools people use are forms of technology. The knowledge and the processes to make new tools are forms of technology too. People use technology every day to make their lives better.

Science and Technology

Science and technology aren't the same, but they go hand in hand. Scientists study the natural world to learn how it works. People use technology to change the world. An **engineer** uses science and technology to find ways to improve people's lives. For example, a scientist studies how a shark's skin helps the shark move through the water. An engineer takes this information and uses it to design swimsuits that help people move through the water faster.

Sometimes technology leads to new inventions. The information scientists discovered about how magnets and atoms interact led to magnetic resonance imaging (MRI). MRI is a way to take pictures of the body. Doctors use MRI to see inside the body. This technology helps doctors and scientists learn more about the body's structure. MRI pictures can also reveal disease.

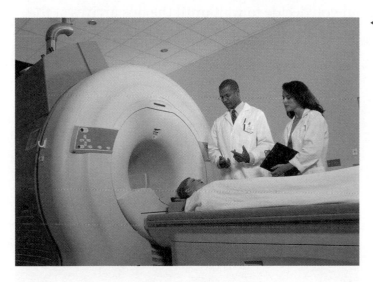
◄ An MRI scanner takes pictures that help doctors learn about the human body.

Technology and Society

Technology can improve people's lives, but it doesn't always offer the best solutions. When technology solves one problem, it may cause a new one. The technology that makes it possible to produce goods in a factory may cause pollution in the air or water. **Pollution** is the act of making something unclean or impure. Living things that depend on fresh air and clean water may be harmed. People must make good decisions about how to use technology.

◄ Technology can lead to pollution.

Lesson Assessment

Review

1. **Summarize** What is technology?

2. **Define** What is an engineer?

3. **Discuss** How do science and technology work together?

4. **Extend** Give three examples of technology you use in school.

Critical Thinking

- You learned that producing technology can cause pollution. What other problems could technology cause?

- Imagine you've invented a new form of technology. Tell how it works and whom it helps.

Writing in Science

Write a short story about a day in the life of a form of technology. Show how the technology changed someone's life.

Reading Skills and Strategies
- Make text connections.
- Decode multipart words.

Lesson 4

Safety in the Laboratory

As YOU Read!

What You'll Learn
- How to be safe in the lab
- What to do if an accident happens

Why It's Important

A lab accident can damage an experiment and injure those performing it.

Key Terms
- investigations
- guidelines

You are riding a bus to the science museum for a school field trip. The bus is crowded and noisy. You're tempted to visit a friend in another seat. But you decide to wait until the bus arrives at the museum. It isn't safe to move around the bus while it's on the road.

▶ Safety is important, no matter where you are.

The Importance of Safety

You know that following rules when you ride a bus keeps everyone safe. The same is true when you conduct **investigations,** or ways of exploring scientific questions, in the science laboratory. Working with animals, plants, chemicals, and heat requires care and special attention. To perform these investigations safely, you must know how to use laboratory equipment. You must also know what to do if there's an accident or an injury.

Preparing for an Experiment

Being prepared is one way to prevent accidents. Before you begin an experiment, read the instructions. Be sure you understand all the steps and the materials and equipment you'll use. Make sure you know safety **guidelines,** or rules. Before you begin, ask your teacher anything you're not sure about.

◄ This is a symbol for general safety awareness.

Performing the Experiment

Always follow the instructions and your teacher's directions exactly. This will help you know what to expect. Take your time as you work through the steps. Rushing your work can lead to accidents. Keep your work area neat and organized. Doing so will help prevent accidents.

Know the safety symbols shown in your textbook or on your lab materials and equipment. These symbols tell you of dangers you may encounter while performing the experiment. Careful work can prevent injuries.

	End-of-Lab Procedures
1.	Turn off equipment.
2.	Unplug equipment.
3.	Put away equipment and materials.
4.	Safely dispose of waste.
5.	Clean workstation.
6.	Wash hands.

Outdoor Safety

Take precautions when you work outdoors "in the field." Don't go out alone. Tell an adult where you're going. Be alert for traffic and severe weather. Use caution when observing wild animals and poisonous plants.

In Case of an Accident

Here's what to do if an accident happens. Notify your teacher right away, even if the accident seems minor. Know where to find emergency and first-aid supplies. If you know basic safety and first-aid procedures, you'll be better prepared if an accident occurs.

Lesson 5

Developing Theories

As YOU Read!

What You'll Learn
■ What a scientific theory is
■ What a scientific law is

Why It's Important
Scientists develop theories and laws to explain how the natural world works.

Key Terms
■ scientific theory
■ scientific law

Scientific Theories

Imagine you're reading a mystery and think you've solved it before the end. Perhaps you form a hypothesis or a prediction of what you think might happen. After you've read several novels by the same author, you notice a pattern in the way her books are written. You develop an idea. This idea says the least likable character always turns out to be the hero. You may call your idea a theory.

A **scientific theory** is an explanation of behavior. It's based on many observations and experiments by many scientists. Do you ever think about why things happen as they do?

If you have a pet, have you ever noticed that when you approach your pet with food, it often greets you? Cat owners say their cats run to the kitchen. Horse owners say their horses gallop to greet them at the barn. Even fish owners say their fish swim to the top of the tank at mealtime. Why do these animals behave as they do? What connects these pets and their behavior?

You may develop a hypothesis to explain why animals act this way. When the cat, the horse, or the fish approaches its owner, what happens? The animal is fed. Your hypothesis may state that if a pet's behavior results in food, the behavior will be repeated. The

▶ A scientist devises a hypothesis, or theory, of what might happen during an experiment.

Scientists develop theories in laboratories. Theories explain why experiments give certain results.

behavior will be repeated because food satisfies a basic need. If you and others observe this behavior many times in many animals, you may call your idea a theory.

Scientific Laws

Theories are usually accepted as true until new information proves them wrong. The results of new experiments can change theories. Unlike theories, scientific laws are less likely to change when new information is gathered. A **scientific law** is a rule applied to the natural world. It's accepted as true. Scientific laws tell us what will take place under certain conditions.

When you give your pet food, your pet seems happy. When you pat its head and praise it, your pet seems happy. When you play with it, your pet seems happy. Your pet comes to you when you call it. When you stop doing these things, your pet changes. If you don't feed it, your pet stops coming to you. If you don't pay attention to your pet, your pet stops paying attention to you. If you and others find the same thing is true for all animals, you develop a law. The Law of Effect states that when an animal is rewarded for a behavior, the behavior will be repeated. When an animal is not rewarded, the behavior stops.

This woman rewards her pet, and the dog rewards her in return.

Lesson Assessment

Review

1. **Explain** How does someone develop a theory?

2. **Compare and Contrast** What is the difference between a hypothesis and a theory?

3. **Compare and Contrast** What is the difference between a theory and a law?

Critical Thinking

- What do theories explain?

- Why do many pets seem loyal to their owners?

Writing in Science

Write a paragraph to explain why theories and laws are important to scientists.

Lesson 1 Living Things

As YOU Read!

What You'll Learn

- The characteristics of living things
- The needs of living things

Why It's Important

Cells are the basic unit of all living things.

Key Terms

- organisms
- cells
- stimulus
- autotrophs
- heterotrophs
- homeostasis

Living things, or **organisms,** can be as large as whales or so small you can't see them without a microscope. All the organisms on Earth are different. What do you think they have in common?

Characteristics of Living Things

All living things share six basic traits, or characteristics. First, living things are made of cells. Second, their cells contain chemicals that carry out various activities. Third, the cells of living things use energy to perform life functions. Fourth, all organisms respond to their environment. Fifth,

living things grow and develop. Sixth, all organisms reproduce.

Cellular Organization

Cells are the smallest parts of living things. They make up the form of an organism and carry out all the functions in the organism's body. Organisms may contain only one cell, or they may contain many cells. In multicelled organisms, cells are specially designed to do certain jobs. For example,

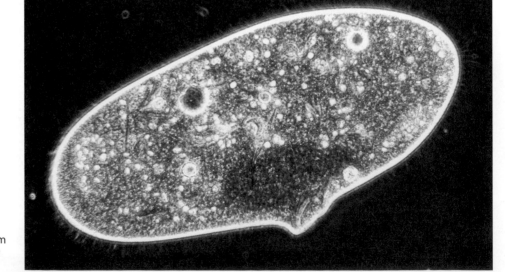

▶ A paramecium contains only one cell.

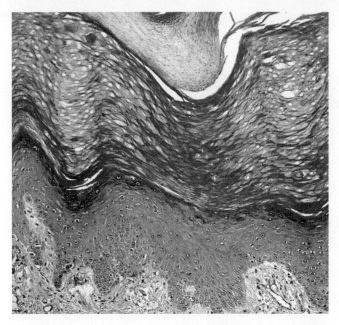
▲ Human skin is made up of many cells.

humans have skin cells, muscle cells, and blood cells that perform specific tasks within the body.

Chemicals

All cells contain chemicals necessary for life. Chemicals in the cell's nucleus, or control center, direct all cell activity. Proteins and fats, or lipids, aid in cell growth and repair.

Energy

Starches, or carbohydrates, provide cells with energy. All the jobs cells do require energy to sustain life for the organism.

Response to Environment

Have you ever looked under a rock in the woods? You probably saw dozens of tiny bugs running in all directions. By lifting the rock, you shed light on their dark environment. The light was a **stimulus,** something that changed the bugs' surroundings and caused them to react. Their response was to run away from the light.

Growth and Development

Living things grow as they progress through their life cycle. They go through a series of changes that make them more complex. When living things are fully developed, they are able to reproduce, or produce offspring.

▼ The drawing shows the life cycle of a frog.

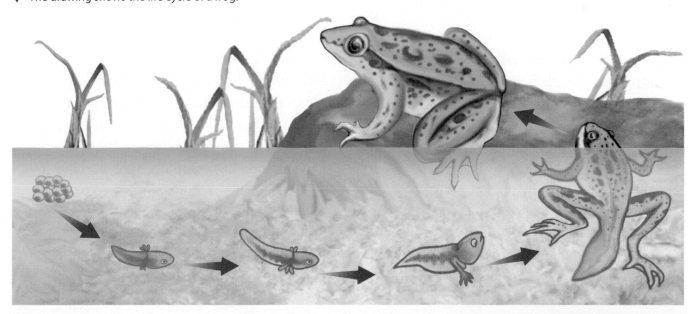

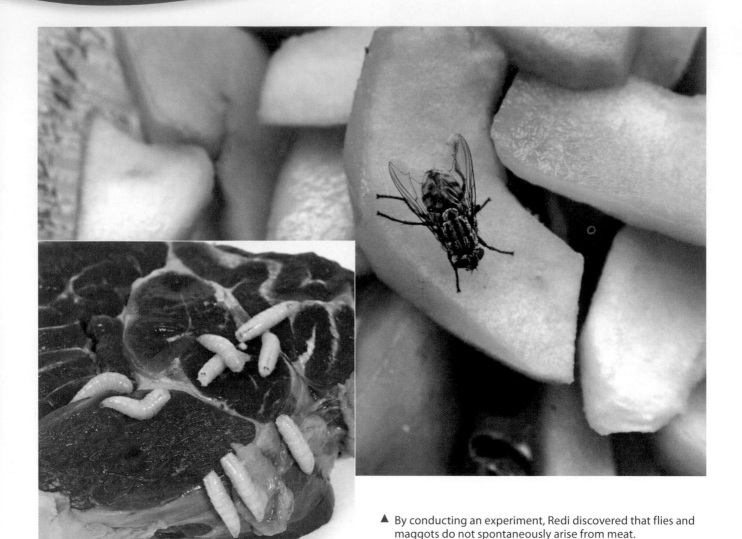

▲ By conducting an experiment, Redi discovered that flies and maggots do not spontaneously arise from meat.

Life Comes from Life

Long ago, people believed living things could come from nonliving things. This idea was disproved in 1668. At that time, people believed flies could spontaneously arise from meat. An Italian doctor named Francesco Redi conducted a controlled experiment. He covered one jar of meat. Another jar was left uncovered. Flies laid eggs on the uncovered meat. The eggs hatched into young flies called maggots. The covered meat showed no signs of maggots because flies could not enter the jar.

Even after Redi's experiment, many people still thought living things could arise from nonliving things. In the nineteenth century, a French chemist named Louis Pasteur set up some experiments. He showed that bacteria must already be present for new bacteria to appear. Pasteur's results convinced people that living things come only from other living things. This happens through reproduction.

The Needs of Living Things

Despite the great diversity, or variety, of life, all living things must meet four basic needs to survive. Every organism must have food, water, a place to live, and stable conditions inside its body.

Food

Remember that organisms are made up of cells, and cells need energy. Living things must get energy from food in order to live. Some organisms, like green plants, can make their own food. They are called **autotrophs.** All other organisms are **heterotrophs.** Heterotrophs cannot make their own food. Heterotrophs must feed on other organisms for the energy they need. For example, a rabbit is a heterotroph. It eats a dandelion, an autotroph. A hawk is another heterotroph. It eats the rabbit.

Water

Water is important to life. Most organisms cannot live more than a few days without it. Living things need water to grow and to reproduce. They need water to break down food and to get other chemicals from the environment.

A Place to Live

For an organism to survive, it must live in a place that meets its needs. Its surroundings must provide food, water, and adequate space. Autotrophs must get enough sunlight to make their own food.

Stable Internal Conditions

An organism's environment provides the resources for survival. However, its surroundings may change. An organism must be able to regulate the conditions inside its cells, even if the environment outside its body changes.

Homeostasis is the ability to maintain stable internal conditions within cells. Without homeostasis, living things could not adjust to changes in temperature, moisture, or chemicals in their environment. For example, desert animals conserve water in their bodies. The stored water helps them survive long periods without rain.

Lesson Assessment

Review

1. List What are the six things all organisms have in common?

2. List What are the four basic needs of all living things?

3. Compare and Contrast How are autotrophs and heterotrophs different?

4. Define What is a stimulus? What is homeostasis?

Critical Thinking

What kinds of living things are autotrophs? What kinds of living things are heterotrophs?

Writing in Science

Describe the experiments of Redi and Pasteur, and explain what they showed.

Reading Skills and Strategies

- Make text connections.
- Identify text structure.
- Decode multipart words.
- Use word-learning strategies.

Lesson 2

Classifying Organisms

As YOU Read!

What You'll Learn

- How scientists name organisms
- What classification is
- How organisms are grouped

Why It's Important

It's easier to study living things that are arranged in groups.

Key Terms

- classification
- binomial nomenclature
- genus
- species

Imagine you're writing a report about a famous scientist. You go to the library to do some research. You find the books aren't in any order. You must look through all the books in the library to find what you need. This will take a long time.

It would also take a long time for scientists to study information about all the organisms on Earth. To solve this problem, scientists put living things in groups. Living things are easier to study if they're organized in groups. The process of grouping things that are similar is called **classification.** Scientists know a lot about an organism based on its group. Taxonomy is the study of how organisms are classified.

The Naming System

An important part of classifying living things is to give each organism a name. The naming system scientists use is **binomial nomenclature.** This system gives each organism a two-part name.

Binomial nomenclature names organisms based on their similarities and special

features. The first part of the name, the **genus,** is a group of very similar organisms. The second part, the **species,** names a certain trait. The trait may tell where the organism lives or what it looks like.

Using Binomial Nomenclature
- Scientific names contain Latin words.
- The first word is capitalized.
- Names are printed in italics or underlined in handwriting.

Levels of Classification

Today's system of classification has eight levels. The highest level is the most general. Each level is smaller than the one above. You can tell how alike two organisms are by the number of levels they share.

Domains are the top level of classification. They contain the most organisms. As you move down through the levels, each group has fewer members. Species is the smallest level and contains only one type of organism.

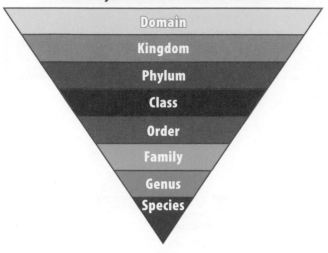

The Major Levels of Classification

Domain
Kingdom
Phylum
Class
Order
Family
Genus
Species

Domains and Kingdoms

Scientists classify organisms in three domains: Bacteria, Archaea, and Eukarya. Living things are grouped in domains based on their ability to make food, the number of cells in their bodies, and their type of cells.

Three Domains

Bacteria cells do not have a nucleus. A nucleus is a dense area in a cell that controls the cell's activities. Bacteria are prokaryotes. They are on everything you touch and inside your body.

Members of the domain Archaea are one-celled prokaryotes that live in extreme environments. They are found in hot springs and in cow intestines.

The domain Eukarya consists of eukaryotes. These organisms have cells with a nucleus.

Six Kingdoms

The three domains are made up of six kingdoms: Archeabacteria, Eubacteria, Fungi, Plantae, Animalia, and Protista.

Some organisms are similar to bacteria but have different cell structures (kingdom Archeabacteria).

Some one-celled organisms have no nucleus at all (kingdom Eubacteria).

Have you ever eaten a fungus (kingdom Fungi)? A mushroom is a fungus. Most fungi are multicelled organisms that live on land. Mold is a fungus. Fungi feed on dead or decaying organisms.

Plants (kingdom Plantae) are multicelled. They use sunlight to make their own food. Plants can be as small as tiny mosses on a rock or as tall as redwood trees.

Like plants, all animals (kingdom Animalia) are multicelled organisms. Animals obtain energy by eating plants or other animals.

Protists (kingdom Protista) are made up of eukaryotes that can't be classified in any other kingdom. Most protists are one-celled, but a few, such as seaweed, are multicelled.

Lesson Assessment

Review
1. **Identify** What are the two parts of an organism's scientific name?

2. **List** Name the eight levels of classification, from largest to smallest.

3. **Define** What does *taxonomy* mean?

4. **Identify** What two domains consist of prokaryotes?

Critical Thinking
What do a mushroom and a fish have in common?

Writing in Science
Write a plan for classifying the objects in your room.

Reading Skills and Strategies

- Make text connections.
- Identify text structure.
- Decode multipart words.
- Use word-learning strategies.

Lesson 3 Cells

As YOU Read!

What You'll Learn	**Why** It's Important	**Key** Terms
■ What cells do ■ How cells were discovered ■ What cell theory states ■ How a microscope works	To learn about living things, you must understand the basic units of life.	■ cells ■ microscope ■ cell theory

The Makeup of Organisms

All living things are made of **cells.** Think of the parts in your body. Every part is made up of cells. Cells are in charge of everything that goes on inside your body.

The structure, or form, of an organism depends on the way its cells are arranged. For example, the cells in a cat form four legs, a tail, and whiskers. Cells are also involved in all the processes in an organism's body. These processes include absorbing nutrients and water, getting rid of wastes, getting oxygen, and growing.

Complex organisms are made up of billions of tiny cells. Individual cells are so small you can't see them with your eyes alone. In fact, no one knew cells existed before the **microscope** was invented. A microscope is an instrument that makes very small objects appear larger so you can study them.

First Observations of Cells

The invention of the microscope allowed people to look at small objects more closely than before. The first microscopes used curved pieces of glass, called lenses, to focus light on an object.

About seventy years after the invention of the first microscope, Robert Hooke (1635–1703) built his own microscope. Hooke looked at a thin slice of bark from a cork oak tree. He observed empty spaces that looked like tiny rooms. He called these "rooms" cells.

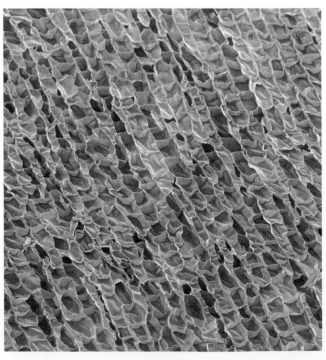

▲ Robert Hooke magnified a piece of cork. He found cells in the cork.

Antoni van Leeuwenhoek (1632–1723) built simple microscopes around the same time Hooke made his discoveries. Leeuwenhoek looked at drops of water and scrapings from teeth and gums. He discovered several types of one-celled organisms.

Development of Cell Theory

Other scientists began to study tiny objects, including cells. Matthias Schleiden (1804–1881) studied plants. In 1838, he stated that all plants are made of cells. Soon after, Theodor Schwann (1810–1882) stated that all animals are made of cells. He then said that all living things are made of cells. Rudolf Virchow (1821–1902) went a step further. He said all cells come from cells that already exist. At the time, many people still believed that living things could come from nonliving things.

What Cell Theory Says

These and other discoveries led to the formation of a cell theory. The **cell theory** explains the link between cells and living things.

Cell Theory
1. All organisms are made up of cells.
2. Cells are the basic units that form the structure and carry out the functions of all organisms.
3. All cells are formed from other cells.

Microscopes and Magnification

Microscopes use lenses to magnify things, or make them appear larger. In a simple microscope, there is one curved lens, called a convex lens. When light passes through the lens, the lens bends the light inward. Thus, when this light hits your eye, the object looks larger.

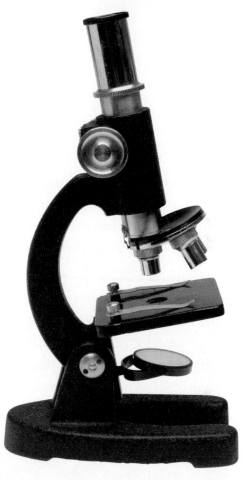

▲ You can use a microscope to view organisms.

Lesson Assessment

Review

1. **Identify** Name two things cells do in an organism.

2. **Explain** How did Hooke come up with the term *cells?*

3. **Explain** How does a simple microscope work?

Critical Thinking

- What contributions did Schleiden and Schwann make to the development of cell theory?

- What did Virchow contribute to cell theory?

Writing in Science

View an object under a microscope. Write a detailed description of it.

Lesson 4 Looking inside Cells

As YOU Read!

What You'll Learn

- The parts of a cell and how they function

Why It's Important

You can learn how living things function by understanding how cells function.

Key Terms

- nucleus
- mitochondria
- chloroplasts
- lysosomes

You know all living things are made up of cells. What goes on inside a cell? Within each cell are smaller structures that carry out the activities necessary for an organism's survival.

Within the Cell

Your brain is in charge of everything that goes on in your body. In a cell, the **nucleus** acts like a brain to control the cell's functions. The nucleus is protected by the nuclear envelope. Materials move in and out through the envelope.

The cytoplasm surrounds the nucleus. It's like thick soup. The other parts of the cell are suspended in the cytoplasm.

Cells must use energy to perform the tasks necessary for survival. **Mitochondria** are shaped like rods and work like a power plant. They convert food energy to energy the cell can use.

Ribosomes are tiny, grainlike structures. They produce proteins to help cell growth and repair.

For plants to make their own food, they must capture the sun's energy. This is the job of large green parts called **chloroplasts.** Chloroplasts use sunlight, carbon dioxide, and water to make food for the plant. Chloroplasts contain chlorophyll, the pigment that makes plants green.

Lysosomes are small, round parts that break large particles into small ones. They function

▲ What makes plants green?

as the cell's digestive and cleaning system. Lysosomes contain digestive enzymes to break down foods. They also break down worn-out cell parts, viruses, and bacteria.

Endoplasmic Reticulum

It would be hard to get from place to place in your school without hallways. Cells also need to move materials from one place to another. This is the function of the endoplasmic reticulum, a network of passageways in a cell. These passageways carry materials between parts of the cell.

Specialized Cells

Plants and animals are made up of many different types of cells. In complex organisms, cells have special jobs. You have different kinds of muscle cells for different jobs in your body. Striated muscle cells, like those in your legs, look and function one way. They are attached to your bones and make movement possible. In contrast, smooth muscle cells, like those around your digestive tract, look and behave differently. They help your internal organs do their jobs.

▼ What cell parts can you find in this diagram?

The Parts of a Cell

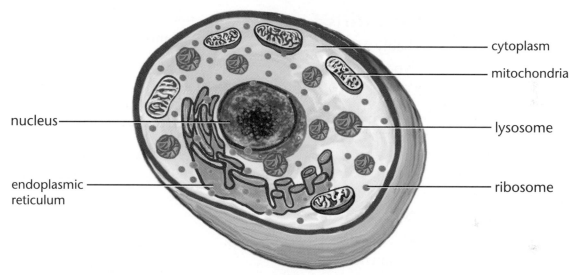

nucleus

endoplasmic reticulum

cytoplasm

mitochondria

lysosome

ribosome

Lesson Assessment

Review

1. **Identify** Which cell part acts as the "brain" of the cell?

2. **Identify** Which cell part converts energy for the cell to use?

3. **Describe** What happens when cell parts wear out?

4. **Compare** To what could you compare cytoplasm?

Critical Thinking

How do ribosomes and the endoplasmic reticulum work together to provide the cell with proteins?

Writing in Science

Draw a simple diagram of a cell. Label the parts, and write a title and a caption for your diagram.

Lesson 5 Viruses

Reading Skills and Strategies
- Use higher-order thinking skills.
- Review text connections and multipart words.

As YOU Read!

What You'll Learn
- What viruses are
- How viruses multiply
- What latent viruses are

Why It's Important
Viruses cause many illnesses. Learning about them can help prevent disease.

Key Terms
- virus
- vaccine
- host cell

Feeling under the Weather

At least once a year, you probably get a runny nose or a sore throat. Maybe you get a cough, too, or even aches and chills. These are symptoms of the common cold. Colds are caused by viruses.

Viruses

A **virus** is a nonliving particle of hereditary material (DNA or RNA) covered with a layer of protein. Unlike cells, viruses don't have a nucleus or a cell membrane.

Structure of a Virus

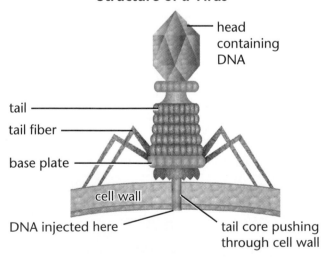

head containing DNA

tail

tail fiber

base plate

cell wall

DNA injected here

tail core pushing through cell wall

▲ Viruses come in many shapes. They don't have a nucleus or a cell membrane. This diagram shows the parts of a typical virus.

Viruses are also too small to see with a light microscope. Scientists couldn't prove viruses existed until the electron microscope was invented. Then they could see viruses and their many different shapes.

Viruses can infect almost every type of organism. In humans, viruses cause polio, rabies, AIDS, chicken pox, measles, and flu.

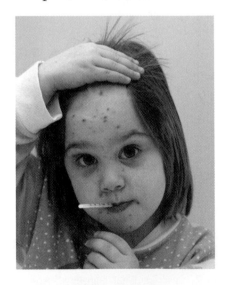

▶ Chicken pox is a virus that causes an itchy rash.

Have you ever had a flu shot? This shot contains a **vaccine.** A vaccine is a weak form of a virus. It helps protect you from catching a flu virus.

Maybe you've had chicken pox. If you've had chicken pox, you're unlikely to get it again. However, the virus remains in your system. It may cause another disease, shingles, at some time in the future. Shingles usually shows up as a rash, which may be painful and itchy.

How Viruses Multiply

Viruses can't reproduce. With the help of a living cell, they make copies of themselves. A living cell that helps a virus multiply is called a **host cell.** A virus inside a host cell can be active or inactive.

Active Viruses

An active virus attaches itself to a host cell. It injects the cell with its hereditary material. Then the cell starts making virus "parts." Some of these parts are proteins. Some are new strands of hereditary material. The parts assemble into new viruses in the cell. The cell makes more copies of the virus. Finally, the cell becomes so full it bursts and is destroyed. The new viruses are then released into the organism's body to find new cells to invade.

Latent Viruses

Sometimes, after a virus enters a host cell, it doesn't make copies of itself right away. After the virus injects its hereditary material

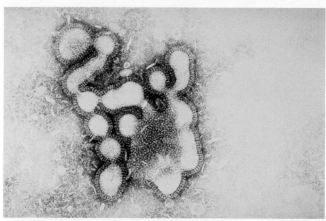
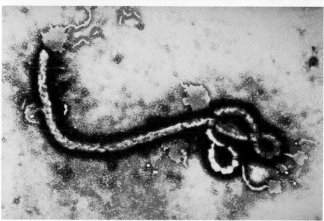

▲ These are viruses under a microscope.

into the cell, it becomes latent, or inactive. When the cell reproduces, it makes a copy of the virus's hereditary material. At some time in the future, certain conditions may activate the virus and start a full-blown viral infection.

Lesson Assessment

Review

1. **Compare and Contrast** How are viruses different from cells?

2. **Define** What is a host cell?

3. **Explain** How do viruses make copies of themselves?

Critical Thinking

- Can a latent virus become active? Explain.

- What happens to the host cell when viruses are released?

- If you were a doctor, what advice would you give a patient with a viral infection such as the flu?

Writing in Science

Describe the steps a virus goes through when it multiplies.

The BELVILLEgazette

Belville's Hometown Paper

OCTOBER 16, 2010

ISSUE 6, Number 3

Fair Winds and Sunny
Mild breezes, temperatures in the 70s with brief showers. Cold front south of the city. Gorgeous sunshine throughout today and into tomorrow.

Lab Explosion Injures Nine

By Lauren Lincoln
Belville Gazette Reporter

A science-class experiment erupted in flames at Belville High School Tuesday morning. The explosion injured eight students and teacher Dan Lippman.

At 9:35 A.M., Lippman was conducting a common experiment that uses methanol, also known as wood alcohol, and mineral salts. The experiment shows how different metals produce different colors of flames. Lippman poured the methanol into a glass beaker, but nothing happened, according to student Tamika Bauer. The teacher began to add methanol a second time. Then the beaker exploded.

"There was a huge fireball that just shot out over everyone," Bauer said. "It was like a blowtorch. Glass flew everywhere."

Glass flew in every direction, scraping cabinets, breaking a plastic ceiling light cover, and ripping the vinyl drapes. Students said that after the explosion Lippman touched the blood on his face. Then he ordered all students to the nurse's office down the hall.

The Belville police and Owen County fire and sheriff's departments responded within minutes.

All twenty-one students in the class were taken to local

Melvin R. Assad | Belville Gazette

The Belville police and Owen County fire and sheriff's departments responded within minutes to Belville High School Tuesday morning after a science-lab explosion.

emergency rooms. Seven were treated for minor cuts and released Tuesday afternoon. One student and Lippman suffered burns. The two were reported in satisfactory condition Tuesday evening.

> "There was a huge fireball that just shot out over everyone," said Belville High student Tamika Bauer. "It was like a blowtorch. Glass flew everywhere."

"Igniting methanol is a frequent and basic experiment in school science classes," said Marian Smith, director of

the Belville Institute of Laboratory Safety, an organization that educates about science safety. Smith said the experiment is usually a safe one. "But accidents aren't unheard of," she said.

"Methanol gives off vapors at a low temperature, around 50 degrees," Smith said. "It has a wide range of flammability. This means a thick concentration of vapors isn't needed for a fire to start."

"The experiment could have gone wrong because there was too much vapor in the glass bottle. Too much vapor could cause a more violent reaction than expected," Smith said. "The experiment is common and normally harmless. Howev-

er, when you're setting things on fire in front of students, the teacher and the students should wear safety goggles. [The experiment] should be done behind a shield."

Only Lippman was wearing safety goggles during the experiment. He was also wearing gloves and earplugs. The classroom safety shield was in another classroom.

"This was an approved demonstration experiment," said Belville High principal Marty Chang. Chang has called for an investigation. "Mr. Lippman is a good teacher. He's very concerned about his students. But we have to know what happened and make sure this doesn't happen again." ■

Extension Activity

You've learned important skills and strategies in the first two units of this program. Using your own classroom science textbook, find the section you're assigned to read next, and follow the instructions below. Write your responses on notebook paper.

a. **Describe** when you would make text connections in your own textbook.

b. **Describe** why you should make text connections in your own textbook.

c. **Answer** the following text-connections questions:

   1. What's the topic of the section?

   2. What's your purpose for reading?

   3. What do you know about the topic?

d. **Describe** when you would use the decoding-multipart-words strategy in your own textbook.

e. **Describe** why you should use the decoding-multipart-words strategy in your own textbook.

f. **Complete** the following steps of the decoding-multipart-words strategy for two multipart words you find:

   Step 1: Underline all the vowel sounds.

   Step 2: Make a slash between the word parts so each part has one vowel sound.

   Step 3: Go back to the beginning of the word, and read the parts in order.

   Step 4: Read the whole word.

Reading Skills and Strategies
• Identify text structure.
• Use word-learning strategies.

Lesson 1 Studying History

As YOU Read!

What You'll Learn

■ The meaning and scope of history

■ The tools and clues historians use to interpret the past

■ How knowing history helps you gain perspective, make connections, and learn skills

Why It's Important

By studying the past, we can better understand our world today.

Key Terms

■ history
■ prehistory
■ primary source
■ secondary source
■ artifacts
■ fossils

Who invented writing? When and where did the first democracy develop? How did early peoples build huge structures without the technology we have today? Ancient civilizations made remarkable advances. Every new invention and idea builds on the achievements of the past.

A Definition of History

History is the study of humans in the past. The people who analyze and write about how humans once lived are called historians. They want to learn about early civilizations and their cultures. Culture includes the beliefs, technology, government, customs, and daily life of a group of people. The pizzas, hamburgers, and other foods you eat are part of your culture. The television shows you watch and the video games you play are part of your culture. Your religion is also part of your culture.

History is commonly divided into four long periods. The first period is called **prehistory.** It's the time before people developed writing. Prehistory lasted until about fifty-five hundred years ago. The period that followed prehistory is known as ancient history. This period lasted until about fifteen hundred years ago. The next thousand years is known as the Middle Ages. Finally, about five hundred years ago, modern history began. This period continues today.

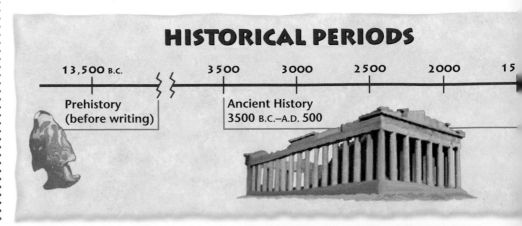

HISTORICAL PERIODS

| 13,500 B.C. | 3500 | 3000 | 2500 | 2000 | 15 |

Prehistory (before writing)

Ancient History 3500 B.C.–A.D. 500

The Petronas Towers in Malaysia (right) reflect modern culture. The temple in Central America (left) reflects Mayan culture more than a thousand years ago.

"Tools" of Historians

Historians rely mostly on written records to tell stories of the past. They search through diaries and letters to find information about how people used to live. They examine markings on clay tablets and temple walls. They look at accounts of business transactions. These types of written records are **primary sources.** They were written by people who witnessed or took part in the events. Other primary sources include drawings on cave walls, legal documents, autobiographies, and photographs and video recordings of primary sources.

Secondary sources summarize or report information from primary sources. Newspapers, textbooks, and biographies are secondary sources. Secondary sources are written later, after the events occurred. They are helpful because they place events in a larger context or time frame. What you are reading now is a secondary source.

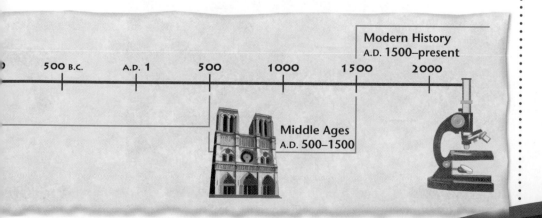

500 B.C.   A.D. 1   500   1000   1500   2000

Modern History
A.D. 1500–present

Middle Ages
A.D. 500–1500

▶ Hieroglyphics were a form of Egyptian writing.

Historians evaluate and interpret information about a historical event. Based on their findings, they propose a theory of what happened. New information is always being found, even about ancient events. When this occurs, historians use the new information to change or strengthen their theories.

As you learned earlier, no written records exist for the prehistory of humankind. How, then, do we know about early humans and their culture?

Clues to the Past

What we know about the earliest people comes from the things they left behind. The field of archaeology, or the study of remains, helps historians piece together clues to the past. Scientists called archaeologists hunt for evidence. They look where ancient settlements might have been located. They dig up and examine

▶ These archaeologists use a grid and other tools to record the exact locations of artifacts they find.

artifacts—tools, pottery, coins, weapons. They also look for **fossils,** or traces of bones, plants, and animals preserved in rock. By examining artifacts, archaeologists may learn that an early society knew how to farm or had military strength. By analyzing bones and plant fossils, archaeologists can tell what foods people ate. They can even tell the climate of the region in the past.

Why We Study History

History includes everything that happens to everyone, including you. As you learn about the past, you see the world from the point of view of other peoples. You discover what they thought was important or beautiful. You learn about the problems they faced and how they solved them. Learning about others helps you broaden your mind, which leads to knowledge and understanding.

Knowing history also helps you make connections. Events that occur today are often based on issues and actions of the past. When you know the past, you can sometimes figure out why certain things are happening now.

Studying history teaches you important skills. Everybody makes mistakes. Most people learn from their mistakes and don't make the same one a second time. In the same way, history teaches what went wrong in the past as well as what went right. It teaches you to ask questions, to analyze facts, and to draw conclusions. You learn the causes and effects of past decisions. You can apply that knowledge to today's world. Knowing the past can help you understand your own role in shaping the future as a citizen and a voter.

Finally, studying history can be interesting and fun. History is full of amazing events and fascinating people. Everything that ever happened and everybody who ever lived are part of history. Science has a history. Mathematics has a history. Music, art, and literature have histories. You, too, are part of history. How will *you* affect history?

◄ Ancient Egyptians thought jewelry and heavy eye makeup were beautiful. This is why Egyptian artwork portrays wealthy men and women with both makeup and jewelry.

Lesson Assessment

Review

1. **Define** What is history?

2. **Define** What is prehistory?

3. **Sequence** Place each event in the correct historical period on the time line: (A) the American Revolution begins (A.D. 1775); (B) farming develops (8000 B.C.); (C) a plague known as the Black Death arrives in Europe (A.D. 1347); (D) a democracy is set up in Athens, Greece (fifth century, B.C.).

4. **Identify** List five elements that make up culture.

5. **Categorize** Make a T-chart in your notebook. Label one side "Primary Sources." Label the other side "Secondary Sources." List at least three examples of each.

6. **Explain** Why must historians sometimes rewrite interpretations of history?

Critical Thinking

Archaeologists a thousand years in the future discover artifacts from your home. What do these artifacts tell them about life in the United States in the early twenty-first century?

Writing in Social Studies

Write a diary entry from the perspective of one of your ancestors.

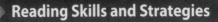

Lesson 2

The Achievements of Sumer

As YOU Read!

What You'll Learn

- The location of Sumer—the world's earliest-known civilization
- What the first writing system was and how it was used
- The Sumerian achievements in technology, math, and science

Why It's Important

The Sumerians invented writing and made other contributions that influence our lives.

Key Terms

- cuneiform

The earliest-known civilization arose on a broad plain bordered by the Tigris River and the Euphrates River. This area is now southern Iraq. In ancient times, the area was called Mesopotamia. *Mesopotamia* is Greek for "the land between the rivers."

The Tigris and Euphrates rivers often flooded. As a result, floods left behind rich soil for farming. The floods were unpredictable, so farmers built dams, walls, and ditches to bring water to their fields. Because of this irrigation, farmers could grow enough food to support large populations. By 3000 B.C., consequently, many cities had formed in southern Mesopotamia in a region called Sumer. The people who lived there were Sumerians.

The Sumerians left a lasting mark on world history. Other peoples copied and improved their ideas and inventions. As a result, Mesopotamia has been called the "cradle of civilization."

The First System of Writing

Probably the most important invention of the Sumerians was **cuneiform.** Cuneiform was the first system of writing. When people lived in villages, they knew everyone. They could remember which goods they exchanged with whom. When cities arose, there were too many people and goods to remember. People in Sumer developed writing to keep track of business deals and other events.

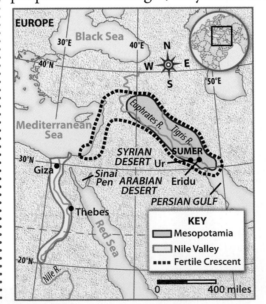

◀ Mesopotamia was part of a large, curved region historians call the Fertile Crescent. It stretched from the Mediterranean Sea to the Persian Gulf.

◀ Sumerian soldiers used wheeled chariots during battles.

Advances in Technology, Math, and Science

The inventiveness of the Sumerians extended to technology. As you read earlier, they developed irrigation systems. They also invented the wagon wheel and the potter's wheel. The wagon wheel helped carry people and goods from place to place. The potter's wheel made it easier to make clay into bowls and other containers. Another Sumerian invention was the plow, which made farming easier. Still another was the sailboat. As a result of this invention, wind power replaced muscle power. The Sumerians were also the first to make bronze out of copper and tin. Bronze was used to craft strong weapons and tools.

Sumerians developed many mathematical ideas. They used geometry to measure fields and construct buildings. They also devised a number system based on 60. We have them to thank for our 60-minute hour, our 60-second minute, and our 360-degree circle. In addition, the Sumerians devised a clock that was operated by drops of water.

Sumerian scholars watched the skies to learn the best times to plant crops and hold religious festivals. They recorded the positions of the planets and stars. They developed a twelve-month calendar based on the cycles of the moon.

Scholars made advances in science too. They studied and categorized thousands of plants, animals, and minerals. They used ingredients from these items to make medicines. They organized their medicines according to the symptoms they relieved and the body parts they affected.

◀ This photograph shows a Sumerian clay tablet from about 3000 B.C.

Lesson Assessment

Review

1. **Identify** Which rivers were important to life in Sumer?

2. **Summarize** What did the Sumerians contribute to the field of mathematics?

3. **Explain** Why did the Sumerians record the positions of stars and planets and develop a calendar?

4. **Support the Main Idea** List four facts that support this statement: Mesopotamia was the "cradle of civilization."

Critical Thinking

Technology made life easier for the Sumerians. In what ways does technology make your life easier?

Writing in Social Studies

You are a visitor in ancient Sumer. Write a letter home in which you describe what you have seen and experienced during your visit.

Lesson 3

The Rise of Democracy

As YOU Read!

What You'll Learn

- Why aristocrats ruled early Athens
- How the first democracy developed
- The difference between the democracy of Athens and the democracy of today

Why It's Important

The democracy that developed in Athens is the foundation of our own democratic government.

Key Terms

- oligarchy
- direct democracy
- representative democracy
- republic

The world's first democracy developed in Athens, a combination city and state in Greece. Democracy is a type of government in which citizens rule themselves.

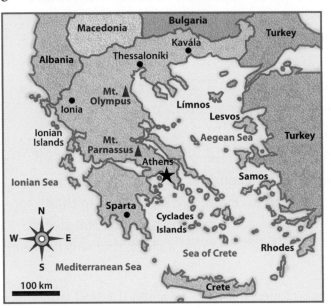

◀ Mountains and seas separated Greek communities from one another. Because of this, Greek city-states like Athens were fiercely independent.

Rule by Aristocrats

Athens did not start out as a democracy. Early Athens was ruled by kings. About 750 B.C., several aristocrats, or rich nobles, overthrew the king. They set up an **oligarchy,** a government in which only a few people rule. Many people were not happy with this arrangement. Over the next 250 years, Athens tried several forms of government.

Democratic Rule

Finally, about 500 B.C., a new leader—Cleisthenes—came to power in Athens. He made the assembly the most important part of the city-state's government. All free male citizens belonged to the assembly and voted on laws. Members of the assembly were given new powers. They had freedom of speech and could debate matters openly. They also appointed military generals. About forty-three thousand male citizens older than eighteen made up the assembly. Usually fewer than six thousand attended meetings, which were held every ten days.

The assembly was large. Speeches and debates were long, noisy affairs. All members were encouraged to voice their opinions. Decision making was slow and difficult. Therefore, Cleisthenes named a new council of five hundred citizens to help the assembly carry out day-to-day governing. The council proposed laws for the assembly to discuss and vote on. The council also dealt with foreign countries and oversaw the treasury.

Athenians chose the members of the council each year in a lottery. The names of five hundred citizens were drawn from a pot. The Athenians believed that choosing council members in this way, instead of by voting, gave everyone the chance to participate in government. Elections, they thought, would favor people who had money or who could speak well in public.

Democracy Today

Like Athens, the United States has a democracy. However, our form of democracy differs from the one developed more than twenty-five hundred years ago. Athens had a **direct democracy.** Every citizen gathered at a single place to discuss and vote on laws. The United States has too many people for direct democracy to work. A mass meeting of millions of citizens would be impossible. In contrast, the founders of our country set up a **representative democracy.** Under this type of democracy, citizens elect officials to represent them in the government. These officials propose and vote on laws for the people who elected them. A representative democracy is also known as a **republic.**

Lesson Assessment

Review

1. **Define** What is an oligarchy?

2. **Explain** Why did Cleisthenes set up the council of five hundred?

3. **Compare and Contrast** How are direct democracy and representative democracy different? How are they alike?

Critical Thinking

Why did Athenians choose council members by lottery? Can you think of drawbacks to this practice? Explain.

Writing in Social Studies

Write a paragraph explaining why the democracy begun by Cleisthenes improved the confidence and prosperity of Athenians.

Unit 3
Social Studies

Reading Skills and Strategies
- Identify text structure.
- Use word-learning strategies.

Lesson 4
The Roman Republic Becomes an Empire

As YOU Read!

What You'll Learn
- How Julius Caesar rose to power in the Roman republic
- How Augustus became sole ruler of the Roman Empire

Why It's Important
The reign of Augustus achieved a new era of prosperity for Rome.

Key Terms
- republic
- triumvirate
- civil war
- dictator

By 60 B.C., Rome had been a republic for almost five hundred years. A **republic** is a form of government in which the rulers are chosen by citizens. A Senate made up of three hundred wealthy aristocrats governed the Roman republic. The republic stretched from Spain to Egypt. A violent situation was brewing. Corrupt senators, power-hungry generals, and thousands of jobless poor had brought the Roman republic to the brink of chaos.

Julius Caesar

In 60 B.C., three generals formed a triumvirate. A **triumvirate** is a government of three people with equal power. One was Julius Caesar. His defeat of Gaul (modern France) made him popular with his troops. He was a hero to lower-class Romans. The second man, General Pompey, ruled Spain. Crassus, the third general, was in Syria.

When Crassus was killed in battle in 53 B.C., leading senators decided Pompey should rule alone. The senators felt Pompey would be easier to control than Caesar. They ordered Caesar to leave his troops in Gaul and return to Rome.

Instead, Caesar *and* his five thousand soldiers marched toward Rome. They crossed the Rubicon, a small river separating Gaul

▶ Caesar and his loyal soldiers cross the Rubicon into Italy. Today, the phrase "crossing the Rubicon" means taking an action that can't be undone.

and Italy. Caesar knew this act would lead to civil war between his forces and Pompey's. A **civil war** occurs when citizens of the same country fight one another.

Pompey fled Italy. Caesar followed him and defeated Pompey in Greece in 48 B.C. When Caesar returned to Rome in 45 B.C., he declared himself dictator for life. A **dictator** is a person who rules with complete power.

Realizing the need for reforms, Caesar provided land and jobs to poor Romans. He increased the Senate to nine hundred members. He filled it with his supporters. Many Romans admired Caesar for bringing order to Rome. Others resented Caesar. They were the aristocratic senators whose powers had been reduced. They feared Caesar would make himself king.

Caesar's opponents were led by the senators Brutus and Cassius. They plotted to kill Caesar. Caesar had received a warning to "beware the Ides of March" (March 15). He ignored it. He entered the Senate on that date in 44 B.C. There, his enemies stabbed him to death.

Augustus

Caesar's murder shocked most Romans. Another civil war erupted. On one side were the men who had assassinated Caesar. On the other side were Octavian, Caesar's grandnephew and heir, and two of Caesar's generals, Antony and Lepidus. Octavian and Antony chased Caesar's killers to northern Greece. In 42 B.C., at the Battle of Philippi, Brutus and Cassius were defeated.

Octavian and Antony then divided Rome. Octavian took the west. Antony took the east. Soon, these two leaders came into conflict. Antony fell in love with the queen of Egypt, Cleopatra VII. He allied his forces with hers. In 31 B.C., however, their army and navy were smashed by Octavian's troops at the Battle of Actium. Antony and Cleopatra fled to Egypt, where they killed themselves.

Octavian, at age thirty-two, stood supreme over the Roman world. He announced to the Senate that he was restoring the republic. In 27 B.C., the Senate gave him a new name— Augustus, or "revered one."

◀ The reign of Augustus began a period of Roman peace, prosperity, and expansion that lasted for almost two hundred years.

Lesson Assessment

Review

1. **Define** What is a triumvirate?

2. **Explain** How did Caesar weaken the power of the Senate?

3. **Summarize** Why did Brutus, Cassius, and other senators kill Caesar?

4. **Identify** Who was Octavian?

5. **Sequence** Using the dates given in the lesson, make a time line of events in the Roman world from 60 B.C. to 27 B.C.

Critical Thinking

Under which ruler would you rather have lived—Caesar or Augustus? Explain your answer.

Writing in Social Studies

Write a newspaper editorial either in favor of or against Julius Caesar's rise to power and his reforms. Include facts from the lesson to support your opinion.

Reading Skills and Strategies
- Use higher-order thinking skills.
- Review of text connections, multipart words, and word-learning strategies.

Lesson 5

The Rise of Feudalism

As YOU Read!

What You'll Learn
- Why feudalism developed
- The duties of lords and vassals
- What a manor was like in the Middle Ages

Why It's Important
During the Middle Ages, feudalism reduced the power of kings and increased the power of nobles.

Key Terms
- feudalism
- fief
- vassal
- serf

In the ninth century, Vikings from northern Europe, Magyars from eastern Europe, and Muslims from Spain threatened the kingdoms of western Europe. The kings' armies were too distant and too slow to stop the attacks of these raiders. Nobles began to defend their own lands. As a result, their power grew.

Land for Loyalty

During the Middle Ages, power shifted from kings to nobles. This happened because of a new social and governing system called **feudalism.** Under this system, landowning nobles protected the people in exchange for services such as fighting or farming. To defend their lands, nobles needed soldiers. The best soldiers of the time were knights. Knights were heavily armored warriors on horseback. Horses, armor, and weapons were expensive, and few people had money at this time. So nobles gave land to knights in return for a pledge of loyalty and military support. The land grant was called a **fief.** With this exchange, the noble became a lord, and the knight became his **vassal**—someone who serves a lord of higher rank.

Lords and vassals followed a set of unwritten rules known as the feudal contract. The main duty of a vassal was to join his lord in battle if the lord went to war. Vassals also had to give money to their lords on special occasions. These included the marriage of

▶ Knights trained for war by participating in tournaments. Here, two knights joust. They ride toward each other and try to knock the opponent off his horse with a lance.

the lord's daughter. Vassals also gave money when the lord's son became a knight. Sometimes a lord was captured in battle and held for ransom. The vassals paid the ransom or became prisoners in the lord's place.

In turn, the lord had duties to his vassals. The main duty was granting a fief to the vassal and giving him permission to rule the people on the land. The lord also sent his knights to help a vassal who was attacked.

Feudal relationships could be complex. A king had his own vassals. These vassals were lords over other vassals. Those vassals, in turn, might also have vassals. At that level, the vassals were simple knights with fiefs barely large enough to provide income. A knight who was granted fiefs from two different lords was a vassal to both.

The Manor

Each lord or knight was responsible for protecting the people on his fief. The lands of the fiefs were called manors. Each manor usually had a castle or a large manor house. A manor also had fields, forests, and a small village where peasants lived. A less important knight or noble would own only one manor. More powerful lords might own several.

In exchange for protection, peasants worked the land and gave some crops and animals to the lord. Some peasants were free men who paid the lord for the right to farm. Others might be blacksmiths or millers. Most peasants, though, were **serfs.** They worked from sunup to sundown. Serfs could not leave the manor or own property. They could not marry without the lord's permission. Yet serfs were not slaves. They could not be sold, and the lord gave them a small piece of land to grow food for themselves.

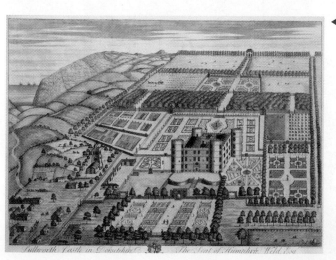

◀ This drawing shows a typical manor in the Middle Ages. Fields and pastures surround a peasant village, a church, and a manor house.

Lesson Assessment

Review

1. **Determine Cause and Effect** Why did feudalism develop?

2. **Define** What is a vassal?

3. **Explain** How could a noble be both a lord and a vassal?

4. **Identify** What duties did a lord have to his serfs?

5. **Categorize** Make a T-chart. Label one side "Lord's Duties." Label the other side "Vassal's Duties." List the duties you read about in this lesson.

Critical Thinking

Why was land the most important gift a lord could give a vassal?

Writing in Social Studies

Use information from the text and the drawing on this page to write a short skit about life on a manor in the Middle Ages.

Reading Skills and Strategies

- Review Description-or-List.
- Review Order-or-Sequence.
- Identify Cause-and-Effect.
- Review Compare-and-Contrast.

Lesson 1

The Italian Renaissance

As YOU Read!

What You'll Learn

- What the Italian Renaissance was
- How the classics led to humanism
- Who the important Renaissance artists and writers were

Why It's Important

During the Renaissance, learning and art reemerged in wealthy Italian city-states.

Key Terms

- Renaissance
- humanism
- classics
- patron
- perspective

In the fourteenth century, several Italian cities were important centers of trade. Ports on the Mediterranean Sea bustled with cargoes of spices and other luxuries from Asia. Italian merchants sold these goods at high prices to nobles in western Europe. Italian cities produced glass, weapons, and silk and other fine cloth. While most Europeans lived on feudal manors in the countryside, artisans flocked to Italian cities.

▶ Under the Medici family, Florence became the center of Italian art, literature, and culture.

A "Rebirth" in Italy

One city in particular, Florence, became wealthy from trade, cloth making, and banking. The city's richest family was the Medici. They were bankers who lent money to Europe's kings and nobles. The Medici became rich by charging interest, or fees, on their loans. They used their wealth to hire architects and artists to build and decorate palaces, churches, and libraries. Rich families in other Italian cities—Venice, Milan, Genoa, and Rome—competed to see who could support more artists and scholars. So many cultural achievements occurred in Italy from 1300 to 1550 that historians call this period the Italian **Renaissance,** a French word meaning "rebirth."

Humanism

The period from 450 to 1450, called the Middle Ages, was a time of warfare and disease. Religion was important. During the Renaissance, people were still religious, but they wanted to balance faith with reason. Their belief in human abilities and actions is called **humanism.** It was based on the study of the **classics.** These are the ancient Greek and Roman works that had long been forgotten in western Europe. Arab scholars, however, had preserved these writings. When Turks conquered the Byzantine Empire in 1453, many scholars fled to Italy. They took the classics with them. Italian scholars and artists studied these works with interest. The Medici and other rich families acted as patrons to these scholars and artists. A **patron** is someone who supports an artist or a scholar who paints, writes, or studies. Art, literature, and learning spread through Italy.

Renaissance Artists

Like the ancient Greeks and Romans, Renaissance artists saw beauty in human beings and in nature. They developed new techniques to make their works look real.

They studied the muscles and bones of the human body and reproduced them accurately. Their figures almost seemed real.

The most important technique these artists developed was perspective. **Perspective** makes a painting look three-dimensional. Before the Renaissance, pictures looked flat. They had no depth. Everything in a picture appeared to be at an equal distance from the viewer.

▲ The house on the left is drawn without perspective. The house on the right shows perspective.

Artists also began to show the emotions of their subjects. They used light, shadows, and color to add drama to their paintings.

Leonardo da Vinci (1452–1519)

Leonardo da Vinci was a master painter. He was also a scientist, an inventor, an engineer, a mapmaker, and a city planner. He was interested in every subject. He designed

▲ *Mona Lisa* is famous for her smile.

Michelangelo Buonarroti (1475–1564)

Michelangelo Buonarroti painted and sculpted many masterpieces. His heart was set on building a tomb for Pope Julius II, his patron. Julius, however, wanted Michelangelo to paint the ceiling of the Sistine Chapel in the Vatican. Michelangelo was a difficult person to get along with. He didn't want to do the painting, but finally he agreed. He demanded sole control over the project. He kept the paintings hidden from all eyes except the pope's until the work was finished. The job took four years. It wore him out. "I was only thirty-seven," he said, "yet friends did not recognize the old man I had become." Visitors still flock to Rome to view the beautiful paintings in the Sistine Chapel.

Renaissance Writers

Writers, too, were inspired by humanist ideas. Until this time, most literature had been written in Latin. To reach a wider audience, writers began to use the language spoken by ordinary people.

Dante Alighieri (1265–1321)

Dante Alighieri wrote *The Divine Comedy* in Italian. *The Divine Comedy* is a long religious poem. In it, Dante tells of a dream in which he travels through Hell, Purgatory, and Paradise. He describes each place and the famous people he meets there. Dante called his poem a comedy, but it is not funny. There is much that's unpleasant in the poem, but it ends well.

weapons, buildings, and machinery. He liked math. He may have been the first person to draw plans for a flying vehicle. Leonardo filled many notebooks with his ideas. Only a few of these notebooks still exist. In 1994, the American businessman Bill Gates paid more than thirty million dollars for one of the notebooks, the Codex Leicester. Leonardo's most famous painting is the *Mona Lisa*. This picture shows a beautiful woman with a mysterious smile. Another famous painting is *The Last Supper*, a religious work.

▲ Dante is famous for *The Divine Comedy*.

▲ Boccaccio wrote the *Decameron*.

Giovanni Boccaccio (1313–1375)

Giovanni Boccaccio's most famous work is the *Decameron*. It's a collection of short stories told by ten people who have fled to the country to escape the plague. The plague is a horrible disease that is almost always fatal. It was called the Black Death because one of its symptoms is the appearance of ugly black lumps on the body. The worst outbreak of this disease killed a third of the people in Europe. The plague is transmitted by the bites of fleas carried by rats. The fleas easily jump from rats to people and from one person to another. Cities were full of rats. You can understand why people would want to go to the country, where there was less chance of being infected.

Lesson Assessment

Review

1. **Identify** Who were the Medici?

2. **Explain** How did the focus of religion change during the Renaissance?

3. **Determine Cause and Effect** How did Arab scholars influence the Renaissance?

4. **Define** What was humanism?

Critical Thinking

Give three reasons the Renaissance began in Italy.

Writing in Social Studies

Write a story you might have told if you had gone to the country with the group of people in the *Decameron*.

Reading Skills and Strategies

- Review Description-or-List.
- Review Order-or-Sequence.
- Review Cause-and-Effect.
- Identify Compare-and-Contrast.

Lesson 2
The Scientific Revolution

As YOU Read!

What You'll Learn

- How the study of science changed during the sixteenth century
- What discoveries Copernicus, Kepler, Galileo, and Newton made

Why It's Important

The Scientific Revolution was the birth of modern science. It changed people's views of the universe.

Key Terms

- theories
- Scientific Revolution
- geocentric
- heliocentric

In the mid-sixteenth century, a change occurred in how people studied the natural world. Before then, Europeans accepted the knowledge of such ancient Greeks as Aristotle. Greek scholars wrote **theories,** or explanations. They based these on observation and common sense. The Greeks, however, had not tested their theories.

Educated people in the sixteenth century also used observation to study nature and the universe. Their scientific methods went further. They tested their theories with experiments. If the results did not support a theory, a scholar would note new facts, make a prediction, and then test the new theory. From about 1540 to 1700, the search for scientific truths overturned many old ideas. This period is known as the **Scientific Revolution.**

Discoveries in Astronomy

Astronomy was the first science affected by the Scientific Revolution. Ptolemy, who lived in the second century, thought Earth was the center of the universe. He theorized that the sun and the planets moved around Earth in circular orbits. Europeans accepted this **geocentric,** or earth-centered, theory for fourteen hundred years.

Nicolaus Copernicus, a mathematician from Poland, thought Ptolemy's theory was too complex. He developed a simpler **heliocentric,** or sun-centered, theory of the universe. Copernicus argued that the sun, not Earth, was the center of the universe. The planets, he thought, moved around the

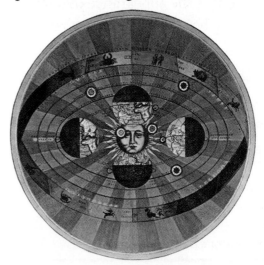

▲ Copernicus developed the heliocentric theory, shown in this diagram.

sun in circular paths. He said the moon revolved around Earth. In 1543, Copernicus published his theories in the book *On the Revolutions of the Celestial Spheres.*

The German astronomer Johannes Kepler agreed with Copernicus's theories. He tried to map the movement of the planets. In doing so, he realized that the planets move in oval, not circular, orbits around the sun.

The Italian Galileo Galilei made other scientific discoveries. He was the first European to observe the skies regularly through a telescope. With this tool, he saw mountains on the moon. He saw sunspots. He also saw four moons revolving around Jupiter. He methodically tested ancient theories. Through careful and thorough research, Galileo disproved Aristotle's theory that the heavier an object is, the faster it falls to the ground. Galileo's experiments proved that objects fall at the same speed no matter what their weight.

Galileo published his research in 1632. His findings angered the Catholic Church. Church leaders, who followed Ptolemy's earth-centered view, thought Galileo's findings went against the Bible. They forced Galileo to withdraw many of his statements. Still, his ideas spread.

Isaac Newton

The most brilliant mind of the Scientific Revolution was the English mathematician Isaac Newton. In 1687, he published *Principia Mathematica.* In this book, Newton used mathematics to explain the motion of objects. He stated that every object is attracted to every other object by a force called gravity. This force keeps the sun and the planets in their orbits. Newton proved his theories so well they became scientific laws.

▲ Some historians believe Isaac Newton "discovered" gravity when an apple fell on his head.

Lesson Assessment

Review

1. **Identify** When did the Scientific Revolution occur?

2. **Contrast** How did the heliocentric view differ from the geocentric view?

3. **Describe** What did Kepler discover?

4. **Explain** Why were Church leaders angry about Galileo's findings?

5. According to Newton, what force holds the solar system together?

Critical Thinking

How did the methods of studying science change in the sixteenth century?

Writing in Social Studies

Write five questions you would like to ask Newton or Galileo about their work.

Reading Skills and Strategies

- Identify Description-or-List.
- Review Order-or-Sequence.
- Review Cause-and-Effect.
- Review Compare-and-Contrast.

Lesson 3

Government and the Enlightenment

As YOU Read!

What You'll Learn

- How Enlightenment ideas changed the way rulers governed
- Who introduced new ideas about government
- What ideas became part of the Declaration of Independence and the U.S. Constitution

Why It's Important

Rights we enjoy today are based on ideas from the Enlightenment.

Key Terms

- divine right
- natural rights

During the seventeenth and eighteenth centuries, Europe experienced an intellectual movement known as "The Age of Enlightenment." The Enlightenment changed the way some people viewed science and philosophy. People who agreed with the ideals of this movement were known as "Enlightenment thinkers." As a result, rulers began to change their views on government and their subjects.

Rulers in the Age of Enlightenment

For centuries, European rulers believed they governed by **divine right.** In other words, they thought God gave them unlimited power. France's King Louis XIV often declared, "I am the state." He meant that his will was law.

Enlightenment thinkers wrote that rulers should share power and wealth with the people. Several rulers used these ideas to win support from the people. For example, Prussia's King Frederick II proposed that all Prussians receive a basic education, and Russia's Empress Catherine the Great granted some powers to nobles.

▶ Unlike Louis XIV of France, Russia's Catherine the Great shared some of her power with the nobility.

Enlightenment Thinkers on Government

John Locke, Charles-Louis Montesquieu, and Jean-Jacques Rousseau wanted even more change. These Enlightenment thinkers claimed that government existed to protect and serve citizens. Their ideas later gave rise to modern republics.

Locke believed all people had **natural rights** to life, liberty, and property. In 1690, he described government as a contract between ruler and people. According to Locke, the contract should uphold people's rights and limit a ruler's power.

Decades later, Montesquieu claimed that separate branches of government would protect people's rights. Each branch would limit the power of the others. No one branch would control the government.

Rousseau thought government should represent the people's will, not the ruler's will. In 1762, he published *The Social Contract*. In his book, Rousseau wrote that when a government no longer serves the people, it should give up its power.

Enlightenment Comes to America

British colonists in North America knew the impact of Enlightenment ideas. They saw that Parliament limited the power of the British king. However, in the 1760s, the colonists felt that both Parliament and the king were against them.

What caused this ill feeling? First, the British parliament imposed a tax on molasses. Then, it passed the Stamp Act. This law taxed newspapers and legal documents. Many colonists concluded that the British government no longer served their interests. Two of these colonists were Benjamin Franklin and Thomas Jefferson.

Enlightenment Leaders in America

In 1766, Franklin applied Enlightenment ideas to the colonists' problems. He argued that the British government should not tax the colonists because the colonists had no representative in Parliament. Franklin's argument sparked protests among the colonists. Their protests persuaded the British to cancel the Stamp Act.

In 1776, Jefferson wrote the Declaration of Independence. This document included many Enlightenment ideas. It stated that people had natural rights to life and liberty, just as Locke had claimed. It also urged colonists to declare independence from British rule because the British government no longer protected their rights. A later document, the Constitution, established three branches of government.

Lesson Assessment

Review
1. **Define** What is divine right?
2. **List** According to Locke, what are people's natural rights?
3. **Describe** How do three branches of government prevent any one branch or person from gaining absolute power?

Critical Thinking
Describe the chain of causes and effects that forced Parliament to cancel the Stamp Act.

Writing in Social Studies
Use information from the lesson to write a conversation between Louis XIV and Enlightenment thinkers.

Lesson 4

The Industrial Revolution

Reading Skills and Strategies

- Review Description-or-List.
- Identify Order-or-Sequence.
- Review Cause-and-Effect.
- Review Compare-and-Contrast.

As YOU Read!

What You'll Learn

- Why machine-made goods replaced handmade goods during the Industrial Revolution
- How factories changed life in Europe and North America

Why It's Important

Modern challenges, such as urban sprawl and global warming, are linked to early industrialization.

Key Terms

- capitalist

What was manufacturing like before 1700? Weavers wove cloth on hand looms. Shoemakers cobbled shoes one pair at a time, and blacksmiths hammered iron into tools. Their businesses were known as cottage industries. They worked in their homes and in small shops and sold their goods mainly to local people.

New Inventions

Making goods by hand required much time and skill. As a result, most goods were scarce and costly. In the eighteenth century, however, inventors introduced new machines that changed the way goods were made.

In 1733, John Kay invented the flying shuttle. This device helped weavers produce cloth faster than spinners could spin thread. Next, James Hargreaves developed the spinning jenny, which sped the production of thread. Then in 1793, Eli Whitney introduced the cotton gin. The cotton gin processed cotton bolls faster than ever.

Changes in Industry

These machines contributed to the rapid spread of British textile, or cloth, factories. The factories housed many machines and manufactured large amounts of low-priced cloth. Early textile factories used water power to run their machines. After 1769, the newly developed steam engine drove the machines in factories even faster.

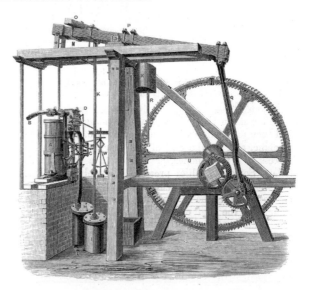

▲ The Scot James Watt invented a steam engine to power factory machines.

The Capitalist System

Bankers, landowners, and other wealthy people saw their chance to become richer. They put up funds for factories, shipping, and railroads. In return, they received a share of the money these businesses earned. People who own or finance businesses are called **capitalists.**

By the nineteenth century, European and American factories were making many kinds of goods, including machines for other factories. Cheap, plentiful factory-made goods replaced handmade products in most people's lives. Cottage industries disappeared.

Changes in Workers' Lives

Machines also changed where and how people worked. Before the nineteenth century, most people lived in the country. Many worked on farms. In the mid-nineteenth century, new mechanical reapers and threshers could do the work of several farmhands. Like craftspeople in cottage industries, farmworkers saw their livelihoods disappear.

Unemployed workers went to factories in the cities to find jobs. City populations grew fast. There was not enough housing for everyone. Newcomers crowded into dark and dirty apartments. Outside the buildings, factory smoke polluted the air. Garbage littered the streets. These run-down areas were called slums.

Few workers could afford better housing. Factory owners paid low wages for long hours. Children took jobs to help their families. Working children could not attend school. Without schooling, they had little hope of ever holding better jobs.

▲ Children of the poor often worked long hours in factories.

Lesson Assessment

Review

1. **Explain** Before the Industrial Revolution, how were goods such as shoes and tools manufactured?

2. **Analyze** Why did people buy machine-made goods instead of handmade products?

3. **Identify** Who were the capitalists during the Industrial Revolution?

Critical Thinking

In 1938, Congress passed a law to limit child labor. Why, do you think, was such a law enacted?

Writing in Social Studies

Write a paragraph telling how life today would be different if farm machines had not been invented.

Reading Skills and Strategies

• Use higher-order thinking skills.
• Review text connections, text structure, multipart words, and word-learning strategies.

Lesson 5

Nation-States and Empires

As YOU Read!

What You'll Learn

■ Who united separate states into modern European nations

■ Why new nations established empires in the late nineteenth century

Why It's Important

Nationalist and imperialist attitudes are the cause of many current conflicts.

Key Terms

■ nation-state
■ nationalists
■ empire
■ imperialism

Look at the world news in today's newspaper. At least one story a day is about fighting between regions or countries. Most likely, nationalism, imperialism, or both sparked the conflict.

Nationalists

One definition of *nation* is "a people with a common past, culture, and language." Most people in 1800 belonged to nations in this sense. However, many nations in Latin America and Europe did not have their own **nation-state,** or self-governing country. Those who feel a strong loyalty to their nation are called **nationalists.**

Nationalists under foreign rule wanted independence and their own nation-state. Mexico as well as Venezuela and other South American states became independent in the 1820s and 1830s. European nations took a few decades longer.

For example, before 1860, Italians were divided among several states. An Italian king ruled Sardinia. Austria controlled the rest of

the northern states. The pope governed Rome and the surrounding area. The Bourbons from France ruled Sicily.

◀ Simón Bolívar freed much of South America from Spanish rule.

Uniting Italy

In 1852, a nationalist named Camillo di Cavour became prime minister of Sardinia. Cavour reorganized Sardinia's army and joined forces with the French. Together they drove the Austrians out of Italy. By 1860, Sardinia controlled all the northern states.

Meanwhile, Italian nationalist Giuseppe Garibaldi and a thousand followers captured Sicily. Soon after, Cavour's armies invaded the papal states. They seized everything but Latium and Rome. Next, Cavour persuaded Garibaldi to give Sardinia control of Sicily. Finally, in 1861, Italy united under Sardinia's King Victor Emmanuel.

One Germany

German-speaking people were divided among many small kingdoms. The largest of these was Prussia. In the 1860s, Otto von Bismarck served as Prussian prime minister. Like Cavour, Bismarck organized a strong army. The Prussians went to war with Denmark and Austria to win control of the northern kingdoms. Next, Bismarck declared war on France. The kingdoms to the south joined him. Prussia and its allies won the war. Then they formed the German Empire.

The New Imperialism

An **empire** is many countries or regions under the control of one nation. Spain, Portugal, England, and France began competing to establish overseas colonies in the fifteenth century. The British were the champions of empire. At one time it was said that the sun never set on the British Empire. That means that wherever the sun was shining, British-ruled land lay beneath it. Great Britain ruled Canada, India, and Australia. Egypt, in northern Africa, and parts of southern Africa also fell under British rule. In the nineteenth century, new nations such as Italy, Germany, and Belgium also began building empires.

A major reason for **imperialism,** or empire building, was industrialization. Factory owners in Europe and North America needed raw materials. Some materials could be obtained only from African, Asian, and Caribbean regions. Nations with strong armies took over these regions and their resources.

In 1898, the United States went to war with Spain. The United States invaded Cuba, Puerto Rico, and the Philippines. The United States wished to remove Spanish influence from the Caribbean. After the United States won the Spanish-American War, Spain agreed to give up all her territory in the area. Later the United States took over part of Panama to build a canal from the Atlantic to the Pacific.

Lesson Assessment

Review

1. **Infer** Why did nationalists reject foreign control?

2. **Summarize** How did Cavour drive the Austrians out of Italy?

3. **Evaluate** Do you think the average Prussian benefited from Bismarck's policies? Explain.

4. **Propose** Suggest a way Europeans could have obtained raw materials without empire building.

Critical Thinking

Compare the unification strategies of Cavour and Bismarck. How were they alike?

Writing in Social Studies

In a letter to the editor, explain why empire building is morally wrong.

Frozen in Time

By Caroline LaFranc

Photos by Maurice Field

How a city was erased in the blink of an eye

On a normal day almost two thousand years ago, citizens milled about the city of Pompeii, busy with their daily activities. It was August 24, A.D. 79. It was nearly noon. The day before had begun and ended like any other day. But at noon on August 24, Pompeii became extinct.

There was no real warning when the eruption occurred. There had been a major earthquake seventeen years before. There had since been a few tremors here and there. But no real volcanic activity had happened for a lifetime. Mount Vesuvius towered six thousand feet over Pompeii. Vesuvius was, and is, a huge volcano. When it exploded in A.D. 79, the people of Pompeii could do nothing to save themselves.

The eruption began as tremendous amounts of dust, ash, and rocks catapulted into the air. The deadly mixture spread over the surrounding area and then fell to the ground. The sky became black; the sunlight was blocked. People scrambled throughout the city, trying to escape the falling debris. But the streets and buildings became covered, making escape impossible.

Twenty feet of ash and rocks soon covered the city and everyone in it. Only the rooftops could be seen. Many buildings collapsed under the weight. Blankets of boiling mud and steam followed the first explosion, further burying Pompeii. Lava did not kill the residents of Pompeii, however. People were suffocated by ash, buried beneath collapsed buildings, or poisoned by volcanic gas. Some say 20 percent of the population died that day, most almost instantly. Others say the percentage is likely more.

Today Pompeii has been excavated. It is one of the most popular tourist attractions in Italy and the world. Ash and rock have been dug away to reveal buildings, still intact, that tell a tale of lives very much like our own. Pompeii holds colorful paintings, roads, restaurants, courtyards, statues, blackened bread in ovens . . . and the forms of the people and animals that perished so long ago.

(Continued on Page 20)

DID YOU KNOW?

Did you know the tallest volcano isn't on Earth? Olympus Mons on Mars is 16.7 miles tall.

Extension Activity

You've learned important skills and strategies in the first four units of this program. Using your own classroom social studies textbook, find the section you're assigned to read next, and follow the instructions below. Write your responses on notebook paper.

a. **Answer** the following text-connections questions:
1. What's the topic of the section?
2. What's your purpose for reading?
3. What do you know about the topic?

b. **Find** one example of text structure. Write the page number, title (or subhead), and paragraph on which you found this example.

c. **Why** did you choose this text structure? Give an explanation.

d. **Complete** the following steps of the decoding-multipart-words strategy for two multipart words you find:

Step 1: Underline all the vowel sounds.

Step 2: Make a slash between the word parts so each part has one vowel sound.

Step 3: Go back to the beginning of the word, and read the parts in order.

Step 4: Read the whole word.

e. **Describe** when you'd use the context-clues strategy in your textbook.

f. **Complete** the following steps of the context-clues strategy for two words—one bold and highlighted word, and one regular word:

When you come across a word you don't know,

Step 1: Read the sentence containing the word.

Step 2: Look for a definition or for examples of the word in the sentence.

Step 3: Read before or after the sentence for a definition or for examples of the word.

g. **Write** the definitions of the two words you researched. Include the page number, title (or subhead), and paragraph where you found each word.

Reading Skills and Strategies

- Review Description-or-List.
- Review Order-or-Sequence.
- Review Cause-and-Effect.
- Identify Compare-and-Contrast.

Lesson 1

Classification

As YOU Read!

What You'll Learn

- How organisms are classified
- How organisms are grouped into domains and kingdoms

Why It's Important

As scientists make new discoveries, they may need to reclassify organisms.

Key Terms

- domain
- kingdom
- Fungi
- Protista
- Bacteria
- Archaea

Changes in Classification

Early scientists placed all living things in two groups: plants and animals. As scientists learned more, they had to reclassify some living things. For example, the giant panda was once classified in the same family as raccoons. By studying the DNA of pandas and other animals, scientists discovered that pandas are more closely related to bears. As a result, pandas were moved from the raccoon family to the bear family.

▶ Pandas were once classified with raccoons but were found to be more closely related to bears.

Domains—A New Level of Classification

Because of new observations, scientists added a new level of classification: domains. **Domains** are the largest classifications. There are three domains: Eukarya, Bacteria, and Archaea. Scientists established these groups based on differences in their cells.

Eukarya have cells with a nucleus. The cells of these organisms are the largest and most complex of all living things. Unlike the cells of Eukarya, the cells of Bacteria and Archaea do not have a nucleus. Cells without a nucleus are called prokaryotic cells. Both Bacteria and Archaea consist of prokaryotes only. However, the cell structure of Bacteria and Archaea is different enough to place them in separate domains.

Kingdoms

The three domains, Eukarya, Bacteria, and Archaea, are divided into six groups called **kingdoms.** Before 1990, scientists used a five-kingdom system to classify living things. Two of the current kingdoms, Bacteria and Archaea, were in the same kingdom. Scientists have since separated them because of differences in cell structure. The six kingdoms scientists use today are Animalia, Plantae, Fungi, Protista, Bacteria, and Archaea.

Animals and Plants

Animals and plants are the organisms most familiar to us. We see them around us every day. Before microscopes, people thought all living things were either plants or animals. Living things that moved were classified as animals. Green, nonmoving organisms were considered plants.

The animal and plant kingdoms display great diversity. Plants range from species as small and simple as mosses to species as huge and complex as redwood trees. Animals are equipped with many adaptations that allow them to live in almost every environment on Earth.

All members of kingdom Plantae are multicellular organisms. They are eukaryotes. Their cells contain a nucleus in which DNA controls each cell's functions. Plant cells have structures that convert sunlight into sugars, which plants use for food. Plant cells are surrounded by tough outer walls that support the plants. Because plants need light to make food, they grow upward toward light.

◄ Redwood trees can grow to 260 feet.

Like plants, animals are multicellular organisms made up of eukaryotic cells. Unlike plants, animals must eat other organisms to obtain energy. At some point in their life cycle, all animals have the ability to move. Animals are complex organisms. Most species have a mouth and a nervous system. There are about four times as many animal species as plant species. Most members of the animal kingdom are insects. Mammals, amphibians, birds, fish, and reptiles make up the rest of the animal kingdom.

Fungi

Fungi are eukaryotes that are either one-celled or multicellular. Like plants, fungi have cell walls and stay in one place. Unlike plants, they do not make their own food. Nor do they eat other organisms. Fungi obtain energy by absorbing nutrients from their surroundings. They break down materials from decaying plants and animals and absorb the nutrients they need. Molds, mushrooms, and most other fungi are multicellular. Yeasts, such as those used in making bread, are typically one-celled.

▶ Yeast is a fungus that makes bread rise. The mold growing on the bread is another type of fungus.

Protists

Protists are a diverse group. Most protists are one-celled, but some are multicellular. Algae are protists that make their own food. Other protists, such as amoebas, get energy by taking in food. Because of the diversity of protists, some scientists believe kingdom **Protista** should be divided into more than one kingdom.

Most protists are microscopic and live in water. Seaweeds are an example of large protists that are easily visible to the naked eye. In fact, giant kelp, a type of seaweed, can grow hundreds of feet in length.

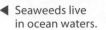
Seaweeds live in ocean waters.

One thing all protists have in common is that they are eukaryotes. They have complex cells that contain a nucleus. However, protist cells are not as complex as plant or animal cells. Some protists are multicellular, but they have few specialized cells. They aren't capable of growing complex structures such as those found in plant, animal, or fungi species.

Bacteria

Bacteria are the most numerous organisms on Earth. They live in nearly every environment. All bacteria are prokaryotes. Their cells lack a nucleus. They are simple one-celled organisms that can produce many generations in a short time.

Some bacteria species are beneficial to other organisms. For example, many types of bacteria live in the digestive tract to help the body break down and absorb nutrients from food. Some types of bacteria cause diseases in other organisms. *E. coli* is a species of bacteria that can live in some of the food we eat. *E. coli* causes illness when humans eat food that hasn't been prepared properly.

Archaea

At one time, there were only five kingdoms. **Archaea** was named after researchers found some important differences among bacteria. Scientists discovered that some bacteria had a unique cell structure. These bacteria resembled eukaryotic cells, but the cells did not have a nucleus. These cells also contained chemicals different from those found in typical bacteria. Scientists named these bacteria *archaea* and gave them a kingdom of their own.

Archaea live in many places where bacteria live. However, archaea stand out in their ability to survive in extreme environments. Scientists have discovered archaea in hot thermal vents at the bottom of the ocean, in the boiling mud around hot springs, and in deep desert sand.

Lesson Assessment

Review

1. What is the main difference between animal cells and bacteria cells?

2. Identify Name a protist that lives in water.

3. Compare and Contrast How are fungi similar to plants? How are they different?

4. Explain What are archaea, and why did scientists give them a kingdom of their own?

Critical Thinking

A new one-celled organism has been discovered. It has a cell wall but no nucleus. In which kingdom would you classify it? Why?

Writing in Science

Make a graphic organizer to show the relationships of the three domains and six kingdoms. Then write a paragraph to explain how domains and kingdoms are related.

Reading Skills and Strategies

- Identify Description-or-List.
- Review Order-or-Sequence.
- Review Cause-and-Effect.
- Review Compare-and-Contrast.

Lesson 2

Bacteria

As YOU Read!

What You'll Learn

- The characteristics of bacteria
- The role of bacteria in the environment
- The pros and cons of bacteria

Why It's Important

Bacteria are found almost everywhere and affect all living things.

Key Terms

- bacteria
- producers
- decomposers

The Simplest Living Things

Bacteria are the smallest and simplest living things on Earth. They are ten to twenty times smaller than the average animal, plant, fungus, or protist cell. They live in water and air. They live underground and inside your body. They live on every surface you touch.

Bacteria are single-celled organisms without a nucleus. Bacteria reproduce by dividing in two. Most one-celled organisms without a nucleus are bacteria.

Classifying by Shape

Bacteria exist in three shapes: spirals, rods, and spheres. Shape is one way scientists classify bacteria. Typically, spiral bacteria appear in single strands. They look something like corkscrews.

Rod-shaped bacteria appear as single individuals or in chains.

Round bacteria may appear as single individuals, in pairs, in chains, or in clusters. They look like little balls or peas.

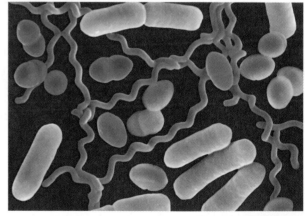

▲ Can you find the three kinds of bacteria—spiral, rod, and round?

The Roles of Bacteria in Ecosystems

Bacteria perform a variety of jobs in the environment. Some bacteria are called producers, and some are called decomposers.

Some bacteria contain chlorophyll. These bacteria use energy from the sun to make their own food. They are **producers.** Like plants, they provide food for other organisms and release oxygen into the environment.

Other types of bacteria do not make their own food. They are **decomposers.** These bacteria obtain energy from dead or decaying organisms. Decomposers break down materials from these organisms and make chemicals other organisms can use. Did you know bacteria can be used to clean water? Bacteria in water-treatment plants break down sewage and help purify the water.

Helpful Bacteria

Producers and decomposers are helpful to other organisms. Producers provide food and oxygen for other organisms. Decomposers break waste materials into a form other organisms can use.

Many types of plants use nitrogen to make proteins. Bacteria inside the plants' roots convert nitrogen into a form plants can use. Bacteria are also used to help clean up oil spills in the ocean. The bacteria break down the oil and convert it to a less toxic form.

▲ Bacteria can be used to lessen the bad effects of an oil spill.

Harmful Bacteria

Some bacteria cause disease. Tuberculosis, cholera, and typhoid are three diseases caused by bacteria. Three other diseases caused by bacteria—whooping cough, rheumatic fever, and tetanus—can now be prevented by a vaccine. All these diseases have almost been wiped out in developed countries. However, in developing nations, these diseases still kill hundreds of thousands of people every year.

Lesson Assessment

Review

1. **Explain** Where are bacteria found?

2. **Describe** How do bacteria reproduce?

3. **Visualize** What three shapes do bacteria have? Draw a sketch of each kind. Label your drawings.

4. **Compare and Contrast** What do producers and decomposers have in common? How are they different?

5. **Explain** How do decomposers help the environment?

Critical Thinking

Are all bacteria bad? Justify your answer.

Writing in Science

Bacteria are sometimes used to clean up oil spills. Write a sentence telling how they do this.

Reading Skills and Strategies

- Review Description-or-List.
- Identify Order-or-Sequence.
- Review Cause-and-Effect.
- Review Compare-and-Contrast.

Lesson 3

Protists

Do you have an "odds and ends" drawer in your house? Maybe you call it a "junk" drawer. It's probably a place where you put various items that don't seem to belong anywhere else. Kingdom Protista is a bit like that drawer. It contains simple organisms that have nuclei and cannot be classified as plants, animals, or fungi.

Protists

Most protists are one-celled organisms. They usually live in water. Many of the organisms you may observe in pond water are probably protists.

Some protists are multicellular, but their structures and functions are simpler than those of plants, animals, and multicellular fungi. A common multicellular protist is seaweed. You may think seaweed is a plant, but seaweed is not as complex as plants.

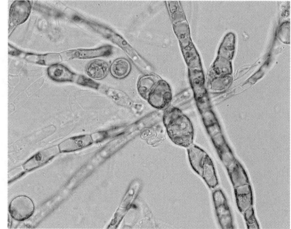

▲ If you took a sample of pond water and examined it under a microscope, you would find several types of protists.

How Protists Get Energy

Protists get energy in different ways. Scientists classify protists in three groups. One group is made up of protists that make their own food. Another group is made up of protists that eat other organisms. The third group is made up of protists that are decomposers.

Plantlike Protists

Algae are protists that have chloroplasts and cell walls like plants. Algae use chlorophyll to get energy from the sun. First, chlorophyll helps algae absorb sunlight. Next, algae use the sun's energy to make their own food. Finally, the algae survive by using the food they produce.

Algae can be one-celled or many-celled. **Diatoms** are one-celled algae that live in salt water, freshwater, or soil. They have hard cell walls made of silica. Volvox are simple, many-celled algae that arrange their cells in a hollow ball. You now know seaweed is a multicellular protist, but did you know seaweed can grow one hundred meters long?

Animal-like Protists

Protozoa are one-celled protists that get energy by eating other organisms. Protozoa can move around to search for food. Some have whiplike tails, or flagella, that push the protozoa through water. Other protozoa wave short strands, or cilia. Still other protozoa have flexible cells that can change shape to wrap around prey.

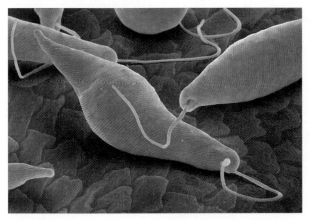

▲ Protozoa with flagella ▲ Protozoa with cilia

Protists as Decomposers

Protists that do not make their own food or eat other organisms get nutrients from soil, living organisms, or dead or decaying organisms. These protists get energy by breaking down materials.

Some types of molds, such as bread mold, belong to the protist kingdom. These molds have simpler structures than fungi molds. Water molds are protists and feed on plant and animal tissues. Slime molds feed on decaying plants and bacteria. Large, plasmodial slime molds get nutrients from rotting logs in damp forests.

Euglena are protists that can get energy in more than one way. They can make their own food if they get enough sunlight. Without sunlight, euglena act like decomposers and absorb nutrients from other sources.

Lesson Assessment

Review

1. **Explain** Why is the protist kingdom sometimes considered a collection of leftovers?

2. **Identify** List three ways protists get energy.

3. **Compare and Contrast** How are algae different from plants?

4. **List** What are three ways protozoa move?

Critical Thinking

Suppose you were going to reorganize the protists in a new classification system. How would you separate and classify them?

Writing in Science

Write a paragraph about protists. Include a sentence describing each type of protist discussed in the text.

Lesson 4 Fungi

As YOU Read!

What You'll Learn
- Characteristics of fungi
- How fungi reproduce
- Types of fungi

Why It's Important
Human life is affected by fungi.

Key Terms
- hyphae
- spores

Living things are either autotrophs (they make their own food) or heterotrophs (they eat other organisms). Fungi are heterotrophs. They do not produce their own food, but they don't eat other organisms as animals do. Fungi absorb nutrients from the remains of other organisms.

Fungi are decomposers. They break down complex materials in dead or decaying organisms. During this process, fungi absorb the nutrients they need. Fungi leave behind simpler materials other organisms can use.

Characteristics of Fungi

Most fungi are multicellular. Most fungi also have strands of cells called **hyphae.** Hyphae release chemicals that break down materials from the soil or from an organism on which the fungus feeds. Then the hyphae absorb the nutrients the fungus needs. Hyphae are often arranged in a weblike network stretching out from the body of the fungus.

Reproduction

All organisms have an instinct to keep their species alive and thriving. Reproduction is the process by which living things produce more of their own species. Different organisms have different ways of reproducing.

A mushroom cap is an example of a fungus reproductive body. This structure produces reproductive cells called **spores.** Each spore a fungus produces is able to grow into a new fungus. The reproductive body releases spores into the air. The spores may drop to the ground, or the wind may carry them away.

Fungi can also reproduce without spores. In multicellular fungi, hyphae can break off. They can then form a new network of cells. One-celled fungi can reproduce by dividing or budding. Budding occurs when an outgrowth of the parent cell separates to form a new cell.

Yeasts, Molds, and Mushrooms

You probably encounter some kind of fungi every day. There are three types of fungi. They are yeasts, molds, and mushrooms.

Yeasts are the simplest types of fungi. These one-celled organisms grow in moist places. They live in plant and animal tissues and in bathroom showers. Some yeasts are mixed with warm water, flour, and, sometimes, sugar to make bread dough. When the yeast breaks down the starches, the yeast releases gas. The gases make the bread dough rise.

Have you ever seen something fuzzy growing on bread or fruit? The hyphae of molds grow down into the food. The fuzzy parts are spores. You would probably throw out food with mold growing on it, but some molds are meant to be eaten. The *Penicillium* fungus is used to make blue cheese and some other cheeses.

The cap of a mushroom is the reproductive body. The cap is held up by a stalk. Both are filled with hyphae. If you see a cluster of mushrooms, those mushrooms probably come from the same mass of hyphae.

◄ One mushroom can produce a billion spores.

Harmful and Helpful Fungi

Fungi play an important role in ecosystems. Without fungi, organic matter would not decay. Wastes would pile up. Plants would not be able to grow without the nutrients fungi return to the soil.

Some molds are responsible for disease in plants and animals. A mold called *Cryphonectria parasitica* arrived from Asia more than a hundred years ago. This mold causes a fungal disease known as chestnut blight. By 1940, the fungus had killed most of the chestnut trees in the United States. In humans, the itchy skin condition called athlete's foot is caused by a moldlike fungus.

Lesson Assessment

Review

1. **Define** What are hyphae, and what do they do?

2. **List** Name three ways a fungus can reproduce. Name three kinds of fungi.

3. **Compare and Contrast** How are yeasts different from molds and mushrooms?

Critical Thinking

You know that fungi can be helpful or harmful. You know a mushroom is a fungus. There are many kinds of mushrooms. Do you think they're all edible? Why or why not?

Writing in Science

How do fungi benefit plants? How do fungi harm plants?

Lesson 5 — Plants

Reading Skills and Strategies

- Use higher-order thinking skills.
- Review text connections, text structure, multipart words, and word-learning strategies.

As YOU Read!

What You'll Learn

- What characteristics plants share
- How plants transport materials
- How plants produce food
- How plants control gas exchange and water loss

Why It's Important

Plants are critical to the survival of humans and other animals.

Key Terms

- vascular system
- xylem
- phloem
- photosynthesis

There are about 260,000 different species of plants. They inhabit every continent, including Antarctica. Some plants are equipped to live in hot, damp jungles. Others are better suited to life in a desert or in the frozen tundra. Plants make up a large part of nearly every type of habitat.

Plant Characteristics

Plants share several characteristics. Plants are multicellular organisms. Plant cells have a cell wall and a nucleus. Plants make their own food.

Transportation

Most plants are vascular. That means they have an internal pipeline that carries materials from one part of the plant to another. Below the ground, the root system absorbs water and nutrients from the soil. Above the ground, leaves make food for the plant. Stems deliver needed materials to different parts of the plant.

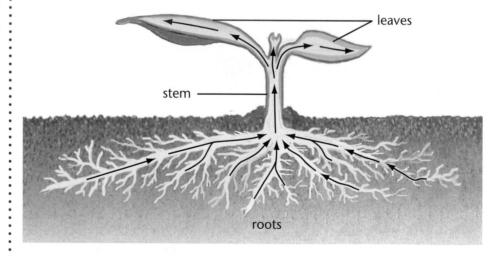

leaves

stem

roots

▶ A plant's root system reaches beneath the soil to absorb nutrients and water. These nutrients are carried up to all parts of the plant.

Plants with roots, stems, and leaves move materials through a network of long, tube-shaped cells. This network is called a **vascular system.** The cells of the vascular system form tissues. These tissues run in bundles from the leaves to the roots.

Materials flow in two directions. They flow up from the roots and down from the leaves. **Xylem** is the tissue that carries water and nutrients up from the roots. **Phloem** transports food produced in the leaves down to other parts of the plant. Phloem cells are smaller than xylem cells, but both types of cells are shaped like pipes. Xylem and phloem tissues have long fibers. These fibers support the plant and the cells that store food.

Food Production

Plants use the energy in sunlight to produce sugars. This process is called **photosynthesis.** Plant cells have chloroplasts, which contain chlorophyll. Chlorophyll absorbs light energy from the sun. Plant cells use carbon dioxide, water, and light to change light energy into sugars. As a result, plants use the sugars for energy to grow and reproduce. Extra sugars are converted to starch and stored in the stems. In addition to sugars, oxygen is also an important product of photosynthesis.

Gas Exchange and Water Loss

Plants need just the right balance of water and carbon dioxide for photosynthesis to occur. Tiny openings allow carbon dioxide, oxygen, and water to move into and out of leaves. The right amount of carbon dioxide must enter the leaves without letting too much water exit the leaves.

Sunny or windy weather causes water to evaporate from the leaves. To help prevent water loss, leaves and stems have a waxy coating that keeps moisture inside the plant. Another way plants hold on to water is by closing the openings in the leaves.

Plant Growth

Most animals stop growing after they reach adulthood. Plants keep growing until they die. Cells at the ends of the roots and stems multiply quickly. New cells cause the roots and stems to branch out and grow longer and thicker. Growth tissue in the stems produces buds that develop into leaves.

◄ A bristlecone pine may live for more than four thousand years.

Lesson Assessment

Review

1. **List** Name three characteristics of plants.

2. **Compare and Contrast** Explain the similarities and differences between xylem and phloem.

3. **Explain** How do plants produce food?

4. **Explain** What helps plants reduce water loss?

5. **Compare and Contrast** How does growth in plants differ from growth in animals?

Critical Thinking

Why are plants important to animals' survival? Give two reasons.

Writing in Science

Observe a plant, and record detailed observations about the plant's structure.

Unit 6
> **Science**

Reading Skills and Strategies
- Monitor comprehension.
- Use word-learning strategies.

Lesson 1 Invertebrates

As YOU Read!

What You'll Learn
- Traits animals share
- Characteristics of invertebrates

Why It's Important
Invertebrates are the most numerous group of animals on Earth.

Key Terms
- invertebrates
- sponges
- sessile
- larva

Types of Animals

There are many different kinds of animals on Earth. There are fish, lions, rats, and lizards. But what characteristics do these organisms have in common that make them animals?

We know animals don't make their own food. They are consumers. We also know animals have specialized cells. Another trait all animals share is the ability to interact with the environment and with other animals.

Invertebrates

Most species in the animal kingdom fall into two main groups. One group is animals with backbones. The other group is animals without backbones. Animals that do not have backbones are called **invertebrates.**

Invertebrates make up more than 90 percent of all animal species. Invertebrates are typically small because they lack a bony skeleton to support their bodies. However, ocean-dwelling invertebrates can grow large

▶ The ocean is home to a great variety of animals.

because their weight is supported by the water. For example, some larger species of invertebrates include squids and octopuses.

Other invertebrates include insects, shellfish, worms, and many other types of organisms. The category of invertebrates is very diverse. It is so diverse it can be divided into six smaller groups, including mollusks, cnidarians, arthropods, worms, echinoderms, and sponges.

Mollusks

Mollusks are able to move around because they have a muscular foot. The mollusk uses this fleshy limb to travel from place to place and to find food. You can find mollusks on land. Snails and slugs are mollusks that live on land. You can also find mollusks in water. Octopuses and clams are mollusks that live in water.

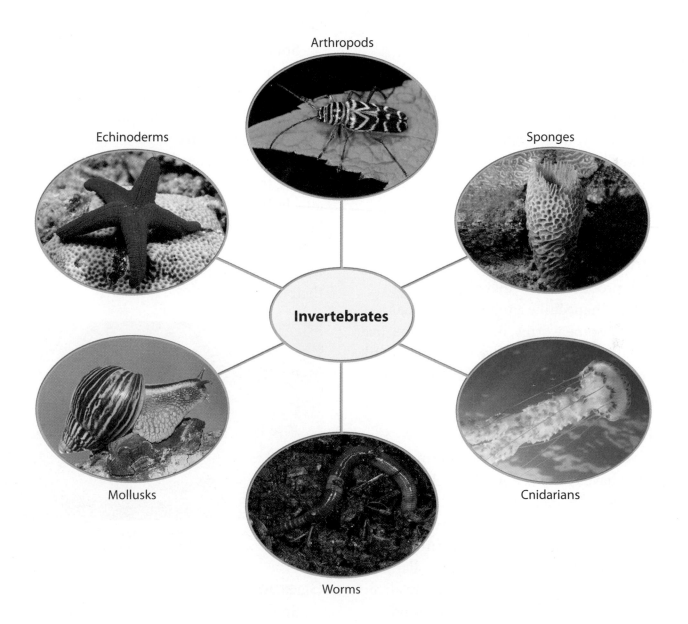

Arthropods

Echinoderms

Sponges

Invertebrates

Mollusks

Cnidarians

Worms

Cnidarians

Have you ever seen jellyfish? They drift in the ocean. Many are almost transparent. But if you look closely, you'll see that jellyfish have a central opening, and this opening is surrounded by tentacles. Jellyfish are one kind of cnidarian. Other cnidarians include corals and sea anemones. Cnidarians use their central opening to eat food and eliminate wastes. All cnidarians live in water.

Arthropods

An arthropod can live in many places. This is because all arthropods have legs. These legs allow arthropods to walk on land and also crawl underwater. Some arthropods also have wings that allow them to fly. Examples of arthropods include spiders, centipedes, insects, and lobsters. A beetle is one kind of insect.

Worms

You probably know that a worm is an organism shaped like a tube. A worm has a soft body. Some worms, like earthworms, live in the soil. Other worms live underwater. Still other worms, called tapeworms, live inside other animals.

Echinoderms

If you've ever seen an echinoderm, you may not have realized it was alive. It may have looked like a seashell. An echinoderm is an invertebrate sea animal with a hard, spiny covering or skin and a central opening that takes in food. For example, a sand dollar is an echinoderm. When sand dollars are alive, they're green, soft, and fuzzy. When sand dollars die, they become hard and white, like seashells. A starfish is also an echinoderm.

Sponges

Of all the invertebrates, sponges are the simplest. Sponges get their food by filtering it from the water they live in. There is a lot more to learn about sponges. You will learn what sponges are made of, where they live, and how they reproduce.

Sponges: Simple Creatures

Sponges are some of the simplest invertebrates. Sponges today look much the same as they did millions of years ago. There are about five thousand species of sponges. They all live in water. Like many simple invertebrates, sponges are **sessile** during their adult lives. That means they attach themselves to one place and stay there. Sponges do not have a mouth, eyes, or legs to help them get food. They filter food particles from the water that passes through holes in their bodies.

▲ A sea sponge attaches itself to one place. The sponge then remains in that place for the rest of its life.

Specialized Cells

Sponges do not have tissues or organs, but they do have special cells to perform certain activities. One type of cell forms the openings, called pores, on the surface of the sponge. Water flows into the pores. Other cells form hairlike structures that move water through the sponge. Another type of cell acts like a filter to gather tiny organisms and to take oxygen from the water. Special cells digest the food particles. Then the water is pushed out of the sponge through a large vent.

Reproduction

Sponges reproduce in two ways. One way they reproduce is to form buds on the parent sponge. The buds break off and float away. The tiny sponge buds attach to an object underwater and grow to adult size.

Sponges can also reproduce by releasing larvae into the water. A **larva** is an immature form of an organism. Sponge larvae swim away from the parent sponge. Then they find a suitable underwater surface and attach to it.

▲ Larvae leave a parent sponge to find homes elsewhere.

Lesson Assessment

Review

1. **List** What four characteristics do animals share?

2. **Describe** What are the six groups of invertebrates?

3. **Define** What does *sessile* mean?

4. **Explain** How do sponges obtain food?

Critical Thinking

What invertebrates might you encounter as a deep-sea diver?

Writing in Science

Invertebrates make up about 90 percent of all animal species.
Make a graph showing the number of invertebrate species compared to all other animal species.

Lesson 2 Fish

As YOU Read!

What You'll Learn
- Characteristics of vertebrates
- Characteristics of fish
- Three types of fish

Why It's Important
Fish are a diverse group of organisms that make up about half of all vertebrate species.

Key Terms
- vertebrate
- endoskeleton
- cartilage
- scales

Vertebrates

If your teacher asked you to name five animals, you would probably name vertebrates. Mammals, birds, reptiles, amphibians, and fish are all vertebrates. A **vertebrate** has a backbone that supports its body.

Vertebrates have bony skeletons inside their body called **endoskeletons.** This makes vertebrates capable of a wide range of movements. Vertebrates have more complex body systems than invertebrates. Vertebrates' special cells form tissues, organs, and organ systems. Bones in the endoskeleton protect organs such as the heart and brain. Although people are more familiar with vertebrates, vertebrates make up only about 5 percent of all animal species.

Fish

There are more than forty thousand vertebrate species. About half of them are fish. All fish live in water. They have several traits that help them survive in this environment. Fish have streamlined bodies and fins. Their bodies and fins help them move through water.

Fish get oxygen from water through their gills. The oxygen then enters the bloodstream. Carbon dioxide is flushed out through the gill slits. Many fish also have a swim bladder. This gas-filled bag keeps fish afloat in the water.

Lampreys and Hagfish

Jawless fish are the simplest type of fish. This group consists of about seventy species of lampreys and hagfishes. Jawless fish have tube-shaped bodies without stomachs. Jawless fish lack hinged jaws. In the mouth is a round sucker surrounded by sharp teeth.

▲ A lamprey is a jawless fish. It attaches its round, sucker mouth to another animal and sucks tissue from that animal for food.

A jawless fish feeds by attaching its mouth to another animal and sucking the tissue. Lampreys are parasites. Hagfish feed only on dead animals.

Sharks, Skates, and Rays

Some types of fish have endoskeletons made of cartilage instead of bone. **Cartilage** is a strong, flexible tissue that provides support. Sharks, skates, and rays have cartilage. These fish are covered with rough, toothlike scales. They have no swim bladder to keep them afloat. They must keep swimming to avoid sinking.

Sharks are some of the most effective predators on Earth. However, the two largest species of sharks filter tiny organisms from water for food. These sharks are the basking shark and the whale shark. Skates and rays have flat bodies. Their fins extend from their bodies like wings. They live mainly on the ocean floor.

Bony Fishes

The most diverse group of fish is the bony fishes. They make up about 96 percent of all fish species. They have bony endoskeletons and swim bladders. They are covered with small, thin, overlapping plates called **scales.** Bony fish range in size from huge, two-ton sunfish to tiny gobies less than half an inch long.

▲ The whale shark is the largest species of shark. Whale sharks are not predators. They filter small organisms from water for food.

▶ Rays have flat bodies and winglike fins that allow them to live mainly on the ocean floor.

Lesson Assessment

Review

1. **Define** What does *endoskeleton* mean?

2. **List** Give one characteristic of each group of fish.

3. **Explain** How do jawless fish eat?

Critical Thinking

Fossils of sharks from millions of years ago look very similar to sharks of today. Why?

Writing in Science

Write a paragraph comparing and contrasting fish with cartilage endoskeletons and bony fish.

Lesson 3

Amphibians and Reptiles

As YOU Read!

What You'll Learn

■ Characteristics of amphibians

■ Characteristics of reptiles

■ What it means to be ectothermic

Why It's Important

Amphibians and reptiles were the first animals to adapt to life on land.

Key Terms

■ amphibians

■ metamorphosis

■ reptiles

■ ectothermic

Amphibians

Amphibians spend at least part of their lives in water. They have sensory organs and legs designed for use on land as well. They take in oxygen through their skin and also use their lungs for respiration.

Amphibians prefer life in damp environments. Some amphibians, like bullfrogs, stay in or near the water all their lives. Other kinds of frogs, as well as salamanders and toads, live in moist, wooded areas, in damp caves, or near streams.

Respiration

In order for amphibians to exchange gases through their skin, their skin must be moist. Most adult amphibians also use their lungs to breathe. Air enters an amphibian's nostrils, which are small openings above the mouth. The air moves into the lungs. Blood cells carry oxygen to tissues in the amphibian's body. The blood carries carbon dioxide back to the lungs, where it is exhaled.

Life Cycle

Young amphibians look quite different from adults. Amphibians go through a **metamorphosis,** or series of changes, as they develop. Amphibians hatch from eggs laid in the water. When they hatch, they are called larvae. They have gills and long tails but no legs. The larvae go through a process of development. They lose their fishlike characteristics and acquire traits better suited for life on land.

▲ Woodland salamanders live in wet areas—in woods, in caves, and near streams. Salamanders need moist skin to survive.

Reptiles

Reptiles are closely related to amphibians. The main difference is that reptiles are completely suited to living on land. Like amphibians, reptiles have sensory organs and two pairs of legs for use on land. Reptiles get oxygen through lungs. They have dry, rather than moist, skin. They lay their eggs on land. Most species don't need to live in or near water to survive.

▲ Alligators lay their eggs on land. What characteristics do all reptile eggs have?

Specialized Traits

Reptiles have thick, dry, scaly skin made of the same substance as your fingernails. Their thick skin helps protect them from predators. Such thick skin prevents them from taking in water through their skin. Thick skin also helps reduce moisture loss.

Because reptiles lay eggs on land, the eggs must withstand hot, dry conditions. Reptile eggs are enclosed in a strong case so the eggs don't dry out. Inside the eggs, offspring have everything they need to survive until it's time to hatch.

Offspring

Reptiles do not go through metamorphosis. Young reptiles hatch from their eggs looking much like adults. Some species, such as alligators, closely guard the eggs and care for their young. Others, such as sea turtles, leave as soon as the eggs are laid.

Body Temperature

Amphibians and reptiles can't regulate their body temperature. They are **ectothermic,** which means their body temperature rises and falls as the temperature in their surroundings rises and falls. These animals are often called "cold-blooded." Amphibians and reptiles tend to stay in places where the temperature is fairly constant.

Lesson Assessment

Review

1. **Identify** What are two ways amphibians obtain oxygen?

2. **Describe** What is the process a frog goes through during metamorphosis?

3. **Explain** What are two benefits of thick, dry reptile skin?

Critical Thinking

- What similarities and differences do amphibian and reptile offspring have?

- Would you expect to see amphibians sunning themselves on a warm day? Why or why not?

Writing in Science

Write a summary of the characteristics that suit amphibians and reptiles for living on land.

Lesson 4 Birds

As YOU Read!

What You'll Learn
- How birds fly
- How birds maintain their internal body temperature
- How birds reproduce and care for their young

Why It's Important
Birds contribute beauty and benefits to the environment.

Key Terms
- migrate
- endothermic
- incubation

Flight

In addition to wings, birds have a number of adaptations that make flight possible. Wing feathers are shaped to help birds take off and glide. Many of the bones in a bird's endoskeleton are hollow. This makes the bones lighter. Flying uses a lot of energy, so birds need a lot of oxygen moving through their bodies. Air flows through air sacs and lungs to give birds a constant supply of oxygen.

Flight gives birds many advantages. They can search for food over a larger area than flightless animals can. They can escape predators on the ground. They can also build nests out of predators' reach. Some bird species **migrate,** or travel long distances, to spend part of the year in an area with more resources. During cold months, birds migrate to warmer climates where more food is available.

▶ An albatross flies for days or weeks at a time over large areas of open water. Its wingspan may reach eleven feet.

Maintaining Body Temperature and Converting Energy

Reptiles and amphibians are ectothermic, which means their internal body temperature depends on the temperature of their surroundings. Birds are **endothermic.** This means they maintain a constant internal body temperature regardless of the temperature in the environment.

Converting Energy

Birds and other endotherms convert the chemical energy in food into heat energy. To maintain body temperature, birds eat more than ectotherms such as snakes and frogs. Birds in colder climates must generate more heat and eat more food than birds in warmer climates. Birds must also eat more in cold weather than in warm weather.

Warming Up, Cooling Down

Birds use both physical adaptations and behavior to maintain their body temperature. An outer layer of feathers protects birds from getting wet. A soft inner layer of feathers keeps birds warm. Birds also warm up by shivering. The muscle contractions generate body heat. When birds are hot, they release heat by fluffing out their feathers. Birds also rest in the shade on hot, sunny days.

Offspring

Before birds reproduce, they select a mate. Typically, the female chooses the male. Many species make elaborate displays to attract a suitable mate. The males of some species have brightly colored feathers. Others perform high-flying aerobatics. Some males bring gifts of food or shiny objects to females.

▲ Male peacocks display their colorful feathers to attract females for mating.

Like reptiles, birds lay eggs in nests. After mating, birds build nests for the eggs. The eggs must be kept warm for the offspring inside to develop. One of the parents sits on the eggs. Its body heat keeps the eggs warm. This process is called **incubation.**

After the eggs hatch, one or both parents care for the young. Birds can't fly when they first hatch. They can't get their own food. Some species of birds hatch without feathers or the ability to see. Other species hatch at a later stage of development. These young require less care.

Lesson Assessment

Review

1. **Identify** What are some traits birds have that enable them to fly?

2. **Explain** How do birds generate body heat?

3. **Describe** Give examples of ways birds control their body temperature.

Critical Thinking

Instead of building their own nests, some birds lay eggs in the nests of other birds. Do you think this is a good strategy? Why or why not?

Writing in Science

- Write a paragraph to compare and contrast birds and reptiles.

- Observe a nest of bird eggs hatching, or watch a video of such an event. How do the young birds look and act? Write your observations.

Reading Skills and Strategies
- Use higher-order thinking skills.
- Review text connections, text structure, multipart words, and word-learning strategies.

Lesson 5: Mammals

As YOU Read!

What You'll Learn
- What environments mammals live in
- How mammals maintain body temperature
- How mammals care for their young

Why It's Important
Humans are mammals. We can learn about ourselves by studying other mammals.

Key Terms
- mammals
- placenta
- gestation

Mammals are animals that are probably most familiar to you. After all, *you* are a mammal. What do you have in common with other mammals? All **mammals** have hair, at least during some part of their lives. Each species of mammal produces milk to feed its young. Most mammals have teeth for chewing certain kinds of foods.

Mammalian Adaptations

There are fewer than five thousand species of mammals. They live in a wide variety of environments on land and in water. Mammals have special traits, or adaptations, to help them survive in different habitats. For example, a beaver's tail is shaped like a paddle that pushes the beaver through the water as it swims. Gibbons, a type of ape, spend almost all their lives in trees. They have long arms that help them swing quickly and easily through the branches.

Special Characteristics

Like birds, mammals are endotherms. They use the food they eat to generate body heat. Endotherms keep a constant internal body temperature. They stay active during cold weather.

▲ Beavers are mammals and have special tails that help them swim.

▲ Gibbons have long, strong arms that aid them in swinging through trees.

Most mammals are covered with hair or fur. Outer hair protects mammals from getting wet. Hairs underneath are soft and fluffy. Other types of hair, called whiskers, are sensory structures that improve a mammal's sense of touch. Some mammals have a small amount of hair. Others have hair at only one stage of development.

Mammals in cold environments need more than a thick coat of hair to keep warm. This is especially true for ocean mammals that don't have fur to protect them from cold water.

▲ A whale is not a fish. It's a mammal! Whales have an extra layer of fat, or blubber, that keeps them warm in frigid water.

Some mammals survive cold or dry conditions by hibernating. These mammals stock up on energy by eating a lot of food in the weeks or months before they hibernate. They store these extra calories as body fat. Hibernating mammals live off this stored fat during their inactive period.

Preparing for Offspring

The offspring of mammals develop inside the mother's body. The offspring receive nutrients and oxygen from the mother's blood through an organ called the **placenta.** The placenta transports necessary materials to the offspring and carries waste from the offspring to the mother's body.

Different species have different periods of **gestation.** Gestation is the time of development within the mother's body. Elephants have a gestation period of almost twenty-two months. In contrast, the gestation period of rabbits is about one month. However, the spiny anteater and the platypus do not give birth to live young. Their offspring develop in eggs.

Mammals feed their new offspring milk produced by the mother. Some young mammals drink their mother's milk for many months. Others nurse for a much shorter time.

Lesson Assessment

Review

1. **List** What are three functions of hair?

2. **Explain** How do mammals stay warm in cold environments?

3. **Describe** How do the young of mammals survive before birth?

Critical Thinking

• Compare and contrast the diversity of mammals with the diversity of fish.

Writing in Science

In a paragraph, summarize how mammals care for their young after birth.

Lesson 1

Ecosystems

Reading Skills and Strategies

- Monitor comprehension.
- Use a glossary.
- Use a dictionary.

As YOU Read!

What You'll Learn

- What an ecosystem is
- The living parts of ecosystems
- The nonliving parts of ecosystems

Why It's Important

Ecology shows how living things depend on one another.

Key Terms

- ecosystem
- ecology
- biotic factors
- abiotic factors

Living Things and the Environment

An **ecosystem** can be defined as all the living and nonliving things in an area. The nonliving parts of an ecosystem are light, air, soil, and water. These nonliving parts support the living things in an ecosystem.

Plants, animals, and other living things form an ecosystem's community. The study of the relationships between living things and their environment is called **ecology,** and this study has resulted in the conclusion that members of a community depend on one another for survival. In other words, ecosystems must maintain a balance of living and nonliving resources.

Imagine you build a tower out of blocks. Each block is placed on another block beneath it until you reach the top and the building is complete. If you removed one of the blocks from the middle of the building, what would happen? The entire building would collapse. This is like the way an ecosystem works. All living things are linked together in an ecosystem—sunlight and soil are linked to plants, which are linked to animals, and so on. If one of these things in an existing ecosystem is suddenly removed or disturbed in some way, the building may come tumbling down.

▲ What living things can you find in this ecosystem?

Organisms in an Ecosystem

The living parts of an ecosystem are called **biotic factors.** Biotic factors include plants, animals, bacteria, fungi, protists, and algae. All consumers depend on other organisms for food. Plants use nutrients in the soil that come from decayed organisms.

In some ways, plants are the foundation of an ecosystem. The plants in an area determine which consumers will live there. Plants also affect some of the nonliving parts of an ecosystem—plant roots hold soil in place, and plants take in carbon dioxide and put oxygen into the air.

Animals also play important roles in an ecosystem. Animals can change an ecosystem by overgrazing, which causes soil to erode. If animals overhunt, this changes the populations of other species in an ecosystem. When a beaver builds a dam, the flow of the river changes, and this affects other organisms in the river ecosystem.

Nonliving Parts of an Ecosystem

Water, light, air, and soil are **abiotic factors,** or nonliving parts of the environment. The temperature of the air or the water is also an abiotic factor. Another is the minerals in the soil. Minerals are important because they are the basic framework of soil. Minerals include substances, such as tin and salt, that are formed naturally in rocks and in the earth. Each abiotic factor affects the organisms in an ecosystem.

Sunlight

It's hard to imagine life on Earth without light. The sun warms Earth's surface and atmosphere. The sun also gives light, which plants use to make food through photosynthesis.

Because of photosynthesis, plants need a certain amount of sunlight to live. For example, a cactus could not live in a cool, dark forest, and a fern could not live in a hot, sunny desert.

Yet there are ecosystems that do exist without sunlight. Deep beneath the ocean's surface, some fish don't even have eyes. There is no light to see by; these organisms have developed other ways to survive. On the other hand, on the sea's surface where sunlight is plentiful, some organisms live by feeding on surface debris that relies specifically on sunlight to exist.

Water

Water is necessary for all living things. Without water, humans will die in a few days. Other animals and plants need water just as badly.

Living things are made of cells, and cells need water to carry out the activities of life. For example, plants need water for photosynthesis to occur. Animals need water for cell functions.

In land ecosystems, more water means more plants will live there. More plants mean more animals. For this reason, tropical rain forests are Earth's most varied ecosystems. Far fewer species live in desert ecosystems, where water is scarce and plants and animals must learn to survive with what little moisture they can find.

► Water is a precious resource. In this African ecosystem, animals gather around a watering hole to sustain life.

Soil

Soil contains minerals and nutrients plants and animals need to live. First, plants obtain chemicals from the soil through their roots. Second, animals obtain these chemicals when they eat plants. Third, humans obtain minerals and nutrients when they eat plants or animals.

The amounts of minerals, nutrients, and water in soil affect plant growth and survival. Soil with a high number of decomposing organisms—that is, living things that break down dead plants and animals—is especially fertile soil. Most plants are best suited for growing in a particular type of soil, whether it is sandy, moist, or clay.

Sandy soil is made up of individualized bits of rock or minerals. These rocks and minerals have been finely ground into the sometimes soft powder you may walk on at the beach. Sandy soil does not hold water well, as the water pours through it too readily.

Moist soil, called silt, contains a great deal of decaying plant matter. This type of soil is a good choice for plants that need lots of water.

The particles in clay soil are very fine, but they are packed so tightly together that it is difficult for water to travel through.

Highs and Lows

Many organisms can survive only within a certain range of temperatures. If the temperature in an ecosystem is too high, certain plants won't grow. For example, in a climate where temperatures never reach freezing, early-flowering bulbs must be chilled in a refrigerator for several weeks before planting. Where temperatures are too low, some plants will die. Orchids, for example, will stop growing and may die if the temperature falls below 50 degrees.

▲ Some like it cold.

▲ Some like it hot.

Because reptiles and amphibians are cold-blooded, they must live in a climate where the temperature does not reach extremes. Reptiles and amphibians must live in ecosystems in which the temperature is high enough to keep their bodies active.

Endotherms, such as birds, whose bodies maintain a constant temperature, have special adaptations that help them live in warm or cold climates.

◄ Reindeer must rely on their abundant fur to protect them in the cold, snowy ecosystem where they live.

Review

1. **Identify** Name three biotic factors that might be found in a forest ecosystem.

2. **List** What are four abiotic factors?

3. **Explain** How do plants affect an ecosystem?

Critical Thinking

- What kind of organisms might live in a cave ecosystem? How could they survive without light?

- What would happen if it did not rain in a rain forest for a month?

- How does a desert ecosystem change during a rainy season?

Writing in Science

Draw a diagram of an ecosystem. Label the biotic and abiotic factors. Write a title for your diagram.

Lesson 2

Energy in Ecosystems

Reading Skills and Strategies

- Monitor comprehension.
- Use a glossary.
- Use a dictionary.

As YOU Read!

What You'll Learn

- The roles of producers and consumers
- What a food chain is
- How a food web works

Why It's Important

In nature, the majority of organisms are food for other living things.

Key Terms

- producers
- consumers
- food chain
- food web

All life functions require energy. The food you digest contains chemical energy that is released when your body digests the food. You use the energy to walk, breathe, think, and sleep. Most of the energy organisms use comes from the sun.

Producers and Consumers

In order for living things to use the energy from the sun, organisms must be able to capture the energy and convert it to a usable form. This is the role of **producers** in an ecosystem. Plants, algae, and some types of bacteria utilize energy from the sun to produce sugars. This process is photosynthesis. When other organisms eat producers, the chemical energy stored in the sugars is released.

Consumers cannot produce their own food. They must eat, or consume, other organisms to live. A consumer that eats producers is called a primary consumer. A consumer that eats a primary consumer is called a secondary consumer. There can be many levels of consumers in an ecosystem. For example, a plant-eating insect is a primary consumer. A bird that eats the insect is a secondary consumer. The bird is eaten by a fox. The fox is a third-level consumer, or a tertiary consumer.

Modeling Energy Transfer

Energy can't be created, and it doesn't disappear. It changes form and moves between parts of an ecosystem. This movement of energy is called energy transfer. Living things transfer some of their energy when other organisms eat them. Models are useful for understanding feeding relationships and energy transfer between organisms.

Food Chains

A **food chain** is a model that shows the path of energy as nutrients move from one organism to another. In a meadow ecosystem, the first link in the food chain is a plant, such as grass.

The next link is a consumer that eats the grass, such as a cricket. The next link in the chain is another consumer that eats the cricket, such as a spider. The last link is a bird that eats the spider.

Food Webs

Ecosystems usually contain several overlapping food chains that together form a **food web.** A food web is a complex model. It shows the different feeding relationships among organisms. Food webs usually have multiple producers, and consumers often eat more than one type of organism. Consumers may also be eaten by more than one type of organism. For example, other producers in a meadow include flowers and shrubs. Many birds, mammals, and insects feed on these plants. Larger birds and insects may feed on the plants and on the primary consumers. A fox may feed on a rabbit, a primary consumer, and also on a secondary consumer, such as a bird.

Availability of Energy

In a food chain, an animal passes on only about 10 percent of the energy it receives from food. The rest is utilized by the animal for its body functions or is released as heat from the animal's body. As energy passes through a food chain, there is less energy available at each level. As the available energy decreases, so does the number of organisms in the feeding level.

A Meadow Food Chain

◀ In this food chain, the arrows indicate the flow of energy from one organism to another.

◀ How do these animals fit into a food chain?

Lesson Assessment

Review

1. **Explain** How does energy enter an ecosystem?

2. **Describe** What is the relationship between producers and consumers?

Critical Thinking

- Why are there fewer hawks than sparrows in a meadow ecosystem?

- What would happen if a primary consumer was removed from an ecosystem?

Writing in Science

Write a paragraph comparing and contrasting food chains and food webs.

Reading Skills and Strategies

- Monitor comprehension.
- Use a glossary.
- Use a dictionary.

Lesson 3 Biomes

As YOU Read!

What You'll Learn

- Characteristics of biomes
- How climate affects biotic and abiotic factors in ecosystems

Why It's Important

Understanding biomes helps you understand why organisms live in certain places.

Key Terms

- climate
- biome
- deciduous
- temperate

What is the climate where you live? **Climate** can be defined as the weather patterns and temperature ranges of a large area. Temperature and rainfall determine the plants, animals, and other organisms that reside in a place. What plants and animals live in your area?

A **biome** is a large area with a common climate; it is home to similar types of plants and animals. A biome is not a particular place but rather a set of abiotic factors that allow certain organisms to live there. Abiotic factors include rainfall, sunlight, and temperature.

Biomes: Cold, Hot, and Wet

The ground in the tundra biome is permanently frozen just below the surface; this layer of frozen soil is called permafrost. The permafrost prevents large plants and trees from taking root. Plants found in the tundra include mosses, grasses, and small shrubs. Rodents and caribou feed on the plants, and snowy owls and arctic foxes are two species that feed on the primary consumers.

▲ The tundra biome is permanently frozen beneath the surface.

▲ Coniferous trees cover the land in taiga biomes.

Temperatures in the taiga biome are nearly as low as in the tundra. However, there is more precipitation. Snow covers the ground much of the year and insulates the soil, which allows coniferous, or evergreen, trees to thrive. Taiga ecosystems support a wider variety of animal life than the tundra.

Desert biomes can be hot or cold. One thing they have in common is a dry climate with little rainfall. Because water is scarce in the desert, plants usually grow far apart. They also have shallow roots to absorb water quickly when it rains. Desert animals survive the dry climate because their bodies are designed to use water efficiently.

◄ Desert biomes may be hot, like the one on the left, or cold, like the one on the right.

The open spaces of grassland biomes receive enough rainfall to support many types of grasses and flowering plants. Compared to deserts, grassland ecosystems are home to a great variety of species, including such grazing animals as bison and zebras. North American grasslands have cold winters and hot summers. African grasslands are located in the tropics.

◄ Bison graze in this grasslands biome.

Forest Biomes

Forest biomes receive more rainfall than any other biome. **Deciduous** trees do well in climates with plenty of rain. These trees drop their leaves and enter a dormant phase during cold, dry weather.

Temperate forests of North America, Europe, and Asia contain many species of broadleaf trees. In regions with cold winters, the leaves change color and drop as winter approaches. Temperatures in this biome tend to be higher than in the grasslands. These ecosystems also support a greater number of species than grasslands.

The tropical rain forest biome receives more rain than any other biome. Rain forests are located near the equator, where temperatures are high year-round. The abundant rainfall and high temperatures support more species than any other biome. Trees may grow to two hundred feet. Some trees may drop their leaves during dry weather.

Lesson Assessment

Review

1. **Define** What is a biome?

2. **Identify** What abiotic factors influence a biome's climate?

3. **List** Name five biomes.

Critical Thinking

• What do tundra, taiga, and desert biomes have in common?

• Explain how a grassland biome could become a desert biome.

Writing in Science

Write a paragraph to compare and contrast temperate forests and tropical rain forests.

Reading Skills and Strategies

- Monitor comprehension.
- Use a glossary.
- Use a dictionary.

Lesson 4

Groups in the Environment

The biotic and abiotic factors in the environment interact in different ways. These various interactions result in different levels of organization within each environment. At the top of this organization is the biome, followed by the ecosystem, the community, the population, and the organism. Let's begin at the bottom of the pyramid.

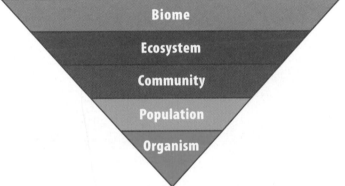

Levels of the Environment

Biome

Ecosystem

Community

Population

Organism

Organism

A **species** is the smallest level of classification of living things. Organisms belong to the same species based on shared traits. Belonging to a species also means organisms can reproduce and their offspring will be able to reproduce.

Population

Members of a species need the same kinds of resources to live. They live in places where they can meet their needs. All individual organisms of a species in a particular area make up a **population.** If some members of the species live in a different area, they belong to a different population.

Populations form spatial and seasonal patterns, which means some organisms in a population are spaced far apart so they don't compete for resources. Organisms of other populations live close together. Living close together helps protect organisms from predators. When many members of a population live together, more individuals are available to raise the young. Populations may increase or decrease depending on the time of year.

Community

All the populations in an area make up a **community.** We usually think of a community as a group of people living in a certain area, but in ecology, a community is composed of *all* the living things in an area. These living things include plants, animals, bacteria, fungi, and protists. Many species interact with one another in a community. A forest community might include trees, owls, chipmunks, mosses, mushrooms, bacteria, and other organisms.

Ecosystem and Biome

An ecosystem is made up of all living things and nonliving things in an area. A biome is a larger area with a single climate. Each biome on Earth contains many ecosystems.

Habitat and Niche

A habitat is the living space of a species. Organisms can find everything they need in their habitat, including food, water, shelter, and mates. Some species can live in more than one type of habitat, but typically there is only one habitat in which a species is most successful. For example, some organisms, such as rock doves, have adapted to city living. Pandas, on the other hand, can live only in bamboo forests.

Living things in a habitat interact. For instance, a population of dragonflies depends on a population of butterflies for food, and the butterflies depend on a population of flowering plants. Each of these organisms fits into its habitat in a particular way. The position an organism fills in its habitat is its **niche.** In a food web, organisms are connected in different ways. An organism's place in a food web is one aspect of its niche in a habitat.

◀ Rock doves can live in a city habitat, but pandas can live only in a bamboo-forest habitat.

Reading Skills and Strategies

- Use higher-order thinking skills.
- Review text structure, comprehension monitoring, multipart words, and word-learning strategies.

Lesson 5 Interactions between Organisms

As YOU Read!

What You'll Learn

- How living things interact in an ecosystem
- How organisms compete for resources
- How organisms benefit from interactions

Why It's Important

To understand how ecosystems work, it's important to learn how organisms interact with each other.

Key Terms

- predator
- prey
- competition
- cooperation

Predator and Prey

A food web shows the movement of energy through an ecosystem. The relationships in a food chain show how organisms interact by eating other organisms or by being eaten. A **predator** is an animal that catches other animals and eats them. **Prey** are animals that are eaten by predators.

The interactions between predator and prey can affect conditions in an ecosystem. The availability of prey affects the population of predators. For example, when the prey population decreases, less food is available. Predator populations sometimes move from an area where prey is scarce to an area where prey is plentiful. Insect populations decrease in autumn in cool climates. For this reason, many insect-eating bird populations migrate to a warmer climate where more insects are available.

▶ These northern birds are migrating south for the winter.

Competition

All living things have the same needs: food, water, air, and space. When these resources are limited, organisms must compete with one another to obtain what they need to survive. **Competition** is the fight for resources that occurs among organisms.

Organisms compete for food when sources of food are limited. Scavengers, such as vultures and hyenas, compete with one another for the remains of dead animals. In a forest community, foxes and badgers compete for small prey, like mice. Elephants compete for trees and other plants in the dry African savanna.

Another type of competition, which occurs within a species, is the competition for a suitable mate. Males of many bird species compete for the attention of females. The male bowerbird builds an elaborate structure called a bower to attract a mate. First, the male gathers items to decorate the bower. Then he waits inside until a female appears. If the female approves of the bower, she will mate with him. After mating, she flies away to build a nest and lay eggs.

When there is competition for food, water, mates, or other resources, some living things claim a territory in which to meet their needs. Large predators, such as grizzly bears, use aggressive displays to keep distance between individuals. The roots of creosote bushes give off toxins that keep other plants from growing too close together in a desert habitat.

Cooperation

Cooperation is an interaction that benefits all the organisms involved. Typically, cooperation occurs only among members of the same species. Individuals work together toward a common goal, such as hunting, avoiding predators, or caring for young.

Some animals cooperate by living in groups. Living in a herd provides prey animals, such as zebras, some protection from predators. Families of monkeys and apes live together and help one another care for

▲ These primates work together to care for their young.

their young. Predators such as wolves and killer whales hunt in groups. Group hunting makes it easier to catch prey.

Insects such as ants live in social groups called colonies. Each member of the group has a specific job to perform to preserve the colony's survival. Tasks include gathering food, protecting the colony, maintaining the hive, and caring for larvae. Cooperation is an adaptation ants use to promote the survival of the colony.

Lesson Assessment

Review

1. Give one example of a predator and one of prey.

2. **List** What are some resources organisms compete for?

3. **Explain** What is one way organisms cooperate?

4. **Compare and Contrast** How does cooperation differ from competition? What do the two have in common?

Critical Thinking

Disease has wiped out most of the antelope population in a grassland habitat. Predict the effect this will have on the lion population in that habitat.

Writing in Science

Write a paragraph about the pros and cons of competition and cooperation.

Reading Skills and Strategies

- Use the SQ3R strategy.
- Use a dictionary.
- Use an online dictionary.

Lesson 1

Matter: Mass, Weight, and Volume

As YOU Read!

What You'll Learn

- What matter is
- The difference between mass and weight
- How to find the volume of solids

Why It's Important

All substances in the universe are made of matter.

Key Terms

- matter
- mass
- gravity
- weight
- volume
- water displacement

Imagine you're spending the day at the beach. You lie in the sand, splash in the water, blow up a beach ball, and shoo a seagull away from your lunch. All these objects—sand, water, air, seagull, and you—have one thing in common. All are made of matter.

▲ All substances are made of matter.

Matter

Every substance in the universe is made of matter, but what is matter? **Matter** is anything that takes up space. Living things, the sun, air, water, and all the objects around you are made of matter. You know something is made of matter if you can measure the amount of matter it contains. For example, you can measure the milk in a carton, the oxygen in a diver's tank, and the weight of your body.

Matter is everywhere, but not everything is made of matter. Light and sound are forms of energy, but they are not matter. You can't measure the amount of matter in light because light does not take up space. The same is true for sound. Both light and sound can travel through matter, but they are not made of matter.

Mass: The Amount of Matter

Mass is the amount of matter that makes up a substance. Objects of the same size do not always contain the same amount of matter. For example, a plastic cup and a glass cup may hold the same amount of milk, but the glass cup contains more matter than the plastic one. Usually a larger object has a greater mass than a smaller object, but sometimes the opposite is true. A bed pillow is larger than a brick, but which one, do you think, has more mass?

▲ Which pan contains more mass?

You can use a pan balance to compare the masses of objects. When objects are placed in the pans, the lower pan holds the object with more mass. Objects of the same mass will balance each other, and the pans will be level.

One way to determine the exact mass of an object is to use a beam balance. It is similar to a pan balance, but instead of comparing the masses of two objects, it compares the mass of a particular object to a standard mass. The object is placed in a pan on one end of the beam. Standard masses are positioned in a pan on the other end of the beam. Standard masses are added or subtracted in small increments until the beam is balanced. The amount of mass it takes to balance the beam equals the mass of the object.

The standard unit of mass is the kilogram (kg). Kilograms are used to express the masses of larger objects. The masses of smaller objects are measured in grams (g). A gram is 1/1000 of a kilogram, or 0.001 kg. The mass of a bag of sugar is about 2 kg; the mass of a paper clip is about 2 grams.

Weight: The Heaviness of Matter

Weight is a property of matter that is closely related to mass. Mass refers to the amount of matter something contains. Weight refers to how heavy something is. We feel the weight of objects because of gravity. **Gravity** pulls everything downward toward Earth, so **weight** is the force of the downward pull of gravity on an object. On Earth, the more mass an object has, the stronger gravity pulls on it. The weight of an object indicates how strongly the force of gravity is pulling on that object.

Now imagine you are on the moon, where the force of gravity is weaker than on Earth. Gravity on Earth is six times as strong as it is on the moon. As a result, objects on Earth feel heavier. Because an object's weight is determined by the pull of gravity on the object, less gravity means the object weighs less. Mass describes only the amount of matter an object has. Therefore, an object's mass is the same on Earth and on the moon, regardless of the pull of gravity.

Weight is measured in standard units called newtons (N). In the United States, the pound (lb) is used in everyday measurements. One newton is equal to about 0.22 pounds. A scale is used to measure weight. A spring scale measures weight by determining how hard an object is pushing or pulling on the spring. An object with a mass of 1 kg weighs 9.8 N, or about 2.2 lb. Therefore, on Earth, we can say that 1 kg equals about 2.2 lb.

Volume: The Space Matter Occupies

Have you ever turned a corner and walked into someone? The two of you bumped into each other because you both have mass, so you cannot occupy the same space. You, like all other forms of matter, take up space. **Volume** is the amount of space an object occupies. Everything that contains matter has volume; even air has volume. A balloon takes

▲ A spring scale measures the pull of gravity on objects.

up more space when it is inflated. The volume of the balloon is greater when the balloon is filled with air than when it's empty.

Unlike mass and weight, volume does not describe the amount of matter an object contains. Objects may have the same volume, even though their masses and weights are different. Imagine two identical shoe boxes.

One is empty, and one full of rocks. The empty box and the full box do not have the same mass or weight. However, the volume of the two boxes is the same because each box takes up the same amount of space.

Using Formulas to Measure Volume

There are two ways to determine volume. One method is used for objects with regular shapes, such as cubes and rectangular boxes. This method involves calculations using the measurements of the shape. You can measure three sides of a box to find the length, width, and height. Then you can multiply these three values to find the volume of the box: Volume = length × width × height.

The volume of a box is calculated by multiplying three dimensions. Length,

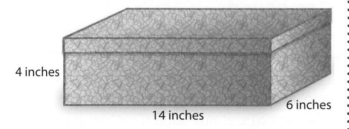

4 inches

6 inches

14 inches

▲ To find the volume of a box, you must know its length, width, and height.

width, and height are often measured in meters (m) or centimeters (cm). To find volume, all measurements must be in the same unit. When you multiply the values for length, width, and height, the unit of measurement is cubed, or raised to the third power. For example, to find the volume of a square block with sides measuring 3 cm each, multiply 3 cm × 3 cm × 3 cm. The volume of the block is 3 cm³, or 27 cubic cm.

The Water Displacement Method

There are formulas for calculating the volume of most regular shapes, such as spheres, cylinders, and pyramids. However, many objects do not have regular shapes. There aren't any formulas for these shapes.

Suppose you want to find the volume of a small rock. You can use the **water displacement** method. Put some water in a container with graduated measurements. Note the marking that shows the volume of the water. Add the rock. Note the marking that shows the new volume. Subtract the original volume of the water alone from the volume of the water and the rock together. The answer is the volume of the rock.

Lesson Assessment

Review

1. **Explain** How do you know that something is made of matter?

2. **Describe** How can you determine the mass of an object?

3. **Identify** What force determines the weight of an object?

4. **Analyze** Why do you need to use displacement to find the volume of an object with an irregular shape?

Critical Thinking

The volume of a 10-cm cube is 1000 cubic cm. A 12-cm cube has a volume of 1728 cubic cm. Each dimension of the larger cube is only 20 percent greater than that of the smaller cube, but the volume of the larger cube is almost 73 percent greater than that of the smaller cube. Why is there such a large difference in volume?

Writing in Science

Write a description of how you would feel on the moon. What could you do on the moon that you can't do on Earth?

Reading Skills and Strategies

- Use the SQ3R strategy.
- Use a dictionary.
- Use an online dictionary.

Lesson 2

Mixtures and Compounds

As YOU Read!

What You'll Learn

- What pure substances are
- How elements, atoms, and compounds are related
- What a mixture is
- How mixtures and compounds are similar and different

Why It's Important

Scientists study mixtures and compounds because most materials on Earth are made from a combination of matter.

Key Terms

- element
- atom
- compound
- mixture

Pure Matter and Mixed Matter

Pure matter is a substance made up of only one type of matter. Most substances are a combination of different kinds of matter. The water you drink is a combination of hydrogen and oxygen. It may also contain minerals and chemicals.

Elements

All matter is made up of elements. An **element** is a pure substance that contains only one type of matter. There are more than a hundred known elements on Earth. Some elements, such as oxygen and iron, occur naturally. Others have been produced only in laboratories. An element cannot be separated into simpler materials. An **atom** is the smallest particle of an element that has all the properties of the element.

Compounds

A **compound** is a substance formed when atoms of different elements bond together. Like elements, compounds are considered pure substances. Compounds form only when specific atoms bond together in specific proportions. Atoms sometimes lose their individual properties when they bond with other atoms. The new compound has its own set of properties. Table salt is a compound of the elements sodium and chlorine.

Mixtures

Matter can be combined in different quantities to produce mixtures. A **mixture** is a form of matter in which two or more substances are combined in no particular proportions. The components of a mixture retain their own properties and can be separated physically.

Some mixtures are easy to identify. You can clearly see the ingredients of a vegetable salad and separate the salad into its parts. The salad does not have the same properties throughout. Some servings may have more tomatoes; other servings may have more cucumbers.

▲ A vegetable salad is a mixture.

Other types of mixtures contain substances that are spread evenly throughout so that it isn't possible to identify the individual parts. When you dissolve table salt in water, the salt water has the same properties throughout. One spoonful of the salt water will be much like any other spoonful. Brass is a solid mixture of copper, zinc, and other materials melted and combined to form a solid mixture that is nearly the same all the way through.

Mixtures and Compounds

Mixtures and compounds have one similarity: both are formed when two or more types of matter join together. However, mixtures and compounds form under different conditions. A mixture is a combination of materials in various amounts. The parts can be separated physically. A compound is a pure substance made from a fixed proportion of atoms bonded together. Compounds can be separated only by a chemical reaction. The ingredients of a mixture keep their own properties, even after they're mixed together. A compound has a set of properties different from the properties of the individual atoms of which it's composed.

Lesson Assessment

Review

1. **Explain** How are elements and atoms related?

2. Give two examples of pure substances.

3. **Compare and Contrast** How are mixtures different from compounds?

4. **Apply** Sodium carbonate is a compound. Its chemical formula is Na_2CO_3. One molecule of sodium carbonate contains two sodium (Na) atoms, one carbon (C) atom, and three oxygen (O) atoms. How many of each type of atom are in three molecules of sodium carbonate?

Critical Thinking

• Simple syrup is a mixture of sugar dissolved in boiling water. How could you separate the sugar and the water in the syrup?

• A vegetable salad is one example of a mixture that contains elements that do not have the same properties. Can you think of another example of a food that is a mixture?

Writing in Science

• Think of a common mixture. Write a step-by-step procedure for making the mixture.

• Create a compare-and-contrast chart for mixtures and compounds.

Unit 8
☆ Science

Reading Skills and Strategies
- Use the SQ3R strategy.
- Use a dictionary.
- Use an online dictionary.

Lesson 3 States of Matter

As YOU Read!

What You'll Learn
- What the three states of matter are
- How the particles in matter behave in each state
- How to distinguish solids, liquids, and gases

Why It's Important
You see and use matter in all its states every day.

Key Terms
- states of matter
- solid
- liquid
- gas

The Three States of Matter

Everything around us is made of matter, including our bodies. Some parts of our bodies are solid, some are liquid, and some are gas. **States of matter** are the forms in which matter exists.

Most matter can exist in any of the three states—solid, liquid, or gas—depending on the arrangement of the particles and their movement. Water flowing in a river is a liquid. The particles are close together but can move around. When the temperature drops to 0°C, water becomes a solid, ice. The particles are packed tightly together and remain in one place. Water exposed to sun and air will evaporate and become a gas called water vapor. The particles are spaced widely apart and move freely in all directions. Clouds are composed of water vapor that has cooled and become liquid again.

Solids

Solids have a definite shape and volume because their particles are packed closely together, allowing no space for the particles to move around. The particles can vibrate, but they stay fixed in one place and retain their shape and volume.

The particles in many solids, such as table salt and snowflakes, are arranged in repeating patterns. These patterns determine the shape of the solid. In other solids, such as glass, plastic, and rubber, the particles are not arranged in a pattern. The particles in these solids somewhat resemble the arrangement

▲ Some solids soften when they are heated. This artist uses heat to shape the glass into a vase.

of particles in a liquid. These solids soften gradually when heated. In contrast, a snowflake melts and becomes liquid as soon as it is heated.

Liquids

Liquids share some similarities with solids. The particles in a liquid are close together. Like solids, **liquids** have a definite volume and can't be squeezed into a smaller space.

Unlike solids, liquids do not have a definite shape. This is due to the arrangement of the particles. The particles in a liquid are not packed as tightly together as the particles in a solid. The space between the particles allows them to move around. As a result, liquids flow and take the shape of the container that holds them.

Gases

Gases have properties that make them unlike solids and liquids. **Gases** are composed mainly of empty space. The particles in gases have so much room to move around that they are never still. Because of all this space and movement, gases have no definite shape or volume. When a gas is held in a closed container, the amount of space between particles will be more or less depending on the size of the container and the number of particles in it. In other words, if more gas is added to a closed container, the particles will become more closely packed. You can feel this increase in gas pressure as you blow up a balloon.

▲ The volume and pressure in a balloon increase as the balloon fills with air.

Gas particles are constantly bouncing off one another and the inside of the container that holds them. As gas particles move faster, they hit one another (and the container) with greater force.

Lesson Assessment

Review

1. **Explain** Why do solids have a definite shape?

2. **Compare** What do solids and liquids have in common that gives them a definite volume?

3. **Describe** Describe the behavior of gas particles as more gas is added to a container.

4. Draw three pictures to show the three states of water.

Critical Thinking

Make a chart with three columns. Label the columns "Solids," "Liquids," and "Gases." Then make three rows. At the left, label the rows "Shape," "Volume," and "Movement of Particles." Then fill in the boxes. For example, in the first box, describe the shape of solids.

Writing in Science

Write a paragraph to compare and contrast the particles in solids and liquids.

Lesson 4 Atoms

Reading Skills and Strategies

- Use the SQ3R strategy.
- Use a dictionary.
- Use an online dictionary.

As YOU Read!

What You'll Learn

- Dalton's atomic theory
- The particles of which atoms are composed
- What atomic mass is and how to determine it

Why It's Important

Understanding atoms and how subatomic particles behave is the basis of chemistry.

Key Terms

- proton
- electron
- neutron
- isotope

Elements and Atoms

Elements are the most basic substances on Earth. Elements are made of atoms—the smallest particles that still have all the properties of an element. All the atoms that make up a particular element are identical and are different from the atoms of any other element.

In the early nineteenth century, John Dalton formulated a theory about atoms. He stated that matter is made of particles called atoms and that atoms of the same element have the same

▶ Much of Dalton's atomic theory is still accepted as true.

properties and the same mass. He also stated that atoms of one element are unlike the atoms of any other element. We know today that all these statements are correct, but one part of Dalton's theory wasn't quite right. He stated that atoms cannot be divided into smaller particles.

Atoms Are Made of Different Parts

Scientists have discovered that atoms do contain smaller particles. Some of these particles are charged and may be positive or negative. **Protons** are positively charged (+) particles. **Electrons** are negatively charged (−) particles. Particles with the same charge repel each other. Particles with opposite charges attract each other. That is, protons repel other protons but are attracted to electrons. Some particles have no charge at all; they are neutral. These neutral particles are called **neutrons.**

Protons and neutrons make up the dense core at the center of an atom. The center of the atom is positively charged: the protons are positive, and the neutrons have no charge. Electrons are found in the space around the center of the atom. The atoms that make up most of the matter in nature are neutral: they contain the same number of protons and electrons.

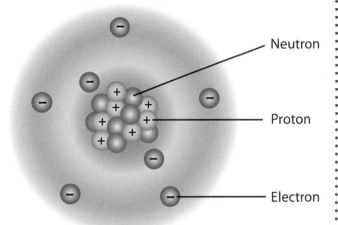

▲ Protons and neutrons are at the center of the atom. Electrons make up the remainder of the atom's volume.

Atomic Numbers

If you've ever looked at the periodic table, you know there are more than a hundred elements. The atoms of each element contain a specific number of protons. This number is the element's atomic number. Each element has its own atomic number. Because every iron atom contains 26 protons, the atomic number for iron is 26.

Atomic Mass

Like all matter, the three types of particles in atoms have mass. Protons and neutrons have about two thousand times the mass of electrons. Because electrons are so small, they don't contribute much to the mass of an atom. The number of protons plus the number of neutrons in an atom equals the atomic mass.

Although the number of protons in an atom is always the same, the number of neutrons can vary. In other words, all atoms of an element may not have the same atomic mass. Each atom of the same element with a different number of neutrons is called an **isotope**. To name an isotope, we write the name of the element followed by the total number of protons and neutrons in the isotope. Carbon has six protons, so the carbon isotope that has six neutrons is carbon-12. Carbon-14 has six protons and eight neutrons.

Lesson Assessment

Review

1. **List** What are the three particles found in atoms?

2. **Explain** What is the difference between atomic number and atomic mass?

3. **Define** What is an isotope?

4. **Compare and Contrast** A chlorine atom has seventeen protons. How are chlorine-35 and chlorine-37 alike and different?

Critical Thinking

- Why do electrons spread out as much as possible in an atom?

- What contributes to the overall mass of an atom?

- What information does the periodic table of elements give you regarding atoms?

Writing in Science

Use the illustration depicting the components of an atom on this page to write a description of the structure of an atom.

Reading Skills and Strategies
- Use higher-order thinking skills.
- Review text connections, text structure, comprehension monitoring, and word-learning strategies.

Lesson 5
Changes in States of Matter

As YOU Read!

What You'll Learn
- How matter changes from solid to liquid to gas and back
- How increases and decreases in energy affect the state of matter

Why It's Important
Understanding states of matter is important in learning chemistry.

Key Terms
- melting point
- freezing point
- evaporation
- condensation

Matter Changes States

Matter commonly exists in one of three states—solid, liquid, or gas. A substance can change states depending on the arrangement of its particles and the energy of the particles. The particles themselves do not change. A solid ice cube left in a glass will eventually change to liquid water. Although the water has changed from solid to liquid, it is still water. Each molecule of water is still made of two hydrogen atoms and one oxygen atom.

▲ Some of the ice has changed from solid to liquid.

Changing from Solid to Liquid

The particles in a solid are held close together and do not move, but they *do* vibrate. These tiny movements make it possible for a solid to change to a liquid under the right conditions. The particles gain energy when the temperature increases. The additional energy makes the particles move faster. The movement of particles causes the solid to become a liquid.

The familiar term for the change from solid to liquid is *melting.* The temperature at which a solid begins to melt is its **melting point.** Solids melt at different temperatures. Some solids have an exact melting point. When they reach a certain temperature, these solids melt and change to a liquid.

Other solids do not have an exact melting point. For such substances, the change from solid to liquid is gradual, and the change in state occurs over a range of temperatures. Suppose you put a chocolate bar in a pan on a cooktop and turn on the heat. As the pan gets warm, the chocolate will soften but still keep its shape. As the pan grows hotter, the chocolate will eventually become a liquid. There is no precise temperature at which melting occurs.

► Some solids melt gradually rather than at an exact temperature.

Changing from Liquid to Solid

The particles in a liquid have more energy than the particles in a solid. Liquid particles lose energy and move more slowly as their temperature decreases. When the particles stop moving, the liquid becomes a solid. The temperature at which this occurs is called the **freezing point.**

The freezing point and the melting point of a substance are the same temperature; a substance can exist as either a solid or a liquid at this temperature. For example, at 0°C, water can be either solid or liquid. Above this temperature, water is liquid. Below this temperature, water is solid.

Changing from Liquid to Gas

Liquid water becomes a gas through a process called **evaporation.** The particles in liquids move at different speeds, with particles at the surface moving fastest. The energy in the particles increases as the temperature increases. The heated particles move faster and faster until they escape the surface of the liquid and become gas particles. The liquid evaporates faster at higher temperatures.

Changing from Gas to Liquid

Gas particles have more energy than liquid particles. When a gas cools, the energy of the particles decreases. Because the particles have less energy, they move more slowly and are drawn together. Eventually the gas particles change to liquid particles. This process is called **condensation.**

Lesson Assessment

Review
1. **Describe** How do the particles in a substance behave when it changes from a solid to a liquid?
2. **Compare and Contrast** What is the difference between a solid with an exact melting point and a solid that does not have a well-defined melting point?
3. **Explain** What happens to particles when they gain and lose energy?
4. Give one example of evaporation and one example of condensation.

Critical Thinking
- A hot frying pan on a stove is a solid. Is it frozen? Why or why not?
- Give some examples of how condensation and evaporation occur in nature. How many examples can you name?

Writing in Science
- Write a description of water as it changes from one state of matter to another.
- Imagine you are in a kitchen and are observing changes in states of matter. Which foods are solids, and which foods are liquids? Where might evaporation or condensation occur? Write about your observations.

Beyond the Book

SEARCH ▶

Insects | **Animals** | People | Plants | Technology | Games

No Longer Endangered

In June 2007, the U.S. Fish and Wildlife Service announced that the *gray wolf* is no longer on the endangered species list.

Grizzly bears in Yellowstone National Park are thriving as of March 2007.

Extinct Species

The *Tasmanian tiger*, which had a pouch for carrying its young, was declared extinct in 1936.

• • •

When the *passenger pigeon* was alive, one flock could contain two billion birds or more.

• • •

The *great auk* resembled the penguin and was hunted to extinction in 1844.

June 12, 2010

Brought Back from the Brink

By Charlotte Yang

The Great Seal of the United States depicts a bald eagle holding arrows and an olive branch. Since Congress adopted this seal in 1782, the bald eagle has been the national symbol of the United States. However, in 1967 the bird was placed on the endangered species list after a count of nesting pairs in 1963 found only 417.

Photograph courtesy Sam Cordoba

The American bald eagle is no longer in danger of extinction.

Yet on June 28, 2007, the U.S. Fish and Wildlife Service officially proclaimed the bald eagle removed from the endangered species list—a great announcement, considering only about 1 percent of endangered animals have ever recovered. Today there are about 10,000 nesting pairs in all lower 48 states and Alaska. You may have seen an eagle high on a tree branch or soaring through the sky if you live in Wyoming or Maryland.

The bald eagle population began to decline in 1870 mainly because of hunting. Though a law was passed in 1940 that made eagle hunting illegal, the bald eagle was threatened further after World War II, when the use of the pesticide DDT was on the rise. DDT contaminated fish, which then poisoned the eagles who ate the fish. DDT also made bald-eagle eggshells weak, so many were broken during incubation.

But the bald eagle bounced back. A law was passed in 1972 that banned the general use of DDT, and over the years conservation groups joined together to protect eagle habitats, begin captive breeding programs, and more.

Page   1 | 2 | 3 | 4 | 5   Next Page ▶

13% of 36K

Extension Activity

You've learned important skills and strategies in the first eight units of this program. Using your own classroom science textbook, find the section you're assigned to read next, and follow the instructions below. Write your responses on notebook paper.

a. **Find** two examples of text structure. Write the page number, title (or subhead), and paragraph on which you found each example so your teacher can find it easily.

b. **Which** of the following text structures best fits the paragraph(s) for each example—Description-or-List, Order-or-Sequence, Cause-and-Effect, or Compare-and-Contrast?

c. **Why** did you choose this text structure? For each example, give an explanation.

d. **Choose** two bold and highlighted words to look up in your **Content Reader** glossary. Write the definitions you find. If you cannot find the definitions in your glossary, use your dictionary.

e. **Write** a sentence using each word you looked up in the glossary (or dictionary).

f. **Choose** a word that is not bold and highlighted, and look it up in your glossary. Write the definition you find. Again, if you cannot find the definition in your glossary, use your dictionary.

g. **Write** a sentence using the word you looked up in the glossary (or dictionary).

Lesson 1

Regions of Latin America

As YOU Read!

What You'll Learn

■ How landforms in Latin America affect the population

■ Why Latin American rivers are important

Why It's Important

The physical features of Latin America help explain the region's cultures and economies.

Key Terms

■ isthmus

■ plateau

■ coral

■ escarpment

■ tributary

■ hydroelectric power

▶ The whole of Central America, not just Panama, forms an isthmus connecting North and South America.

Latin America consists of all the land in the Western Hemisphere south of the United States. Mountains and bodies of water divide Latin America into three regions—Mexico and Central America, the Caribbean, and South America.

The Regions of Latin America

KEY

Mexico and Central America

Caribbean Islands

South America

Major Political Regions

Political regions are determined by people. Governments decide their boundaries. However, political boundaries often follow natural features such as rivers and mountain ranges.

Look at the map above. The Rio Grande forms part of the boundary between Mexico and the United States. South of Mexico is Central America. Central America is an **isthmus.** An isthmus is a narrow strip of land that has water on either side and connects two larger regions. South of Central America is South America. It is bigger than Mexico, Central America, and all the Caribbean Islands put together.

Now find the Caribbean Islands. They are located in the Caribbean Sea. Both the islands and the sea are named after the Carib people. The Caribs were living in the region when Columbus arrived in 1492.

Regions within Regions

Each major political region of Latin America includes various other kinds of regions. Mountains, plains, and plateaus make up landform regions. Tropical rain forests, grasslands, deserts, and highlands make up climate regions, and the ways land is used form regions of land use.

Landform Regions

The principal landforms in both Mexico and Central America are mountains. These mountains are part of a great network of ranges. The mountain ranges stretch from Alaska to the southern tip of South America.

In Mexico, the Sierra Madre Occidental loom over a narrow plain on the west coast. The Sierra Madre Oriental extend along a narrow plain on the east coast. These mountain ranges join to form the Sierra Madre del Sur in southern Mexico.

Amid the mountains lies the Central Plateau. A **plateau** is a vast flat-topped highland. Mexico's Central Plateau covers more than half of Mexico. Most of Mexico's people live there, even though the surrounding mountains make reaching the coasts difficult.

Unlike Mexico, Central America has mountains that run through the central area rather than along the coasts. Several mountains in Mexico and Central America are volcanoes. Ashes from the volcanoes have produced rich soil. The low temperatures and rich soil in the mountains of Latin America are ideal for growing coffee.

The mountains of the Caribbean are mainly underwater. Many of the islands are actually mountaintops. Other Caribbean islands are made of **coral**. Coral is a rock-hard material formed by the skeletons of tiny sea animals.

The mountains of Mexico, Central America, and the Caribbean are impressive. The greatest range is the Andes. The Andes Mountains extend forty-five hundred miles along the western coasts of Chile, Peru, Ecuador, and Colombia and into Venezuela. Some of the peaks reach twenty thousand feet. Yet, for hundreds of years, farmers have cultivated the rich mountain soil.

East of the Andes lie the rolling hills of Brazil, Guyana, and other South American countries. Other South American landforms include the Guiana Highlands in the northeastern part of the continent and the Brazilian Highlands along Brazil's east coast. The easternmost part of the Brazilian Highlands drops sharply to the sea, forming an **escarpment,** or tall cliff.

Latin American Bodies of Water

The mightiest Latin American river is the Amazon. It flows four thousand miles from Peru in western South America to the Atlantic Ocean in the east. In length, the Amazon River is second only to the Nile River in Africa. However, it carries more water than any other river—one-fifth of all the freshwater in the world. More than a thousand tributaries feed water into the Amazon. A **tributary** is a river or a stream that flows into a larger river. The Amazon and its tributaries drain millions of square miles. This drainage area is known as the Amazon Basin.

People who live in the Amazon Basin depend on the Amazon River and its tributaries for their livelihood and basic needs. They fish for food, drink the water, and travel from one place to another in boats. They even wash their clothing on the riverbanks.

The second largest river system in South America is the Rio de la Plata, or "river of silver." It is composed of the Paraná, the Paraguay, and the Uruguay rivers. The Rio de la Plata forms the boundary between Argentina and Uruguay. Although not as large as the Amazon River system, the Rio de la Plata has heavier traffic. It carries barges of goods from place to place in the continent's interior.

South America's largest lake is Lake Maracaibo in Venezuela. It covers more than five thousand square miles and is the site of Venezuela's most productive oil field. Also in Venezuela is Angel Falls. This waterfall drops three thousand feet, making it the longest waterfall in the world. Waterfalls provide hydroelectric power for many countries in Latin America. **Hydroelectric power** is electricity generated by rushing water.

Climate Regions

Southern Mexico, eastern Central America, some Caribbean islands, and the Amazon Basin have high temperatures and heavy rainfall year-round. These conditions make up a tropical rain forest climate. In tropical rain forests, tall evergreen trees form a canopy. This covering blocks the sun so few plants can grow on the forest floor.

A tropical savanna climate prevails in most of Central America and the Caribbean islands and in parts of Colombia, Venezuela, Brazil, Bolivia, and Paraguay. Most of the year, these areas are hot and wet, but they also have cooler, drier seasons.

Much of southeastern South America has a humid, subtropical climate. Summers are long and wet, and winters are short with mild temperatures. These conditions produce grasslands like the pampas of Argentina and Uruguay.

The southern tip of South America, called Tierra del Fuego, has a climate much like that of Iceland. It is cold and wet year-round with temperatures averaging between 32°F and 48°F. Plants and animals are few.

▲ The Atacama Desert in northern Chile is one of the driest places on Earth and an example of a desert climate region. In parts of this desert, no rainfall has ever been recorded.

Lesson Assessment

Review

1. **Categorize** What term describes mountains, plateaus, and hills?

2. **Identify** Why do few plants grow on the floor of the rain forest?

3. **Locate** In which political region of Latin America are the Andes found?

4. **Analyze** How do South American rivers benefit people?

5. **Explain** Why do farmers settle in the mountains of Central America?

Critical Thinking

Contrast the Amazon River and the Rio de la Plata.

Writing in Social Studies

Write a travel brochure briefly describing must-see features of Latin America.

Reading Skills and Strategies
- Use the SQ3R strategy.
- Use an online dictionary.

Lesson 2

The Panama Canal

As YOU Read!

What You'll Learn
- Why building the Panama Canal posed challenges
- How the United States obtained control of the Panama Canal

Why It's Important
The story of the Panama Canal shows how economic and military considerations affect government decisions.

Key Terms
- canal
- lock

Everyone likes shortcuts. They save time and effort. As early as 1850, shipping companies and American presidents were pushing for a shortcut between the Atlantic and the Pacific Oceans.

Early Efforts

For years, any ship sailing from New York to San Francisco had to go around the tip of South America—a voyage of thirteen thousand miles. A **canal,** or artificial waterway, through Central America would eliminate 60 percent of the distance. The best locations for a canal were Nicaragua and Panama.

Every American president since Ulysses S. Grant considered building a canal through Central America. A canal would save businesses time and money, and it would help the military. Battleships had no quick route between the Atlantic and the Pacific. The navy would face critical delays if the United States ever fought a war on both oceans. However, the French, not the Americans, were the first to try building a canal.

Since 1821, Panama had been part of Colombia. In 1881, Colombia sold land in Panama to a French company for a canal. Once the work began, the builders faced many challenges. A mountain range stood in the way, and mud slides erased much of the workers' progress. Worst of all, tropical diseases, such as malaria and yellow fever, killed twenty-five thousand workers. After a few years, the company ran out of money, and the canal was left unfinished.

The United States Steps In

In early 1902, President Theodore Roosevelt asked the House of Representatives for $140 million to build a canal across Nicaragua. Instead, Congress approved funds to buy the land from the French company and complete the route through Panama. Roosevelt offered $10 million and an annual rent of $250,000 to Colombian officials for the right to build the canal. Colombia refused the offer.

Roosevelt decided to support a rebellion in Panama. A rebellion is a violent action by a large group of people to change a country's government.

An agent of the French canal company gathered a small army of Panamanians. On November 3, 1903, this group took over Panama City and declared independence from Colombia. Two days later, an American warship reached the coast of Panama and sent four hundred marines ashore. Eight more American warships formed a blockade to keep out Colombian ships. Roosevelt recognized the rebels as the new leaders of Panama, and the rebels gave the United States the right to build and control a canal.

Overcoming Difficulties

Building the canal might have been impossible if tropical diseases had gone unchecked. Fortunately, doctors had recently discovered that mosquitoes spread malaria and yellow fever. Mosquitoes need swamps or other standing water to multiply. The canal company hired a crew to fill swamps, cover water containers, and kill mosquitoes. Even so, of the 5,609 people who died while building the canal, many were victims of disease.

About 45,000 workers, most of them from the Caribbean, dug the canal. In addition to digging, they built locks and a dam. The **locks** adjusted water levels to raise and lower ships. Locks were necessary because the canal went through mountains. A dam was necessary to construct a lake for ships to sail across to the other side of Panama. The canal took eight years to complete. The dream of a passageway between oceans was realized.

◀ The canal is roughly fifty miles long. A ship can cross it in about eight hours.

Lesson Assessment

Review

1. **Explain** How would a canal help businesses and the military?

2. **Describe** How do locks help ships cross the Panama Canal?

3. **Summarize** What challenges did canal builders face?

4. **Conclude** Why did more workers die of tropical diseases during the canal project in the 1880s than during the project in the early twentieth century?

5. **Judge** Do you approve or disapprove of Roosevelt's support for the rebellion in Panama? Give reasons for your answer.

Critical Thinking

Why, do you think, did the French canal company organize the rebellion in Panama?

Writing in Social Studies

Write lyrics for a song about the Panama Canal to the tune of one of your favorite songs.

Reading Skills and Strategies
- Use the SQ3R strategy.
- Use an online dictionary.

Lesson 3 · Caribbean Islands

Picture a vacation paradise. Do you imagine white beaches, tropical breezes, and clear blue water? Your paradise sounds like the Caribbean.

Tourism

Millions of tourists visit the Caribbean each year. One-third of all islanders are part of the tourist industry. They work as shop owners and clerks, hotel managers and maids, and restaurant cooks and servers.

Some island nations base their whole economy on tourism. This becomes a problem during hurricane season when winds and waves level trees and buildings. On other islands, tourism is not enough to support the population. Many people are unemployed or **underemployed.** This means they do not make enough money to meet their basic needs. In Jamaica, riots by the poor during the 1960s and 1970s discouraged tourism. Fewer tourists resulted in more poverty.

▶ Hurricanes in the Caribbean cause damage that reduces the tourist trade.

Agriculture

Agriculture is even more important than tourism to Caribbean economies. More than one-half of the islanders are farmworkers. The leading employers are large sugar cane plantations. Other plantations on the islands raise bananas, coffee, and cotton. These crops are **exported,** or shipped, to other countries, including the United States.

For years, some of the island nations had a **one-crop economy.** In other words, they relied on only one crop for most of their income. If a disease wiped out the main crop or the crop's price fell, the economy suffered. Today islanders grow a variety of crops to protect their economies.

Independent Island Nations

All Caribbean nations were colonies at one time. Some are still controlled by other countries. Others, such as Haiti and the Dominican Republic, have been independent for a long time.

Haitians became the first self-governing people in the Caribbean. A former enslaved African named Toussaint-Louverture led a revolt against Haiti's French rulers. The French captured and imprisoned Toussaint, but his movement continued. Haiti declared its independence in 1804.

Haiti in Turmoil

After independence, Haiti endured a long series of presidents who became dictators. A **dictator** takes total control of a government. In 1990, Haitians held a democratic election for the first time in many years. They chose Jean-Bertrand Aristide, a former Catholic priest, as president.

After seven months, Haiti's military forced Aristide out of office and set up a military dictatorship. In 1994, the United States government helped Aristide return to office and restore democracy. The next year's elections put Aristide's ally, René Préval, in the presidency, and in 2000, Aristide was reelected.

Four years later, Guy Philippe, a Haitian criminal exiled to the Dominican Republic, returned to Haiti. He took over a band of rebels who had captured Cap Haitien, Haiti's second-largest city. The rebels threatened to march into Port-au-Prince, Haiti's capital.

United States officials wanted to restore calm in Haiti, so U.S. Marines took Aristide out of the country. The next day, Philippe and his crew occupied the capital. They later surrendered their arms to a United Nations

peacekeeping force. Support for Aristide and his party remained strong, and in 2006, René Préval was reelected president.

Lesson Assessment

Review

1. **Explain** How was tourism in Jamaica affected by underemployment?

2. **Infer** Why, do you think, did some Caribbean nations with plantation-based economies have food shortages?

3. **Identify** Who was Toussaint-Louverture?

4. **Theorize** How does an elected official become a dictator?

5. **Assess** Did American intervention help or hurt Haitian democracy in 2004? Explain.

Critical Thinking

What are possible causes for the failure of a one-crop economy?

Writing in Social Studies

You are the master of ceremonies at a meeting of Caribbean leaders. Write an introduction for Jean-Bertrand Aristide.

◀ Jean-Bertrand Aristide has tried to bring democracy to Haiti.

Reading Skills and Strategies
- Use the SQ3R strategy.
- Use an online dictionary.

Lesson 4

Rural and Urban Mexico

As YOU Read!

What You'll Learn
- Why Mexican farmers move to cities
- How rapid growth in Mexico City has increased pollution

Why It's Important
Similar trends occur in other countries, increasing pollution worldwide.

Key Terms
- campesinos
- subsidies
- squatters
- subway

The Mexican Plateau is a flat-topped highland in the middle of three mountain ranges. It is also the site of the country's richest farmland and the national capital, Mexico City.

Changes in Rural Mexico

Wealthy landowners and big companies control most of the farmland on the Mexican Plateau. **Campesinos,** or rural people who own no land, work on the large farms. Many campesinos are migrant workers. They travel from one farm to another picking crops.

Migrants may make as little as a dollar a day. Often, a whole family, including children, works in the fields to earn a living wage. However, there is not enough work for all the migrants who need jobs.

How did this situation come about? In 1993, leaders in Mexico, Canada, and the United States signed the North American Free Trade Agreement (NAFTA). This agreement undermined government protections for Mexican farmers. For example, their government guaranteed a minimum price for farmers' corn. After NAFTA, American agricultural companies sold their crops in Mexico for less than Mexican farmers could. Why? The companies received millions in **subsidies,** or financial aid, from the United States government. After 1993, tons of cheap corn from the United States poured into Mexico.

The first Mexicans to suffer were small farmers. They could not compete, so they sold their land. Many became migrants. Large companies bought Mexican farmland and introduced farm machines. As a result, fewer jobs remained for migrants. Two million farmworkers have been forced to leave rural Mexico since 1993.

Life in Urban Mexico

Thousands of farmworkers have moved to Mexico City to find work. Many settle on the edges of the city. Usually, they cannot afford to buy land. They build ramshackle shelters of scrap metal and rock on the mountainsides. If they do not have permission to build there, they are known as **squatters.** Squatters have little access to clean water or electricity.

Many women and children in squatter communities take part in the informal economy of Mexico City. They sell handicrafts, food, drinks, and other things on city streets. Most start early in the morning, selling to workers on their way to the central city.

Because newcomers live on the city outskirts, many travel a long way to work. Thousands of people take the **subway,** or underground railway system, to jobs in factories, offices, and restaurants. Well-to-do city workers drive cars through congested streets.

◀ Many farmworkers who have moved to the city must live in substandard housing.

▲ The Metro is a popular way to get around in Mexico City.

Pollution in Mexico City

Traffic jams occur daily in Mexico City. Millions of cars, trucks, taxis, and buses emit exhaust fumes. Factories add smoke to the fumes, and the surrounding mountains trap the pollution in a cloud over the city. This heavy air pollution increases illness, especially among children.

Lesson Assessment

Review

1. **Name** Who benefits when poor Mexican farmers sell their land?

2. **Explain** Why can United States companies sell crops in Mexico at a lower price than Mexican farmers can sell their crops?

3. **Generalize** How do people get around Mexico City?

4. **Summarize** What challenges do poor people face in Mexico City?

5. How might officials in Mexico City reduce air pollution?

Critical Thinking

Many migrant farmworkers cannot find jobs in Mexican cities. Where do you think they then go to find work?

Writing in Social Studies

Write a picket sign for a campesino protesting NAFTA.

Lesson 5

Brazil's Rain Forest

Reading Skills and Strategies

- Use higher-order thinking skills.
- Review text connections, text structure, comprehension monitoring, SQ3R, and word-learning strategies.

As YOU Read!

What You'll Learn

■ How Brazil's economy is altering the rain forest

■ Why rain forests are vital parts of the environment

Why It's Important

Some scientists believe the destruction of rain forests may contribute to global climate change.

Key Terms

■ deforestation
■ slash-and-burn
■ photosynthesis

▶ Almost two-fifths of all the world's tropical rain forest is located in Brazil.

The rain forest in Brazil is twice the size of Alaska and five times the size of Texas. The forest was even larger before 1970. Since then, Brazil has lost 232,000 square miles of rain forest. That is an area larger than France.

Agriculture and Deforestation

Both cattle ranchers and farmers contribute to **deforestation,** or forest destruction. Ranching alone is responsible for two-thirds of the total. According to Brazilian law, ranchers get title to all the forestland they clear and put cattle on. Cattle offer a better return than crops because crops may fail or fall in price. The price of cattle, on the other hand, stays high because of the demand for beef in other countries. Europeans, for example, buy most of their imported beef from Brazil.

Demand has also given rise to Brazil's large soybean plantations. Plantation owners make use of large tracts of grassland. This forces ranchers and farmers into the rain forest.

During the 1990s, the Brazilian government gave away forest lots to thousands of poor farmers. These farmers used **slash-and-burn** methods (cutting down and burning trees) to clear the land. They planted bananas, maize, and other crops where the trees once stood. The crops wore out the forest's thin soil after only a few seasons. Then farmers moved deeper into the forest and cleared new fields.

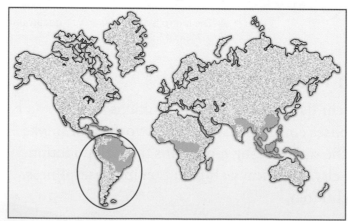

Other Economic Causes of Deforestation

Roads have contributed directly and indirectly to deforestation. Brazilians bulldozed thousands of miles of trees for the Trans-Amazonian Highway. Loggers and miners then used the road to get into the forest.

Tropical hardwoods in the Amazon rain forest are worth about $600 billion on the world market. To reach the oldest, most valuable trees, loggers have cleared miles of minor roads off the main highway. Brazil limits logging to certain parts of the forest, but laws are hard to enforce in remote areas. So loggers continue to clear acres of old-growth timber.

In the 1980s, miners discovered gold in Brazil's rain forest. Additional miners arrived and felled acres of trees for buildings and fuel. They polluted streams with arsenic, a by-product of gold mining and a harmful poison. The forest's native people depend on the streams for water, and the arsenic has made many of them sick. The government has since passed strict laws regulating mining.

Deforestation and the Environment

People around the world are alarmed about the rapid destruction of Brazil's rain forest. Why? Rain forests stabilize Earth's atmosphere. Through a process called **photosynthesis,** green plants absorb carbon dioxide and give off oxygen and water vapor. The trees of the rain forests produce about one-third of the world's oxygen. They also prevent drought by returning moisture to the air that later falls as rain. Finally, carbon dioxide may contribute to global climate change. Plant regions like rain forests "scrub" carbon dioxide from the air. However, slash-and-burn farmers have added tons of carbon to the atmosphere.

◄ Deforestation peaked in the 1990s after Brazil gave land to slash-and-burn farmers.

Lesson Assessment

Review

1. Use *deforestation* in a sentence.

2. **Conclude** Do slash-and-burn farming methods contribute to global climate change? Explain.

3. **Restate** Describe photosynthesis in your own words.

4. **Synthesize** What role does trade play in deforestation?

5. **Summarize** How do rain forests affect climate?

Critical Thinking

What can you infer from the fact that Brazil has passed strict laws regulating mines in the rain forest?

Writing in Social Studies

List three actions that people in your community can take to help stop deforestation in Brazil.

Lesson 1

Egypt and Its Culture

Reading Skills and Strategies
- Use the SQ3R strategy: question.
- Use the SQ3R strategy: read.
- Use the SQ3R strategy: reflect.

As YOU Read

What You'll Learn
- The role Islam plays in Egyptian culture
- How life differs in rural and urban Egypt

Why It's Important
Americans must understand Arab nations to evaluate policies in the Middle East.

Key Terms
- monotheism
- calligraphy
- mosque
- sharia
- fellaheen
- hieroglyphics

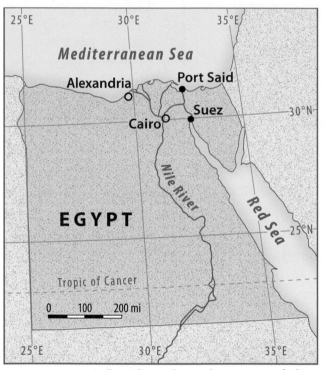

▲ Egypt lies in the northeast corner of Africa.

The word *Egypt* suggests pyramids, mummies, and sphinxes. All these things express ancient religious beliefs. Five thousand years ago, Egyptians worshipped many gods, including their pharaohs. Today, most Egyptians follow a very different kind of religion.

Origins of Islam

Islam is the official religion of Egypt. More than 74 million of Egypt's 80 million people are Muslims, or followers of Islam. The first principle of Islam is **monotheism,** or belief in one God.

Islam's founder, the prophet Muhammad, came from what is now Saudi Arabia, across the Red Sea from Egypt. Muslims believe that in A.D. 610 an angel revealed God's words to Muhammad. At first, the prophet simply told these revelations to his followers. Later, he asked his followers to write down the sayings. In 655, several years after Muhammad's death, the written words were collected in the Koran.

Islam and Egyptian Culture

The Koran is the holy book of Islam. Muslims look to it for guidance, comfort, and protection. Over the centuries, artists have raised **calligraphy,** or beautiful writing, to a fine art by copying the Koran. In Egypt, calligraphy decorates coins, clothing, and buildings, especially **mosques.**

A mosque is a Muslim place of prayer. Muezzins at the mosques call the faithful to prayer. Their calls fill the air in Egyptian cities and villages five times a day. Islam requires its followers to pray at dawn, noon, midafternoon, sunset, and evening. When Muslims pray, they face the city of Mecca, the birthplace of Muhammad and the location of Islam's holiest shrine.

Islam also requires Muslims to fast. During the month-long observance of Ramadan, Muslims go without food from dawn to dusk. Restaurants stand empty, and many shops are closed until dark. Then the streets of Egypt come alive. People carry on as they would during the day at other times of the year.

Many Egyptian Muslims believe that Egyptian law should be based on **sharia,** or Islamic law. Sharia draws mainly from the Koran and hadiths. Hadiths are traditions handed down from the Prophet. For example, the following hadith quotes Muhammad:

> "All people are as equal as the teeth on a comb. There is no claim of merit of an Arab over a non-Arab, or of a white over a black, or of a male over a female. Only a God-fearing people will rate a preference with God."

This hadith makes clear that men and women are equal and that God and sharia favor religious people.

However, other interpretations of sharia consider women inferior to men. For this reason, some Egyptians resist the idea of adopting sharia. In Islamic courts, a Muslim's testimony is considered more credible than a non-Muslim's. A pious Muslim is believed

▲ This Cairo mosque, built in 970, houses the oldest university in the world.

before a nonpracticing Muslim, and a man is believed more truthful than a woman. Many women and non-Muslims fear they would be at a disadvantage under sharia.

Egypt's Economy

Egyptian religion is rooted in centuries-old traditions. In contrast, Egypt's economy resembles those of modern industrial nations. Egypt's leading industries include textiles, chemicals, and petroleum. Millions of Egyptians hold jobs in factories and oil fields.

Other Egyptians work in the main port cities—Alexandria, Port Said, and Suez. There, dockhands load and unload cargo. Outgoing ships take cotton, yarn, metal products, chemicals, petroleum, and petroleum products around the world. Ships from the United States, Germany, France, and China bring in food, machinery, wood products, and fertilizer.

Another huge industry in Egypt is tourism. Thousands of visitors arrive each year to view the pyramids and the mummies. They spend billions of dollars and provide income for guides, shopkeepers, restaurant owners, and hotels.

Rural Life in Egypt

One-third of all Egyptians work as farmers and live in villages. They are known as **fellaheen.** Many rent small plots along

▲ Most of Egypt's farmland is located in the six hundred miles of the Nile River Valley.

the Nile River and the Suez Canal. Others raise rice and cotton in the fields of large landowners.

Rural families build their houses with stones and mud bricks. The typical house has one to three rooms and a courtyard. Families share the courtyard with their animals. Egyptians own about 95 million chickens, 4.5 million cattle, 4 million goats, and 5.2 million sheep.

Thousands of fellaheen move from the country to cities each year. Some hope to find better-paying jobs in factories or ports. Others seek more or better education.

City Life in Egypt

Cairo is Egypt's largest city and the national capital. It has a population of more than 11.1 million people. Unsurprisingly, traffic jams and housing shortages are common.

Cairo is also Africa's oldest city. Some of its buildings are a thousand years old. Its bazaars, or open-air markets, recall ancient times. Other parts of Cairo resemble Miami or Los Angeles. High-rise apartments and offices line the streets.

People from the country have a hard time finding places to live. Some live in rowboats. Others have made homes in graveyards on the edges of the city. These graveyard communities are so populous the government considers them suburbs and provides electricity for the people who live in them.

Egyptian Antiquities

A popular attraction in Cairo is the Egyptian National Museum. Tourists flock to see mummies and tombs of pharaohs of long ago. Golden objects from the tomb of Tutankhamen, the boy king, also draw crowds.

In 1835, the Egyptian government established what is now called the Supreme Council of Antiquities. Its purpose is to protect and preserve the ancient artifacts of Egypt. The government began its own collection of objects from tombs and temples. These are now on display in the national museum. However, many valuable artifacts were already in foreign museums.

An important example is the Rosetta stone. In 196 B.C., a scribe chiseled the same message in Greek and **hieroglyphics** on a stone slab. Hieroglyphics are ancient Egyptian picture writings. Two thousand years later, French soldiers unearthed the Rosetta stone in lower Egypt. The discovery caused a sensation. Historians finally had a key to understanding the writing on Egyptian temples and pyramids.

The Rosetta stone is now in the British Museum. However, the head of Egypt's Supreme Council of Antiquities claims it belongs in Egypt. Other artifacts Egypt wants returned are the bust of Queen Nefertiti on display in Berlin, Germany, and a temple ceiling now in Paris, France.

▲ This sculpture of Nefertiti, the wife of an Egyptian pharaoh, is more than three thousand years old.

Lesson Assessment

Review

1. **Explain** How does Islam differ from the religion of the pharaohs?

2. **Define** What is calligraphy?

3. **Infer** What was found on the Rosetta stone that helped historians understand hieroglyphics?

4. **Judge** Is Islam a force for unity or division in Egypt? Explain.

5. **Analyze** Why, do you think, does Cairo have such a large population?

Critical Thinking

Do you think fellaheen have high incomes? What facts in the lesson help you reach your conclusion?

Writing in Social Studies

Write an argument for or against basing Egyptian law on sharia.

Lesson 2

One Nigeria, Many Cultures

As You Read

What You'll Learn

- Why Nigeria has many languages
- How groups in Nigeria differ

Why It's Important

An appreciation of many cultures contributes to a more peaceful world.

Key Terms

- ethnic group
- cacao
- pidgin

Imagine a classroom in which each person, including the teacher, speaks a different language. Learning would be difficult. For a similar reason, living and working in Nigeria can also be difficult.

▲ Nigeria is located in the bend of the west coast of Africa.

Roots of Nigerian Cultures

Two hundred fifty languages are spoken in Nigeria. Each language represents a different **ethnic group.** An ethnic group consists of people who share a common culture. In other words, they have the same history, language, religion, and traditions or some combination of these. The largest ethnic groups in Nigeria are the Hausa-Fulani, the Yoruba, and the Ibo.

These groups have not always been part of the same nation. The oldest Nigerian cultures go back 2,800 years or more. For centuries, each ethnic group inhabited and governed a separate territory.

The land of the Hausa lay along trade routes between Europe and Asia. The Hausa built seven kingdoms with walled cities at the center. Each kingdom had its own ruler, and each city had a market.

As part of the Hausa-Fulani, you were either a nomad, or wanderer, or a trader who settled among the Hausa in the early thirteenth century. Some traders were

◀ Kano, the former center of a trading kingdom and the oldest city in West Africa, is still a central market for the Hausa-Fulani.

Muslims, and they introduced Islamic ideas about law and religion to Hausa kings. Many of these rulers converted to Islam. As a result, a Muslim culture developed in what is now northern Nigeria.

European Influence

After Islam took root, Spanish and Portuguese slave traders arrived. They bought or kidnapped Yoruba and Ibo people and then sold them in the Americas. Later, the British came and seized territory instead of people. In 1861, they took over the port of Lagos and gradually moved inland. By 1902, they controlled the Muslim kingdoms in the north and, by 1914, had established the present-day boundaries of Nigeria.

In 1960, Nigerians declared independence from Great Britain. All the ethnic groups joined to form one government. To promote unity, the government moved Nigeria's capital from Lagos to the centrally located city of Abuja in 1991.

Nigeria's Ethnic Groups Today

The Hausa-Fulani make up one-third of all Nigerians. They form the majority in northern Nigeria, and most practice Islam. Many leaders in the region would like to see all of Nigeria under Islamic law. Presently, twelve of Nigeria's thirty-six states have adopted sharia. You read about sharia in Lesson 1.

One-fifth of all Nigerians belong to the Yoruba ethnic group. Five hundred years ago, the Yoruba founded Lagos. Today it is Nigeria's most populous city. However, many Yoruba are farmers who live in the country surrounding Lagos. A principal crop there is **cacao**—the source of cocoa and the country's most important export after oil.

The Ibo make up the smallest of the three major groups. They have not established large population centers as the Hausa-Fulani and the Yoruba have. Instead, the Ibo live in villages that are models of democracy. All the villagers participate in governing the community.

Scores of smaller ethnic groups make up the remainder of Nigeria's population. Most groups have their own language. They communicate with one another by speaking **pidgin,** which combines English words with the grammar of Nigerian languages.

Lesson Assessment

Review

1. **Restate** Complete the following definition of *ethnic group* in three words or less: people with _____.

2. **Examine** How did Europeans exploit the people of Nigeria?

3. **Identify** Who included the territories of so many different ethnic groups within the same boundaries?

4. **Infer** Why, do you think, is Nigerian pidgin based on English?

5. **Deduce** Which ethnic group do you think has the most influence in Nigeria? Explain your answer.

Critical Thinking

Compare the Yoruba and the Ibo. What do the two groups have in common?

Writing in Social Studies

Investigate cacao farms in Africa, and write a two-page report on your findings.

Reading Skills and Strategies

- Use the SQ3R strategy: question.
- Use the SQ3R strategy: read.
- Use the SQ3R strategy: reflect.

Lesson 3

Chinese Politics and Economics

As YOU Read

What You'll Learn
- How Mao changed the lives of Chinese farmers
- How Chinese imports affect Americans

Why It's Important
Americans should know the workers' rights records and safety standards of the nations that make the goods in U.S. stores.

Key Terms
- communes
- free enterprise
- boycott

How would you help millions of needy people? In the 1950s, the new leader of China looked to industrialized nations for answers.

The Great Leap Forward

Mao Zedong and his Communist Party took control of China in 1949. At the time, most Chinese were very poor. Factories were outdated. Farmers still used animals to pull plows.

Mao tried to improve conditions by developing agriculture and industry at the same time. His government seized factories and the land of large landowners. Then in 1958, Mao began the "Great Leap Forward"—a five-year plan to speed up production on farms and in factories.

During the first year, the government reorganized rural life. It settled 700 million people on 26,758 **communes,** or government-owned farms. Farmers on communes were expected to do more than raise crops. More than 600,000 farmers also made steel in backyard furnaces.

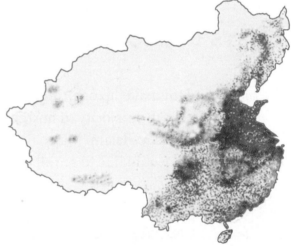

▲ China's best farmland lies in the most densely populated areas, allowing little land for each family.

A Failed Policy

Meanwhile, factories in urban China were having problems. Thousands of untrained workers assembled farm machines. When farmers tried to use the machines, the machines fell apart.

On the communes, buildings made from homemade steel were falling down. Crops were rotting in the fields because farmers were busy making steel. In 1959 and 1960, floods and drought destroyed more crops.

The government rationed the available food, but steelmaking used so much coal that little was left to run China's trains. As a result, food could not be shipped where it was needed, and 20 million Chinese starved to death.

Mao shouldered the blame and resigned as head of state. More moderate leaders took over the economy. They allowed farmers to own land again and made the remaining communes smaller. After Mao died in 1976, the new leaders permitted limited **free enterprise.** Individuals could start businesses and earn profits.

Free Enterprise in China

Today, China is an industrial powerhouse. Coal fuels most of its factories and power

▲ In recent years, skilled workers in China have commanded relatively high wages—two hundred to four hundred dollars per month. Most unskilled workers, however, make less than a living wage.

plants, but these businesses make little effort to capture harmful emissions. Instead, they release tons of gases that may contribute to global climate change.

International companies pour money into Chinese factories. Yet many men, women, and children who work there earn less than a dollar a day. Chinese law does not guarantee workers' rights to a fair wage and a safe workplace.

Relations with American Consumers

Presently, the United States imports billions of dollars in Chinese goods each year. In 2007, American consumers learned that some dog food and certain kinds of toothpaste from China contained poisons. Consumers also discovered that millions of Chinese-made toys included toxic lead paint.

Companies pulled the harmful products off store shelves. Even so, many Americans demanded that their government guarantee the safety of all Chinese-made goods. In response, the Senate held hearings on safety inspections for imports. Meanwhile, Americans who support workers' rights and consumer safety **boycott,** or refuse to buy, products made in China.

Lesson Assessment

Review
1. **Contrast** How is free enterprise different from China's economic system under Mao?

2. **Analyze** Should Americans be concerned about air pollution in China? Why or why not?

3. Which group do you think was more productive—farmers on communes or farmers with their own land? Explain.

Critical Thinking
Predict Americans' reactions if the United States government seized American land and factories.

Writing in Social Studies
Write an e-mail message encouraging readers to buy or to boycott Chinese-made toys.

Reading Skills and Strategies
- Use the SQ3R strategy: question.
- Use the SQ3R strategy: read.
- Use the SQ3R strategy: reflect.

Lesson 4

Manufacturing in Japan

As YOU Read

What You'll Learn
- Why Japanese companies have been so successful
- How Japanese companies treat workers

Why It's Important
Successful principles of Japanese business may help other countries develop their industry.

Key Terms
- subsidies
- discrimination

Where would you like to work someday? Many Japanese consider a factory a secure and satisfying place to work. Read on to find out why.

History of Industry

By the 1920s, Japan was a major manufacturing nation but lacked important resources. Japanese military leaders convinced the emperor that the best way to obtain raw materials was to expand Japan's

▲ Resources that Japan wanted from China included iron ore for making steel and bauxite for making aluminum.

Iron ore
Bauxite

CHINA
JAPAN

territory. In 1931, Japan's army invaded a part of China called Manchuria. In 1937, Japan launched a war on all of China that lasted throughout World War II.

During World War II, American planes bombed Japan's manufacturing centers. Little remained but rubble. After the war, the U.S. government sent aid to rebuild Japan's factories. Japanese industries continued to grow with the help of **subsidies,** or money, from the Japanese government.

Economic Strategy

The Japanese market has always been too small to absorb the entire output of Japan's factories. Consequently, businesses focused on exports. However, they imported designs and technology from the West. Instead of using engineers to develop products, managers put engineers on the factory floor. The engineers kept costs low and productivity high. This strategy saved enough money to offset the costs of shipping goods overseas and paying tariffs.

By 1960, Japanese products were widespread but considered poor imitations of Western goods. For example, Japanese television sets did not work as well, last as long, or look as stylish as American television sets. Japanese companies decided to change this situation. They set new standards for quality and reliability that went beyond the standards of Western companies.

Japanese Success

By the 1970s, Japan was the world's largest producer and exporter of television sets. Japan also produced more watches and cameras than the Swiss or the Germans, who had been the leading producers for decades. By the 1980s, Japan was also exporting large numbers of automobiles and electronic devices of high quality.

Japanese auto companies have even exported assembly plants to the United States. They save the cost of shipping whole automobiles by having American workers assemble Japanese-made parts. Then they sell the cars to American buyers.

Japanese Workers

After World War II, an important goal of Japanese government and business was full employment. Many Japanese companies guaranteed employees jobs for life. In the 1990s, economic downturns forced companies to lay off workers, but by 2007, the economy had recovered, and employment was high again.

◄ Japanese companies spend more on education and training than companies in other industrialized nations.

Japanese companies today try to keep worker morale high. They invest in robots to do boring tasks and free human workers for more interesting jobs. They hold competitions to encourage workers to think of new ideas.

Many single women in Japan work in business but quit after they marry. One reason for this may be that Japanese companies appoint few female managers. Women who do become managers face **discrimination.** They receive less money and fewer benefits than men who do the same work.

Lesson Assessment

Review

1. **Explain** Why did the Japanese go to war with China?

2. How has the Japanese government helped Japanese industry?

3. **Generalize** Why might women give up jobs at Japanese companies?

4. **Summarize** How did Japanese companies become successful in the 1960s?

Critical Thinking

Analyze ways in which Japanese companies save money. How do savings help them export more goods?

Writing in Social Studies

Compose a want ad describing an opening at a Japanese factory.

Reading Skills and Strategies

- Use higher-order thinking skills.
- Review text connections, comprehension monitoring, SQ3R, and word-learning strategies.

Lesson 5

Society in India

As YOU Read

What You'll Learn

- How the caste system divides the people of India
- How the Indian government has tried to change Indian society

Why It's Important

The struggles of Indians offer lessons in how to change unfair systems.

Key Terms

- caste
- dalit
- quota
- literacy rate

Have you noticed that students sometimes form cliques? For example, athletes stick with athletes, and musicians hang out with other musicians. In some ways, cliques in schools are similar to the caste system in India.

Religious Traditions in India

The main religious groups in India are Hindus, Muslims, Christians, Sikhs, and Buddhists. The largest group by far is the Hindus. They make up more than four-fifths of all Indians.

For thousands of years, Hindus have been divided into social groups called **castes.** Each caste has been associated with certain occupations. Traditionally, Brahmans, members of the highest caste, were teachers and priests. Just below them were the soldier and merchant castes. Below them were hundreds of subcastes, including farmers, shopkeepers, hairdressers, and barbers. At the very bottom were casteless people known as **dalits.** They did the dirtiest work, sweeping streets and cleaning toilets. Other Hindus avoided contact with dalits, also called "untouchables."

▲ India's people are also divided into language groups.

Changes in the Caste System

In the 1940s, Mohandas Gandhi, a great religious and political leader, championed the cause of the untouchables. He opened a school for dalits and called his students Harijans, or "children of God."

With Gandhi's help, India won its independence from Great Britain and became a democracy in 1947. The country's new leaders drew up a constitution that protected the rights of dalits. New laws set aside 15 percent of government jobs for dalits and guaranteed them 15 percent of places at public universities. Such guarantees are known as **quotas.**

The quota system was put in place to break down the caste system. However, Indian traditions change slowly, especially in rural areas. Four out of five dalits live in villages, where caste discrimination remains strong. Dalits must live in areas separate from the rest of the villagers. Some dalits challenge tradition by running for village council or by voting. They are sometimes threatened or beaten for these actions.

Cities are the best places to escape discrimination. People there are more tolerant than in villages, and dalits blend in with everyone else. Thanks to the quota system, dalits in cities have become police officers, engineers, professors, and members of parliament. A dalit woman was once governor of India's largest state, and from 1997 to 2002, a dalit man served as president of India.

Other Changes

Women have also traditionally suffered discrimination in India. Mohandas Gandhi encouraged women to participate in boycotts against the British. After independence, women demanded more rights and began voting and running for office. In 1966, Indira Gandhi became India's first female prime minister.

India's government has tried to provide food and health care for millions of poor Indians. Through an agricultural program known as the green revolution, the government increased crop yields to try to

▲ India's green revolution increased farmers' use of pesticides and fertilizers that pollute the water and endanger people's health.

prevent famine. Other government programs have sent doctors to rural areas and reduced deaths from malaria.

Another challenge the Indian government faces is educating its people. One measure of education is a nation's **literacy rate.** This is the percentage of people fifteen years and older who can read. In 1991, India's literacy rate was about 50 percent. By 2007, it was 61 percent.

Lesson Assessment

Review

1. **Define** What are castes?

2. **Describe** What kinds of discrimination do dalits face?

3. **Conclude** How do quotas help dalits?

4. Choose one word from the lesson to describe Mohandas Gandhi.

Critical Thinking

Evaluate improvements in education in India between 1991 and 2007. Rate the government's success on a scale from one to ten with ten as the highest rating.

Writing in Social Studies

Write a story about a dalit who goes from a village to a seat in parliament. Base your story on facts in the lesson.

Beyond the Book

Top Ten CREEPIEST JOBS

By Matilda Juarez

How to make a living searching for spider nests, building haunted houses, and digging up mummies.

#1 Ask archaeologists if they've ever had one of their mummies wake up and chase them around the room—in old horror-movie fashion—and you'll probably get an annoyed glare. The fact is that a day in the life of an archaeologist can be spent in many ways. It can be in the library amongst piles of books. It can be in the lab analyzing bits of cloth. Or it can be in an Egyptian pyramid. Most of the time, archaeologists aren't actually in the field. Instead they're in a lab completing the painstaking analysis of chips of ancient pottery. Yet those days in the field—the days when great discoveries are made and mummies are unearthed from ancient crypts—are when all sorts of old horror movies nearly come alive. An archaeologist may spend her nights in a tent twenty miles from freshwater or air-conditioning. She may shake out her boots each morning to make sure no scorpions are inside. And she may cover every inch of her body in clothing and scarves—even in blistering heat—to protect herself from millions of buzzing insects native to the area. The bugs, however, are probably what she thinks are the creepiest part of her job. The dusty, forever-sleeping, fabric-wrapped mummy she discovers in a sarcophagus that hasn't been opened in three thousand years . . . that's not creepy—that's just cool.

(continued on page 40)

Extension Activity

You've learned important skills and strategies in the first ten units of this program. Using your own classroom social studies textbook, find the section you're assigned to read next, and follow the instructions below. Write your responses on notebook paper.

a. **Survey** the section you're assigned, and describe what you did.

b. **Find** two examples of text structure. Write the page number, title (or subhead), and paragraph on which you found each example so your teacher can find it easily.

c. **Which** of the following text structures best fits the paragraph(s) for each example—Description-or-List, Order-or-Sequence, Cause-and-Effect, or Compare-and-Contrast?

d. **Why** did you choose this text structure? For each example, give an explanation.

e. **Choose** two bold and highlighted words to look up in a dictionary. Write the definitions you find.

f. **Write** a sentence using each word you looked up in the dictionary.

g. **Choose** a word that is not bold and highlighted, and look it up in an online dictionary. Write the definition you find.

h. **Write** a sentence using the word you looked up in the online dictionary.

Reading Skills and Strategies

• Use the SQ3R strategy: reflect.
• Use the SQ3R strategy: review.

Lesson 1 Measuring Motion

As YOU Read

What You'll Learn

■ How we observe motion using reference points

■ How speed and velocity differ

■ Types of acceleration

■ How speed, velocity, and acceleration are related

Why It's Important

Understanding speed, velocity, and acceleration is important in physics.

Key Terms

■ motion
■ reference point
■ speed
■ velocity
■ acceleration
■ centripetal acceleration

Observing Motion

How can you tell something is moving? You can observe some objects moving. You can see a leaf blown by the wind or a ball thrown at you. Objects are moving all around you, even if you can't see the movement. For example, you can't see Earth rotating or gas particles moving in the air. We recognize the movement of an object by observing a change in its position. **Motion** is a change in position.

We detect motion by observing an object change position compared to another object that stays in one place. The object that stays in one place is a **reference point.** Common reference points include the ground and other nonmoving objects, such as trees and buildings. A reference point can also be a moving object. When you ride in a car, you can observe the motion of a car driving past you.

► The poles are reference points for observing the motion of the car.

Speed

The motion of an object is measured by observing the distance the object travels and the time it takes to travel that distance. The distance traveled divided by the time that elapses equals the object's **speed.** A car that travels 100 meters (m) in 5 seconds (s) has a speed of 100 meters per 5 seconds (100 m/5 s), which equals 20 m/1 s. Speed is usually measured in m/s for scientific purposes. You can measure speed in any unit as long as the speed is expressed as

A speedometer shows the speed a car is moving at a particular moment.

distance divided by time. Speed is often expressed as miles per hour (mi/h), kilometers per hour (km/h), or feet per second (ft/s).

When you go for a walk or ride your bike, you probably don't maintain the same speed the whole time. On a long car trip, you may make stops along the way. Objects do not typically travel at a constant speed. Instead of calculating the speed during each minute or each second, it's more useful to find the average speed. Average speed is figured by dividing the total distance traveled by the total time an object was in motion. Suppose it takes 8 hours to drive a car 400 miles. The average speed for the whole trip is 50 mi/h.

Velocity

You may think velocity is the same as speed. Speed and velocity are related, but they aren't the same. Speed expresses only the distance an object travels during a specific period of time. To figure an object's velocity, you must know its direction. **Velocity** describes an object's speed as well as the direction it travels. For instance, a

These two trucks have the same speed, but their velocities are different because their directions are different.

runner's average speed is 7 miles per hour (mi/h), but her average velocity is 7 mi/h north. Her velocity is equal to her speed in a particular direction. Two cars driving 80 kilometers per hour (km/h) in opposite directions have the same speed but do not have the same velocity.

Velocity Changes

You can think of velocity as speed with a direction. Velocity measures speed—the rate at which the position of an object changes. Rate is a measure of one quantity in relation to another quantity. In this case, rate is the distance an object travels divided by the amount of time that passed while the object was in motion. Keep in mind that velocity is dependent on both speed and direction. It is constant only if an object's speed *and* direction don't change. If one of these factors changes, the object's velocity also changes. A woman walking at a constant speed of 1 m/s on a treadmill maintains the same velocity. If she walks on a sidewalk at a constant speed and turns a corner, her speed remains the same, but her velocity has changed because she changed direction.

Velocities Can Be Combined

Sometimes the motion observed from one perspective is different from the motion observed from another perspective. Suppose you're watching a boat heading down a river. The boat travels at a velocity of 20 mi/h down the river. The current is flowing at 5 mi/h down the river. When two velocities are in the same direction, you can add the two velocities. What you observe is that the boat is traveling at 25 mi/h.

20 mi/h
5 mi/h

▶ The combined velocity of the boat and the river current equals 25 mi/h.

You can also combine the velocities of objects that are moving in opposite directions. When two velocities are in opposite directions, you combine them by subtracting the smaller velocity from the larger velocity. For example, a plane is flying west, heading into the wind at 600 mi/h. The wind is blowing 20 mi/h eastward. The plane's velocity is 580 mi/h west.

Acceleration

In everyday language, *accelerate* means "to speed up." In scientific terms, **acceleration** is the rate at which velocity changes. In other words, it's the rate at which an object's speed or direction changes. Acceleration can also express the rate at which both speed *and* direction change. You can find the average acceleration by dividing the change in velocity by the elapsed time, or the time it took for the velocity to change. The change in velocity equals the final velocity minus the starting velocity. Acceleration is expressed in units of velocity per time. Because velocity is typically expressed in meters per second (m/s), acceleration is usually calculated as m/s^2.

Positive and Negative Acceleration

Velocity can increase or decrease, depending on how the speed of an object changes. As a result, acceleration of an object can be positive (increasing velocity) or negative (decreasing velocity). Acceleration measures two properties of velocity: how much velocity changes and the rate, or how fast, velocity changes. Acceleration is greater when velocity changes faster. When the velocity changes more slowly, the acceleration is less.

Constant Acceleration

Objects experience constant acceleration when the velocity changes by the same amount at set intervals. For example, a cyclist traveling east increases his speed by 2 m/s each second. Because the velocity of the cyclist changes by the same amount each second, the cyclist has constant acceleration. A person or an object with constant acceleration does not have constant velocity. If a person or an object has constant velocity, speed and direction are not changing, and the person or object is not accelerating.

Acceleration along a Curved Path

Acceleration does not always occur in a straight line. In fact, you can experience acceleration without really going anywhere at all. On a Ferris wheel, you travel up, around in a circle, and back to the place where you started. But because the motion is circular, the direction you are traveling is always changing. When an object in motion changes direction, it is accelerating. Acceleration in a circular path is called **centripetal acceleration.**

Lesson Assessment

Review

1. **Define** What is a reference point?

2. **Explain** How do you calculate the speed of an object?

3. **Compare and Contrast** How are speed and velocity alike and different?

4. **Describe** How are velocity and acceleration related?

Critical Thinking

What does a race car's speed tell you? What does its velocity tell you? Which information is more useful? Why?

Writing in Science

Draw a diagram that shows the combined velocities of two objects. Label all the parts of your diagram. Then write a title and a caption for your diagram.

Reading Skills and Strategies
- Use the SQ3R strategy: reflect.
- Use the SQ3R strategy: review.

Lesson 2 Forces

As YOU Read

What You'll Learn
- How forces act on objects
- How to determine net force
- The difference between balanced and unbalanced forces

Why It's Important
Studying how forces act on objects helps us understand the forces we exert and the forces that act on us.

Key Terms
- force
- net force
- unbalanced forces
- balanced forces

How Force Acts on Objects

A **force** is a push or a pull that acts on an object. A force can change the motion of an object by causing the object to speed up or slow down. A force can make an object in motion stop moving or make a stationary object start moving. A force can also change the direction of an object. Scientists measure force in Newtons (N).

Net Force

Most of the time, there is more than one force acting on an object. Gravity is a force that pulls objects toward the center of Earth. Even the air around us is held close to Earth's surface by gravity. When more than one force acts on an object, the forces combine. The combination of forces acting on an object is called the **net force.**

▶ The net force equals the sum of the two forces acting on the wagon: 15 N + 20 N = 35 N.

Forces in the Same Direction

Recall that when velocities combine, you add them together if they are in the same direction. The same is true for *forces* that act in the same direction. The forces of a push and a pull in the same direction can be combined. For example, suppose you are trying to move a wagon full of rocks. You are unable to move it very far by pulling alone. A friend comes along to push the wagon while you pull. The net force of your pull and your friend's push is in the same direction. When forces act in the same direction, they combine to make a greater net force. These forces can act on an object to push or pull it a greater distance, in the same amount of time, than one force acting alone. Together, you and your friend can move the wagon easily.

Forces in Different Directions

Forces that act in different directions can also be combined. When one force is smaller than the other force, you subtract the smaller force from the larger force to determine the net force. The net force is always in the same direction as the larger force. Picture a football player

30 N   25 N

◄ The net force equals 5 N in the direction the player with the ball is moving.

running with the ball and a player on the other team trying to stop him. The player with the ball pushes forward while the other player pushes back. The net force equals the larger force minus the smaller force.

Unbalanced Forces

A change in motion occurs when the net force acting on an object is greater than zero. The forces that combine to produce the net force are called **unbalanced forces.** The motion of an object will not change unless the forces acting on it are unbalanced. In other words, the forces acting on an object must be unbalanced for the object to start moving, stop moving, change speed, or change direction.

Balanced Forces

Balanced forces produce a net force of zero. Because the net force is zero, there is no change in motion. Balanced forces do not cause an object to change direction or speed. Balanced forces cannot cause a stationary object to start moving. Any nonmoving object you see has balanced forces acting on it. Your chair, for example, has balanced forces acting on it. The force of gravity pushing the chair toward the floor equals the force of the floor pushing up on the chair.

Lesson Assessment

Review

1. **Define** What is net force?

2. **Explain** How do you find the net force of forces acting in the same direction? In opposite directions?

3. **Compare and Contrast** How are balanced and unbalanced forces alike and different?

Critical Thinking

Why is it important to know the direction of the forces when you calculate net force?

Writing in Science

Write a description of some pushes and pulls you exert every day. Describe the kinds of force you use and how each force causes a change in motion.

Reading Skills and Strategies
• Use the SQ3R strategy: reflect.
• Use the SQ3R strategy: review.

Lesson 3 Friction

As YOU Read

What You'll Learn

■ Why friction occurs

■ The effect of friction on different surfaces

■ The difference between kinetic and static friction

■ How to reduce and increase friction

Why It's Important

Understanding how friction works can help you increase or decrease friction to make your life easier.

Key Terms

■ friction

■ kinetic friction

■ static friction

▶ This girl must overcome friction to move forward on her skates. When she wants to stop, friction between the wheels and the pavement will slow her down.

Friction Opposes Motion

A runaway skateboard may seem as if it will roll forever. How do you know it will stop? The skateboard wheels turn more and more slowly until eventually the skateboard comes to a stop. What makes it slow down?

You learned that the motion of an object changes when an unbalanced force acts on it. A surface exerts a force called **friction** on an object that moves across it. Friction opposes the motion of objects. Friction occurs when two surfaces are pressed together. Friction causes moving objects to slow down and stop moving. Friction also makes it difficult for objects to start moving.

Friction on Various Surfaces

All surfaces are covered with tiny bumps and cracks. The contact between the bumps and cracks on two surfaces results in friction. Bumps and cracks on the wheels of the skateboard and the pavement cause friction between the two surfaces. As a result, the skateboard slows down and stops. The amount of friction is less between smooth surfaces with fewer bumps and cracks. The amount of friction is greater between rough surfaces.

Force and Friction

The amount of friction that occurs between two surfaces is also dependent on the force that pushes the surfaces together. Suppose you slide a book across your desk. Friction results when the book and the desk are in contact with each other. The more force the book exerts on the desk, the more friction there will be between the two surfaces. If you push down harder on the book or if the book is heavy, it will exert more force on the desk. A book that weighs less exerts less force on the desk, and there is less friction.

Kinetic Friction

Friction occurs when surfaces are moving and when they're stationary. Friction between moving surfaces is called **kinetic friction.** The word *kinetic* means "moving." Surfaces move by either sliding or rolling. Two surfaces sliding past each other results in sliding kinetic friction. Pushing a box across the floor causes sliding kinetic friction. Pushing the box on a cart causes rolling kinetic friction. The wheels of the cart roll over the floor. Which do you think is easier—sliding a box across the floor or pushing the box on a cart with wheels? Typically, sliding kinetic friction requires greater force to move an object. Less force is needed to move an object that rolls.

Static Friction

Sometimes the force applied to an object is not enough to make it move. The type of friction that balances the force applied to a surface is called **static friction.** *Static* means "nonmoving." When forces are balanced, there is no change in motion. Static friction balances the force applied to a nonmoving object. As a result, the object does not move. As soon as the object starts to move, static friction disappears and kinetic friction occurs.

Pros and Cons of Friction

Friction has many important uses in our daily lives. The friction that occurs between a car's tires and the road makes it possible for the car to move. Without friction, the car's tires would spin in place. We need friction to walk without slipping. Friction is also necessary for writing. Without friction, a pen or pencil would move across a paper but would leave no mark.

There are also negative aspects of friction. Friction between surfaces causes wear. Car parts wear down when they rub together, and clothes wear out when they rub against other surfaces. That's why your socks get holes. Friction also makes it difficult to push or pull heavy objects.

Lesson Assessment

Review

1. **Describe** How does friction act against the motion of an object?

2. **Identify** Is the force required to move an object greater for sliding kinetic friction or for rolling kinetic friction?

3. **Infer** Why is the force of friction greater on rough surfaces than on smooth surfaces?

4. **List** List three ways friction is helpful.

Critical Thinking

Static friction can be used to hold objects in place. Give one example of static friction. What would happen if a large enough force was applied to overcome static friction?

Writing in Science

Write about some of the ways you use rolling kinetic friction. Then write about what it would be like if you could use only sliding kinetic friction for these activities.

Lesson 4 Gravity

Reading Skills and Strategies
- Use the SQ3R strategy: reflect.
- Use the SQ3R strategy: review.

As YOU Read

What You'll Learn
- The meaning of gravity and the law of universal gravitation
- How mass and distance affect gravitational force
- How gravity is measured

Why It's Important

All objects in the universe are attracted to one another by gravitational force.

Key Terms
- gravity
- gravitational force
- law of universal gravitation
- weight

The Attraction of Gravity

Have you ever wondered why objects fall toward the ground or how Earth stays in its orbit around the sun? You probably know the answers have something to do with gravity, but what exactly is gravity? **Gravity** is a force that attracts objects to each other. All matter has mass. Objects are attracted to each other by gravity because of their mass.

You and all the matter around you exert a pull because all matter has mass. Small objects exert a small pull; large objects exert a large pull. This pull is the force of gravity, or **gravitational force.** You've probably never noticed objects like a book and a pencil being pulled toward each other. That's because their masses are so small. An object as large as Earth has enough mass to make gravitational force easy to observe. A dropped object falls toward Earth because of the strength of the pull Earth exerts on it.

Try this simple experiment to show how gravity affects an object. First, place a small rubber ball on top of your desk. Second, place an open jar over the ball, and spin the jar in a circular motion. Third, after the ball starts spinning, lift the jar from the desk. The ball will remain spinning until it loses speed and gravity pulls it back to the desk.

Newton's Discovery

Sir Isaac Newton wasn't the first person to observe the effects of gravity on objects and planets. However, he was the first person to realize that these two ideas are connected. Unbalanced forces act on both falling objects and orbiting planets. Newton reasoned that the same force that determines the motion of falling objects on Earth also keeps planets and moons in their orbits.

Newton discovered that the force of gravity between two objects depends on the masses of the objects and the distance between them. He developed mathematical equations to explain his ideas about gravity in a theory now called the **law of universal gravitation.** The relationships between gravitational force, mass, and distance apply to everything in the universe.

Gravity and Mass

Newton's law states that all objects are attracted to one another by the force of gravity. The amount of gravitational force between objects depends on two things: mass and distance. There is a small amount of attraction between objects with small masses. Larger

◀ The moon's gravitational force is about one-sixth of Earth's gravitational force.

masses exert a greater gravitational force. For example, the force of gravity between a piece of paper and Earth is less than between a table and Earth. The moon has less mass than Earth, so it has less gravitational force. The moon exerts a weaker pull, which allows astronauts to bounce on the moon's surface.

Gravity and Distance

Newton determined that gravitational force decreases as the distance between objects increases. Gravitational force increases when the distance between objects decreases. In other words, the force of gravity is stronger when objects are closer together. The gravitational force exerted by Earth on all of us is strong. The mass of the sun is about 300,000 times that of Earth. However, the gravitational force between the sun and objects on Earth is weak because the sun is so far away.

Measuring Gravitational Force

When you think of the size of an object, you may think of **weight** as a measure of its size. Weight is actually a measure of the gravitational force exerted on an object by a larger object, such as a planet or a moon. Because weight is a measure of force, it is expressed in Newtons (N).

An object's weight changes depending on its location in the universe. A student who weighs 500 N on Earth would weigh about 80 N on the moon. The moon has less mass and exerts less gravitational force than Earth. On Jupiter, which has more mass than Earth, the student would weigh about 1150 N.

Lesson Assessment

Review

1. **Define** What is gravity?

2. **Explain** What ideas about gravity did Newton first connect?

3. **Identify** What two things determine the amount of gravitational force between objects?

4. **Apply** Mass is a measure of the amount of matter an object has. How does mass differ from weight?

Critical Thinking

Venus and Earth have similar masses. Venus is closer to the sun than Earth is. Is the gravitational force greater between Venus and the sun or between Earth and the sun?

Writing in Science

Plants respond to gravity. Roots grow down, and stems and leaves grow up. Look up *geotropism,* and write a paragraph explaining what you learn.

Lesson 5

Newton's First Law

Reading Skills and Strategies

- Use higher-order thinking skills.
- Review text connections, text structure, comprehension monitoring, SQ3R, multipart words, and word-learning strategies.

As YOU Read

What You'll Learn

- How forces affect the motion of objects
- Newton's first law of motion
- How mass affects inertia

Why It's Important

Learning about Newton's first law of motion makes the relationship between force and motion easier to understand.

Key Terms

- force
- motion
- friction
- inertia

Force and Motion

You learned that a **force** is a push or a pull. Forces cause objects to change speed or direction. When an unbalanced force is applied to an object, you know the object will change position by speeding up or slowing down. When forces are unbalanced, there is more push or pull in one direction than in another. Recall that an object's change in position is called **motion.** When you kick a soccer ball, the ball changes position as a result of the force applied to it by your foot. The force you exerted is related to the motion of the ball.

◄ The soccer ball starts to move because of the force applied by the kick.

Laws of Motion

Have you ever seen a stationary object start to move without a force acting on it? Have you ever seen a moving object stop without a force acting on it? Do you think such things can't happen? You're right. All objects follow rules of force and motion.

More than three hundred years ago, Isaac Newton wrote laws of motion to explain how force and motion are related. The first law of motion states two important ideas. First, an object at rest stays at rest. Second, a moving object continues to move in a straight line and at a constant speed. Objects, whether they are moving or not moving, do not speed up, slow down, or change direction unless acted on by an unbalanced force.

Objects at Rest

The first part of Newton's law deals with nonmoving objects. It states that an object at rest remains at rest unless acted on by an unbalanced force. A shopping cart will stay in one place until you push it or pull it.

Objects in Motion

Like the first part of Newton's law, the second part of Newton's law involves an object; however, in this case, the object is moving. A moving object will remain in motion at a constant speed and in a straight line unless acted on by an unbalanced force. In other words, an object in motion maintains its velocity—speed and direction—until an unbalanced force acts on it. Suppose you're playing a game of miniature golf. When you hit the ball with the club, the ball slows down because of friction and then changes direction when it bumps into a wall. The unbalanced forces exerted by friction and the wall change the ball's speed and direction. Rolling uphill or downhill would also change the ball's velocity. If you hit the ball along a straight, flat path, would it move at the same velocity forever?

Motion and Friction

If there is no unbalanced force exerted on an object, the object will stay in motion forever. You know that doesn't happen in real life. **Friction** is a force that opposes motion. Under ordinary conditions, it's impossible to prevent friction. No matter how or where you hit that golf ball, friction will act on the ball. Friction will slow it down and cause it to stop. The second part of Newton's law is hard to observe because objects in motion are always acted on by friction.

Inertia

All objects have a tendency to resist a change in motion. An object at rest will resist being moved, and a moving object will resist a change in velocity. This tendency is called **inertia.** Have you ever been in a car that stopped suddenly? While the car came to a stop, your body continued to move forward. Your body resisted the change in motion until an unbalanced force overcame inertia.

An object's inertia largely depends on the mass of the object. An object with less mass has less inertia. An object with more mass has more inertia. In other words, it's easier to change the motion of an object with a small mass than an object with a large mass. This becomes obvious if you try to push an empty box and a box full of books. For the same reason, it's easier to stop a rolling soccer ball than a rolling bowling ball.

Lesson Assessment

Review

1. **Identify** According to Newton's first law of motion, what is needed to change the motion of an object?

2. **Explain** What effect does friction have on Newton's first law of motion?

3. **Define** What is inertia?

4. **Describe** When you're riding in a bus, why does inertia cause you to fall forward when the bus stops?

Critical Thinking

What effect does wearing a seat belt have on your inertia? How does the unbalanced force applied by the seat belt change your motion if the car suddenly stops or makes a sharp turn?

Writing in Science

Write a summary of Newton's first law of motion. Give an example for each part of the law.

Reading Skills and Strategies
• Use the SQ3R strategy: review.
• Review text connections, comprehension monitoring, and word-learning strategies.

Lesson 1

Electric Charge and Static Electricity

As YOU Read

What You'll Learn
- How charged objects interact
- How objects can become charged
- What static electricity is
- How electric discharge occurs

Why It's Important
Knowing about electric charges will help you understand how electricity works.

Key Terms
- electrical force
- electric field
- conduction
- induction
- static electricity
- electric discharge

Electric Charge

You know that matter is made of atoms. Atoms, in turn, are made up of protons, electrons, and neutrons. Protons and electrons are charged particles. Protons are positive, and electrons are negative. Neutrons have no charge. Because of the interaction between charged particles, objects, too, can become charged. Like atomic particles, objects can have a positive charge, a negative charge, or no charge.

The Force of an Electric Charge

Charges exert a force, a push or pull. Two identical charges repel, or push, each other. Opposite charges attract, or pull toward, each other. Charged objects behave in the same way. An object with a charge exerts a force on another charged object. This type of force is called **electrical force.**

The size of an electric charge depends on the amount of charge and the distance between two charged objects. Electrical force is greater when the amount of charge is greater. Electrical force is also greater when the charges are closer together. Charges that are smaller or farther apart exert less electrical force.

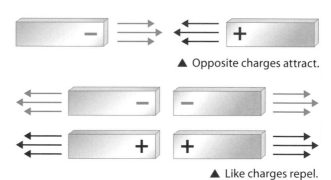

▲ Opposite charges attract.

▲ Like charges repel.

The electric charge exerted by an object is limited to its **electric field.** The electric field is the area around a charged object where it exerts its electrical force. If a charged object is within the electric field of another charged object, it will be attracted or repelled by the other object, depending on the electrical force applied to it.

Changing Charges

When the number of protons and electrons is equal, an atom has no charge. When atoms gain or lose electrons, they become charged. A gain in electrons results in an overall negative charge. A loss of electrons results in an overall positive charge. An object thus becomes charged when its atoms gain or lose electrons.

Electrons move between objects in three ways. Objects can become charged by friction. When objects rub together, the electrons from one object move to the other object. This causes the objects to have opposite charges. When objects are oppositely charged, they exert a pull and attract each other. If you rub a balloon on your hair, electrons move from your hair to the balloon. Your hair then has a positive charge, and the balloon has a negative charge. As a result, hair "sticks" to the balloon when you pull the balloon away.

Another way electrons travel is through contact between a charged object and an uncharged object. This contact is called **conduction.** Electrons travel from a negatively charged object to give the uncharged object a negative charge. When a positively charged object touches an uncharged object, electrons move from the uncharged object to the positively charged object. Then the uncharged object becomes positively charged.

Friction and conduction both cause charging when objects touch. Objects change their charge by friction because they rub together. The objects then acquire opposite charges. In contrast, conduction requires only that two objects touch. Unlike friction, conduction results in both objects having the same charge.

Electrons can also move between objects when the objects do not touch. Uncharged metal objects can become charged just by being near a charged object. **Induction** occurs when the charges in an uncharged object rearrange without actually touching a charged object. If you hold something metal near a positively charged object, the electrons in the metal are attracted to the positively charged object. The electrons move toward the positively

▲ Friction causes the charges in the balloon and the charges in the cat's hair to attract each other.

charged object. The movement of electrons produces a negatively charged area on the surface of the metal object. When you place an uncharged aluminum plate on a negatively charged foam plate, electrons on the bottom of the aluminum plate are repelled. The bottom surface of the aluminum pan becomes positively charged. Pull the aluminum plate away from the foam plate, and the overall charge becomes neutral again.

It's important to note that although charges can move between objects, they cannot be created or destroyed. The charge an object has changes because electrons move from one atom to another. The electrons themselves do not spontaneously appear or disappear.

Static Electricity

Electric charges may move or they may stay put. Conductors allow charges to move freely between objects. Insulators prevent the movement of charges. Electric charges that are not moving are said to be at rest. This condition is called **static electricity.** Have you ever noticed that clothes sometimes stick together when you take them out of the dryer? Clothes rub together as they tumble around in the dryer. Friction causes the charges to move among the clothes. Cloth is an insulator, so the charges stay on the clothes when the dryer stops. The result of all that friction is static cling.

Loss of Static Electricity

As you know, your clothes don't stick together forever. Even if you don't pull the clothes apart, eventually they separate on their own. The static electricity that was built up in the clothes is lost. This loss of charges is called **electric discharge.** Electric discharge can happen slowly or quickly. Two socks stuck together by static electricity may release their charges gradually if left alone. If you pull the socks apart, you may feel the effect of a quick electric discharge: a shock.

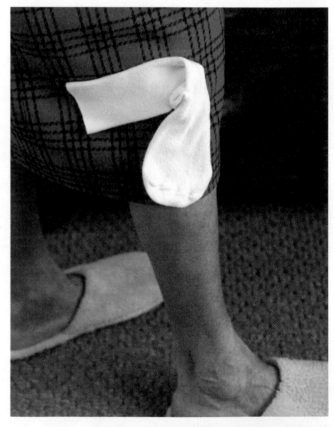

▲ Has this ever happened to you? Did you feel a little shock as you pulled the clothing apart?

Lightning

Lightning is a large-scale example of electric discharge. During a thunderstorm, lightning occurs because of a buildup of static electricity in clouds. The movement of air, water, and ice causes negative charges to accumulate at the bottom of a cloud. Members of the scientific community have not determined how a cloud acquires these charges. Positive charges move to the top of the cloud. When the bottom of the cloud nears the ground, the negative charges in the cloud cause the ground to become positively charged. As the electric field intensifies, the electrons at the ground's surface are pushed deeper into the ground by the strong negative charge at the bottom of the cloud. Thus, the ground acquires a strong positive charge. A quick electric discharge—a bolt of lightning—results from the difference in charge between the cloud and the ground.

During electric discharge, charges travel the shortest path between objects. When you reach for a metal doorknob, your hand receives a shock because your hand is the object closest to the doorknob. Lightning behaves in the same way. The shortest path to the ground is from the cloud to the object that is closest to the cloud, in other words, the object that is highest from the ground. Trees, buildings, and people can all provide a path for lightning to travel.

◀ Lightning travels from a cloud to the nearest object.

Lesson Assessment

Review

1. **Identify** What force exists between charged objects?

2. **Explain** How does an object become positively charged? How does it become negatively charged?

3. True or False: When an object becomes positively charged, the negative charges are destroyed.

4. Give two examples of electric discharge that happen quickly.

Critical Thinking

Lightning happens because of induction. The charges from a cloud can make a path to the ground, although the cloud does not touch the ground. Why is it dangerous to be near an object that is struck by lightning?

Writing in Science

Use the headings in the lesson to write an outline. Then write a summary of the lesson based on your outline.

Lesson 2 Magnets

Reading Skills and Strategies

- Use the SQ3R strategy: review.
- Review text connections, comprehension monitoring, multipart words, and word-learning strategies.

As YOU Read

What You'll Learn

- The properties of magnets
- What magnetic domains are
- How to make a magnet

Why It's Important

Although people have used magnets for thousands of years, scientists continue to learn more about the nature of magnetic force.

Key Terms

- magnetic pole
- magnetic force
- magnetic field
- domain

Magnets and Magnetic Poles

A magnet is any substance that attracts iron or steel. You know from experience that magnets pick up some metal things, such as paper clips and pins. A magnet's power to attract objects is strongest at each end of the magnet. The ends of the magnet are called **magnetic poles.**

All magnets have two poles—a north pole and a south pole. You can find which pole is the north pole by hanging a magnet from a string. The north pole of a magnet always points north. The needle of a compass is a magnet that is free to spin around, like a magnet on a string. A compass helps you find your way by pointing north.

Magnetic Forces and Magnetic Fields

The poles of a magnet have opposing magnetism. Opposite poles attract, and like poles repel. When two magnets are brought close together, the north pole of one magnet is attracted to the south pole of the other magnet. If you try to bring two north poles or two south poles together, the magnets will repel each other. The force magnets exert on each other is **magnetic force.**

Magnetic force acts only in a certain area around a magnet, known as the **magnetic field.** Although a magnetic field is invisible, you can see its shape by sprinkling bits of iron around a magnet. The magnetic force of the magnet arranges the iron filings in lines called magnetic field lines. The lines are closer together around the poles because that is where the magnetic force is strongest.

▲ The magnetic field is strongest in the areas with the greatest concentration of iron filings.

Domains

As you know, atoms contain tiny particles called electrons. As an electron moves around an atom, it makes a magnetic field. As a result of the magnetic field, the atom has a north pole and a south pole. In some substances, such as iron, atoms group together to form domains. **Domains** are very small areas within a substance where the magnetic fields in the atoms line up. When the domains are randomly arranged, the magnetic fields cancel each other out. The material does not act as a magnet. When the north poles in most of the domains point in the same direction and the south poles point in the opposite direction, the material becomes a magnet.

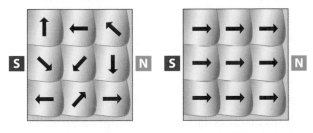

▲ The domains in the iron on the left are randomly arranged. It is not a magnet. The iron on the right is a magnet. Its domains are aligned in the same direction.

Metals such as iron, nickel, and cobalt contain domains in which the poles of the atoms can align. These metals are magnetic. Not all metals can be magnetized or attracted by magnets. Some of these are silver, gold, aluminum, and copper. Many other materials, such as paper, plastic, and glass, cannot be made into magnets.

Making Magnets

You can make a magnet. An object made of iron, nickel, or cobalt can become a magnet if its domains line up. You can align the domains by using a single pole of a magnet to stroke the object repeatedly in the same direction. The magnetic force of the magnet causes the domains in the object to line up. As you continue to stroke the object, more domains line up, and the object becomes a more powerful magnet. After the object becomes magnetized, it will attract other objects made of iron, nickel, or cobalt. For example, if you stroke an iron nail several times with a magnet, you can use the nail to pick up a paper clip.

Lesson Assessment

Review

1. **Identify** What are three metals that magnets attract?

2. **Explain** How does a compass help you find your way?

3. **Define** What is a magnetic field?

4. **Analyze** How do domains act like tiny magnets within an object?

Critical Thinking

A piece of iron can become a magnet only if its domains line up. Why might the object become demagnetized if it's dropped?

Writing in Science

Investigate the history of magnets. Write a paragraph about the ways people used magnets long ago.

Lesson 3

Electromagnetism

Reading Skills and Strategies

- Use the SQ3R strategy: review.
- Review text connections, comprehension monitoring, and word-learning strategies.

As YOU Read

What You'll Learn

- How magnetism and electricity are related
- How solenoids and electromagnets are constructed
- Some applications of electromagnetism

Why It's Important

Electromagnetism has many important applications that affect our quality of life.

Key Terms

- electromagnetism
- solenoid
- electromagnet
- electric motor

The Relationship between Magnetism and Electricity

A compass needle is a magnet. The needle points north because of Earth's magnetic field. If the compass is in a different magnetic field, the needle will not point north. In 1820, Danish scientist Hans Christian Ørsted experimented with magnetism and electricity. He held a compass near an electric current flowing through a wire. He saw that the needle did not point north. After more experiments, he concluded that the current in the wire produced a magnetic field.

The action between magnetism and electricity is called **electromagnetism.** Ørsted's experiments showed that the direction of an electric current's magnetic field depends on the direction of the current. Electric current flowing in one direction causes a compass needle to turn clockwise. Current flowing in the opposite direction causes the needle to turn counterclockwise.

The magnetic field produced by such current is weak. It's strong enough to turn a compass needle, but it can do little more. Two devices can increase the magnetic power of an electric current. They are solenoids and electromagnets.

Solenoids

The current flowing through a loop of wire generates a weak magnetic field. If the wire is looped many times, its magnetic power is increased. This coil of wire is called a **solenoid.** When electric current flows through it, a solenoid generates a magnetic field like that of a bar magnet. The ends of a solenoid exert greater magnetic force than the

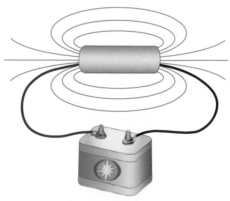

▲ An electric current flows through a solenoid connected to a battery.

middle. The magnetic field of a solenoid can be strengthened in two ways. The number of loops in the coil may be increased, or the current flowing through the coil can be increased.

Electromagnets

The magnetic field of a solenoid can be made hundreds of times stronger by placing an iron bar inside the coil of wire. An **electromagnet** is simply an iron bar with a solenoid wrapped around it. When the wires are connected to a battery, electric current flows through the coil to produce a magnetic field. The magnetic field of the solenoid aligns the domains in the iron core. The iron core becomes magnetized. The resulting magnetic field equals the magnetic field of the solenoid plus the magnetic field of the iron core. The combined magnetic fields are far more powerful than a solenoid alone.

Using Electromagnets

Electromagnets have many useful applications. They are used in things as small as a doorbell or as large as an electric generator in a power plant. Electromagnets are temporary magnets. They can be turned on and off. At a salvage yard, an electromagnet is turned on to pick up huge metal objects such as cars and refrigerators. When the electromagnet is turned off, it releases the object.

◀ The crane operator turns on the current to the electromagnet to pick up objects and shuts off the current to drop them.

Many machines use electric motors. An **electric motor** can convert electrical energy into mechanical energy. Current flows through a coil of wire between the two poles of an electromagnet. The electromagnet exerts a magnetic force on the wire and makes it rotate. The rotating wire starts the motor. A ring attached to the wire causes the electric current to change directions. The repeated change in direction of the current keeps the motor running.

Lesson Assessment

Review

1. **Explain** Why did Ørsted's compass needle fail to point north?

2. **Compare and Contrast** What do solenoids and electromagnets have in common? How are they different?

3. **Identify** What are two ways to increase the magnetic field of a solenoid?

4. **List** Give three examples of devices that use electromagnets.

Critical Thinking

• How would you go about making a simple electromagnet? What will happen if you change the size of the battery?

• Can you think of any other practical uses of electromagnets that were not provided in the text?

Writing in Science

• Design an experiment to test the strength of a simple electromagnet. Write a list of materials you will need. Then write steps for performing the test.

• Write a procedure a scientist could follow for creating an electromagnet.

Reading Skills and Strategies
- Use the SQ3R strategy: review.
- Review text connections, text structure, comprehension monitoring, and word-learning strategies.

Lesson 4 Electronic Devices

As YOU Read

What You'll Learn
- The role of circuit boards in electronic devices
- How semiconductors are used in electronic devices
- How diodes are put together

Why It's Important
Electronic devices have changed the world and play an important role in modern life.

Key Terms
- circuit board
- semiconductor
- diode

The Development of Electronic Devices

Can you imagine life without cell phones? What if a computer was so big it wouldn't fit on a desk? Years ago, cell phones didn't exist, and computers filled entire rooms. Over the years, engineers have developed many new electronic devices. Engineers use scientific knowledge to design smaller, faster electronic devices. These devices use electrical energy to send and receive information.

Think about the electronic devices you use every day. Computers, calculators, remote controls, cell phones, and digitized music players such as MP3s are all electronic devices. They perform different functions, but they have many of the same parts.

The Role of Circuit Boards

Electronic devices contain many small connected parts. Each part has a particular role in processing information. The parts are put together on a sheet of green insulating material called a **circuit board.** The circuit board supplies electric current to the device.

It also sends signals to all the parts of the device. When you push a button on a television remote control, a signal is sent to the circuit board. The parts on the circuit board sort out the signal you sent when you pushed the button. Then the parts send information to the television set to increase or decrease the volume or change the channel.

▲ The circuit board of this electronic device controls all its functions.

Semiconductors

The parts of an electronic device must conduct electricity, but the parts must also be able to change their conductivity. A conductor allows electric current to flow easily. An insulator does not allow electricity to flow. An element or a compound that conducts electric current better than an insulator but not as well as a conductor is a **semiconductor.** A semiconductor changes its conductivity when an impurity is added to it. Usually, a small amount of another substance, such as an element or a compound, is added to change the conductivity.

The element silicon (Si) is the typical semiconductor used in electronics. The conductivity of silicon changes when some of its atoms are replaced by atoms of another element or compound. Arsenic and gallium often replace some of the silicon in a semiconductor. Arsenic has one more electron in its outer shell than silicon. Gallium has one less electron than silicon. When an arsenic atom replaces a silicon atom, there is an extra electron. This is called an n-type semiconductor. When a gallium atom replaces a silicon atom, there is one less electron. A hole is left in the place of the missing electron. This is a p-type semiconductor.

Diodes

N-type semiconductors and p-type semiconductors are joined in layers to form **diodes.** Diodes control the flow of electrons between the two types of semiconductors. Extra electrons from the n-type layer move to the p-type layer to fill the gaps. The n-type layer acquires a positive charge, and the p-type layer becomes negatively charged. When a diode is connected to a battery, a current is produced if the p-type layer is connected to the positive (+) terminal. There is no current if the p-type layer is connected to the negative (–) terminal of the battery.

▲ Despite its small size, this transistor can process a lot of information.

Lesson Assessment

Review

1. **Define** What is a semiconductor?

2. **Identify** Which element, when added to silicon, adds an extra electron?

3. What does a diode do?

Critical Thinking

Why, do you think, are circuit boards made from materials that are insulators?

Writing in Science

Write a paragraph about the influence of semiconductors and electronic devices in the world today. How would your life be different without these devices?

Lesson 5

Electronic Communication

Reading Skills and Strategies

- Use higher-order thinking skills.
- Review text connections, comprehension monitoring, SQ3R, and word-learning strategies.

As YOU Read

What You'll Learn

- How signals send and receive information
- How analog signals function in telephones
- How digital signals work
- How radio and television are transmitted

Why It's Important

Communication technology helps people stay informed.

Key Terms

- signal
- carrier
- analog signal
- digital signal

Signals

Many electronic devices send and receive information. Telephones, radios, and television sets are three of these devices. Information is sent by **signals.** Signals include sounds, numbers, letters, movements, and anything else that sends information. The signals are sent by a **carrier,** such as an electric current or a radio wave. Communication devices use two types of signals to send information—analog signals and digital signals.

Analog Signals

An **analog signal** is a changing electric current that carries information. Analog signals change based on the information they carry. When you speak into a telephone, the sound waves change into an electric current in the telephone's transmitter. This analog signal is similar to the sound of your voice. The signal changes as your voice changes. The electric current travels along wires to

the telephone of the person to whom you're speaking. The current is changed back into sound waves in the receiver of the other person's telephone. Because the analog signal is based on changes in the original sound waves, the sound the listener hears is very similar to the actual sound of the speaker's voice.

Digital Signals

A digital signal sends information in a different form than an analog signal does. The information carried on a **digital signal** is a series of separate numerical values. These values are made up of a sequence of 1s and 0s, where 1 represents an electric pulse and 0 represents a missing pulse. Electronic devices process digital signals by detecting the pattern of electric pulses.

Unlike analog signals, digital signals do not change continuously based on the information they carry. Instead, the information is measured many times per second. Each measurement is a sample of the information. It doesn't closely match the original information as an analog signal does. In a digital recording, a digital signal measures the amplitude of a sound wave. These values do not match the original sound wave. By taking many samples of the sound waves each second, the digital sound comes close to the original.

▲ The information from a digital recording is stored on a compact disc.

Electromagnetic Waves

Another type of carrier is an electromagnetic wave. Electromagnetic waves contain electric and magnetic fields. They transmit signals from radio and television stations. These signals may be either analog or digital. The electromagnetic waves are sent from the station through the air and are picked up by an antenna.

Radio

At a radio station, a microphone picks up sound waves and produces an electric current. A device called a modulator produces an analog signal that acts as a carrier for the sound waves. The antenna on a radio tower changes the electric current into electromagnetic waves and sends them through the air. The antenna on a radio receives the electromagnetic waves. The radio's receiver separates the electromagnetic waves from the analog signal. Finally, the radio's speakers change the analog signal back into sound waves.

► The antenna on top of a radio tower sends electromagnetic radio waves through the air.

Lesson Assessment

Review
1. Give four examples of information sent by signals.
2. **Compare and Contrast** What do analog and digital signals have in common? How do they differ?
3. **Explain** What happens in a digital recording to make the signal come close to the original sound?

Critical Thinking
Why does a cell phone sometimes stop transmitting or receiving signals in the middle of a conversation?

Writing in Science
Reread the paragraph about radio waves. Use the text to make a flowchart showing how radio signals are transmitted and received.

Unit 13
Science

Reading Skills and Strategies

• Review text connections, comprehension monitoring, SQ3R, and word-learning strategies.

Lesson 1 Waves

As YOU Read

What You'll Learn

■ How waves transfer energy

Why It's Important

Learning about waves will help you understand more about forms of energy such as light and sound.

Key Terms

■ wave
■ medium
■ transverse wave
■ longitudinal wave

If you mention the word *waves,* most people picture waves of water at the beach. However, a wave can be much more than just energy moving through water. A **wave** is the transfer of any type of energy. You encounter waves constantly in your daily life. Both light energy and sound energy move in waves.

Wave Energy

The waves that transfer energy act much like the waves in the ocean. Waves move up and down, just as ocean waves do, and just as ocean waves carry energy from the ocean to the shore, other types of waves carry sound or light energy from one place to another.

▶ Just as ocean waves carry surfers toward the shore, energy waves carry energy to a new location.

Work Effects of Waves

Because waves carry energy, they do work. You can see the direction in which work is being done by finding the direction of the wave. In waves in the ocean, energy moves from the ocean toward the shore. As a wave moves, it carries energy and does work on the things in its way. For example, an energy wave that carries heat makes things warmer as it passes through them.

Energy Transfer through a Medium

Energy waves can carry energy through many different substances. The substance an energy wave moves through is called a **medium.** Common mediums that energy waves move through include air, water, and even sediment and rocks beneath our feet. Although the medium carries the wave, it is not considered part of the wave. Many energy waves, such as sound waves, need a medium in order to travel.

Energy waves move through a medium by transferring energy from particle to particle in the medium. Each particle receives energy and then transfers it to the next particle. You can visualize this movement by picturing a line of tennis balls in a tube. If you hit the tennis ball at one end of the tube, it will bang into the next tennis ball. That ball will bang into the next, and so on, until the last tennis ball has moved. Although each ball has moved very little, the energy you used to hit the first ball moved from one end of the tube to the other. The energy traveled through the medium, the tennis balls, to move from the start to the finish.

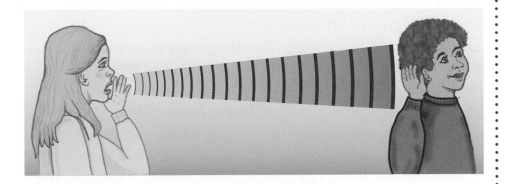

◀ These sound waves are the movement of energy from one person's mouth to another person's ear. Sound waves must have a medium—in this case, the air—in order to move from one place to another.

Energy Transfer without a Medium

Not all energy waves need a medium in order to move. Many forms of energy, such as light, can travel through outer space, where there is no air. Waves that require a medium, such as sound waves, cannot travel through outer space. That is why we can see objects in space but we cannot hear them. Television and radio waves can also travel through empty space without a medium. Other types of waves that do not require a medium are X-rays and microwaves. Although these energy waves do not need a medium to travel through, they can still move through a medium, such as air or water, if it's present.

We can see these stars from Earth because light waves can travel through space without a medium.

Transverse Waves

Waves can be divided into two types, depending on the direction in which they move. The first type of wave is called a **transverse wave.** The energy in a transverse wave moves in a horizontal direction, at right angles to the up-and-down motion of the particles that make up the wave. You can see an example of a transverse wave in the diagram below. Notice how the particles of the wave move up and down while the energy travels at a right angle to the up-and-down motion. If you could watch the wave in motion and look at just one spot, you would see that spot moving up and down. The whole wave moves energy in one direction while the particles move up and down. Light is an example of a transverse wave. The different lengths of the waves in light cause us to see colors. When colors are described in terms of light energy, we identify them by their individual wavelengths.

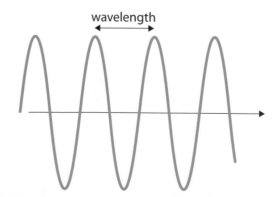

▶ This diagram shows a transverse wave.

Longitudinal Waves

The second type of wave is a **longitudinal wave.** The particles in a longitudinal wave move back and forth in the same direction as the wave. Sound waves are longitudinal waves. They move by compressing and expanding to produce different sounds as the wave travels through the air. The back-and-forth motion of the wave produces the sounds you hear when the wave hits your ears.

You can see what a longitudinal wave looks like in the diagram below. A longitudinal wave looks like a spring. In fact, the longitudinal wave behaves much like a coiled spring. When you pull the spring apart or push it together, the coils move toward or away from one another, carrying energy.

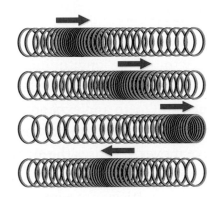

▶ The particles in a longitudinal wave move back and forth in the same path as the energy of the wave.

Sound Waves

The most common example of a longitudinal wave is a sound wave. Sounds move in longitudinal waves from the person or thing making the sound to the listener. Particles of the medium of the sound wave press together and spread apart, depending on the energy used. A sound wave performs work on the air as the wave travels through the air. The movement of the particles of the medium of the sound waves, as they press together and spread apart, produces sounds.

You can picture the motion of the sound wave as one particle bumps another in the direction of the wave. As the particles collide, they push the particles in front of them forward. After a particle bumps into the particle in front of it, it loses energy and stops moving.

Another Type of Wave

Although waves on the ocean may look like transverse waves, they are actually surface waves. Surface waves occur when the wind transfers energy to the surface of the water. The friction between the water and the air allows the water to gain energy from the air.

Unit 13
Science

Reading Skills and Strategies

• Review text connections, comprehension monitoring, SQ3R, multipart words, and word-learning strategies.

Lesson 2 Sound

As YOU Read

What You'll Learn

■ How vibrations cause sound

■ How sound is transmitted and received by the human ear

Why It's Important

Sound is an important part of daily life.

Key Terms

■ sound wave

■ outer ear

■ middle ear

■ inner ear

Sound is an important part of our daily lives. We use sound to learn about our environment and to communicate. Most of us take sound for granted without thinking about how it's made.

Making Sound

The sound we hear travels in the form of **sound waves.** The waves that carry sound are longitudinal waves. Longitudinal waves move like the coils of a spring. Vibrating particles of a longitudinal wave travel back and forth and expand and compress as the sound wave moves in one direction. Sound waves often travel through the air. As the wave moves, it causes the air particles to collide with one another. Sometimes the air particles collide close together; at other times, the air particles are spread out. The different levels of collisions between the air particles cause vibrations in the air that make different sounds.

▶ This illustration shows how the particles of sound waves stretch and compress as they travel. The tuning fork produces sound by causing air molecules to collide.

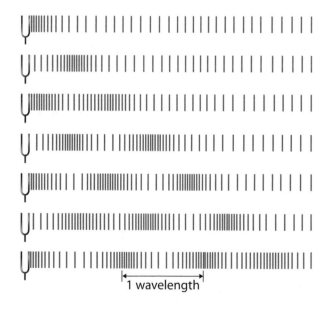

1 wavelength

Sound and Media

Because producing sound depends on the collision of molecules, sound waves must have a medium in order to move. A medium is any substance that waves travel through. Air is not the only possible medium for sound waves. Sound can travel through water and even through solid substances such as wood and glass. Consequently, when someone shouts from behind a door or a window, you can often still hear the person. The sound waves travel not only through the air but through the solid medium as well.

How You Detect Sound

Your ears are precise instruments that allow you to collect sound waves and interpret the sounds so they're recognizable to you. Your ear is made up of three specialized areas that perform specific functions in detecting sound. Your **outer ear** is basically a cone or funnel that collects sound waves and directs them into your ear. Your **middle ear** is made up of three bones that receive the sound waves. The sound waves make the bones vibrate. The vibrations increase and pass the sound on to the **inner ear.** Your inner ear changes the vibrations into electrical signals that travel to your brain, and your brain interprets the sounds.

Hearing Loss

It's easy to take your hearing for granted, but damage to the parts of your ear can cause difficulty in hearing. If there's too much damage, you can lose your hearing altogether.

Damage to the ear is often caused by exposure to very loud sounds. These loud sounds can destroy hairs and nerve cells in your ear that are important for hearing. If the cells are heavily damaged, they will not recover, and hearing loss becomes permanent. Your ears can be damaged either by a single exposure to a very loud noise or by repeated exposures to loud sounds over a long period of time. Ear infections can also cause permanent hearing loss.

Fortunately, you can take some easy steps to protect your hearing for life. Avoid loud places whenever you can. If you know you will be somewhere loud, such as a concert, you can protect your ears by wearing earplugs. Always make an effort to keep radios and television sets tuned to a reasonable sound level. Finally, have your hearing tested regularly.

◄ An audiologist, a person who specializes in hearing problems but is not a physician, can test your hearing and make treatment recommendations.

Lesson Assessment

Review

1. **Describe** Draw a diagram to explain the role each of the three parts of the ear plays in hearing.

2. **Define** Explain the movement of a longitudinal sound wave.

3. Describe the activity of air particles that are being used as a medium for sound waves.

4. **Relate Cause and Effect** Why, do you think, do people's voices sound muffled when heard through a closed door or a wall?

5. **Compare and Contrast** Describe some of the differences you might expect to find in the ears of people with excellent hearing and the ears of people who have hearing loss.

Critical Thinking

Why is it common for rock musicians to develop hearing problems as they get older?

Writing in Science

Some of your friends are buying a new radio. Write a warning label that will help them use the radio properly to protect their hearing.

Unit 13
⫸ Science

Reading Skills and Strategies

- Review text connections, comprehension monitoring, SQ3R, and word-learning strategies.

Lesson 3 — Properties of Sound

As YOU Read

What You'll Learn

■ How sound differs in pitch and frequency

■ How to describe sound in loudness and amplitude

Why It's Important

By learning about the properties of sound, you will understand what makes sounds different from one another.

Key Terms

■ pitch
■ Doppler effect
■ loudness
■ decibel

The sounds the human ear can hear are almost endless. You know sounds can be loud or soft, high or low. In addition, the same note, played on different instruments or sung by different voices, may have a different quality or tone.

The Speed of Sound

Sound travels in waves. One factor that determines how fast a sound wave travels is the medium through which the wave is moving. You might think that sound travels fastest through the air. Actually, the opposite is true. Although sound waves travel at approximately 343 meters per second in the air, the same sound waves will travel at 1,482 meters per second through water. When sound travels through a solid medium, such as steel, it moves at an astounding 5,200 meters per second.

The temperature of the medium also affects the speed of sound. As the temperature falls, a sound wave travels slower. As the temperature increases, a sound wave moves faster. This is true no matter what medium—air, water, or steel—the sound wave is traveling through.

Pitch and Frequency

Most people describe musical notes as high or low. When people compare sounds in this way, they are referring to the **pitch** of the sound. The pitch of a sound is caused by the frequency of the wave. The frequency is a measure of how fast the waves are moving. In a low frequency, sound waves move slowly. A sound wave with a low frequency will have a low pitch, like the sound of

▶ The sounds of a flute are produced by high-frequency waves. The sounds of a bass guitar are produced by low-frequency waves.

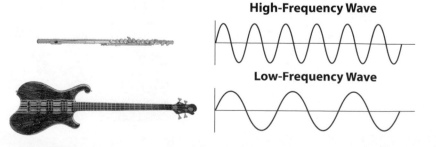

High-Frequency Wave

Low-Frequency Wave

a bass guitar or a tuba. With a high frequency, sound waves move faster. A sound wave with a high frequency will have a high pitch, like the sound of a flute or a piccolo.

The Doppler Effect

If you stand on a train platform and close your eyes, you can hear a train coming. Without seeing the train, you hear it approach, whiz by, and travel away into the distance. Even though the train makes the same noise the whole time, it sounds different to you as your position in relation to the train changes. These changes in sound are called the **Doppler effect.** The Doppler effect is produced because the frequency of the sound waves changes as a sound moves toward or away from a listener. The pitch increases as the train approaches and decreases as the train moves away, and the listener hears the difference.

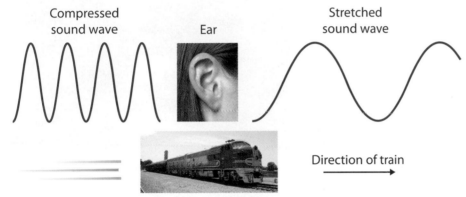

Compressed sound wave   Ear   Stretched sound wave

Direction of train

▲ As a train approaches a person at the station, the sound waves are compressed, and the pitch increases. As the train moves away, the sound waves expand, and the pitch decreases. This is called the Doppler effect.

Loudness and Amplitude

The **loudness** of sound refers to the amount of energy a sound wave carries. If you blow into a horn very softly, the sound is not very loud. On the other hand, if you blow into the horn with force, you add extra energy to the sound waves, and the sound is louder. The energy you add increases the amplitude of the wave. The amplitude is the height of the sound wave.

Measuring Loudness

We measure the loudness of sound in **decibels** (dB). Louder sounds have higher decibel levels. Sounds at 0 dB can barely be heard by humans. Normal speech is about 60 dB. A power lawn mower would have a level of approximately 90 dB. Sounds start to become painful to humans at about 120 dB, which is the sound level of some airplane engines at close range.

Lesson Assessment

Review

1. **Contrast** Tell how sounds can differ in pitch and amplitude.

2. **Define** Draw or describe in words how a change in frequency affects a sound wave.

3. Draw a picture of a sound wave that experiences an increase in amplitude.

4. **Relate Cause and Effect** Explain why the sound of a siren on a police car seems to change as the car drives toward you and then away from you.

5. **Explain** Why is the word *frequency* used to describe the changes in sound waves as they move toward or away from a listener?

Critical Thinking

Describe how air particles might be affected when sound waves pass through them at different amplitudes.

Writing in Science

Think of a sound you have experienced. Write a few sentences that describe the sound as a writer or a musician might describe it. Then write a few sentences to describe the sound as a scientist would describe it.

Reading Skills and Strategies

• Review text connections, text structure, comprehension monitoring, SQ3R, and word-learning strategies.

Lesson 4 Light

As YOU Read

What You'll Learn

■ How light travels in wave form

Why It's Important

Light energy in some form provides energy for everything we do on Earth.

Key Terms

■ electromagnetic wave
■ radiation

What exactly is light? The characteristics of light are some of the most important and complex subjects scientists study. The shortest explanation is that light is energy.

▶ A flashlight is a helpful tool to illuminate dark areas. Light, however, is much more than a tool. Light is energy.

Light Travels

Light energy moves as an **electromagnetic wave.** An electromagnetic wave does not need a medium to move through. It can travel through empty space where there is neither air nor any other gas. This is why you can see light from stars that are billions of miles away in outer space. The electromagnetic wave that makes up light is so named because it is made up of electric and magnetic fields.

How Electromagnetic Waves Are Produced

An electric field surrounds electrically charged particles. When a particle vibrates, the field around it picks up the vibration and begins to vibrate as well. The vibrations produced by the electric field produce a magnetic field. You are probably familiar with the weak magnetic fields that surround magnets. These magnetic fields attract metal and have poles that repel like the poles of other magnets. When an electric field and a magnetic field vibrate together, they produce an electromagnetic field. This field emits **radiation.** Radiation is energy that moves as an electromagnetic wave.

The Speed of Light

Scientists have measured the speed of light as it travels. The electromagnetic waves that carry light move at a speed of approximately 300,000,000 meters per second. This is the speed that light waves move in a vacuum, such as space. When light waves move through a medium, such as air or water, they slow down.

Nothing we know of moves faster than light. Sound waves move much more slowly, approximately 344 meters per second through dry air at room temperature. This is why you see lightning before you hear thunder during a storm. Although the lightning and thunder occur at the same time, the sound waves are slower to reach you than the light waves are. Sound waves travel faster when they travel through a solid medium such as steel instead of air. Unlike light, sound waves require a medium and cannot travel through outer space.

You can count the seconds between a lightning flash and the sound of the thunder to estimate how far away the lightning is. As soon as you see a lightning flash, begin counting seconds. If you hear the thunder at five seconds, the lightning is a mile away. If you hear the thunder before five seconds, the lightning is less than a mile away. If you hear the thunder at ten seconds, the lightning is two miles away.

◀ The next time you see lightning, count the seconds until you hear thunder to learn how far away the lightning is.

Light from the Sun

In space, light must often travel great distances to reach a destination. There is a special unit, called a light-year, for measuring distances in space. A light-year is the distance light travels in one year. This distance is almost six trillion miles. The sun is only ninety-three million miles away.

Some stars you see in the night sky may no longer exist. You may be seeing light they gave out before they died.

Lesson Assessment

Review

1. **Compare and Contrast** Compare and contrast light waves and sound waves.

2. **Define** What two things make up an electromagnetic wave?

3. Tell how the speed of a light wave will be affected as it moves through different mediums.

4. **Explain** What does a light-year measure?

Critical Thinking

Many scientists think the dinosaurs became extinct when a meteorite hit Earth and produced clouds of dust that blocked the sun. Why might this cause mass extinction?

Writing in Science

Write a poem about a form of light. You may choose sunlight, starlight, light from a fire, an electric light, or any other form of light.

Lesson 5

Light and Sight

Reading Skills and Strategies

- Use higher-order thinking skills.
- Review text connections, text structure, comprehension monitoring, SQ3R, multipart words, and word-learning strategies.

As YOU Read

What You'll Learn

- How your eyes detect light in order to supply you with vision

Why It's Important

Most people use vision to supply much of the information about their environment.

Key Terms

- visible spectrum
- nearsightedness
- farsightedness

▶ The eye detects and interprets light so you can see.

How Eyes Detect Light

Your eyes detect electromagnetic light waves and send the information to your brain, which interprets the images. The range of light your eyes can detect is called the **visible spectrum.** Light is received and interpreted by your eyes in these four steps:

1. Light waves are reflected off an object you're viewing. These waves pass through the cornea of the eye. The cornea is a clear covering that directs the light as it enters the eye.

2. The light is directed to pass through an opening called the pupil. The iris causes the pupil to open or close to let in more or less light as needed.

3. The lens focuses the light and projects the image onto the back of the retina at the back of the eye. The lens flips the image so that it's upside down.

4. Optic nerves interpret the image and transmit it to the brain.

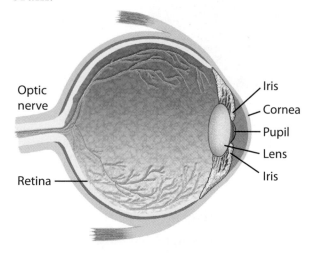

Common Vision Problems

Problems with vision can occur when parts of the eye do not focus light correctly. When this happens, a person may need corrective lenses (eyeglasses or contact lenses) to assist in focusing light.

Nearsightedness and Farsightedness

The most common vision problems caused by improperly focusing light are **nearsightedness** and **farsightedness.** A person who suffers from nearsightedness can see clearly things that are close by but cannot make out things far away. This condition occurs when the shape of the eye is too long. The lens of the eye focuses the image too far in front of the retina.

A person who suffers from farsightedness has trouble seeing clearly things that are close but can easily make out images that are farther away. Farsightedness is the opposite of nearsightedness. Farsightedness occurs when the shape of the eye is too short. The lens focuses the image behind the retina.

Color Deficiency

Another type of vision problem is color deficiency. Most people commonly refer to this lack of ability to distinguish certain colors as color blindness. Color blindness is a condition in which a person can't distinguish between two colors. Color deficiency is more common among men than women, and the colors most often associated with color blindness are green and red. This problem is not caused by the shape of the eye. Instead, it's caused by problems with receptors called cones in the retina. When cones work properly, they detect different colors of light. The cones of people with a color deficiency respond weakly or wrongly to colors.

Surgical Eye Correction

Although people have traditionally corrected vision problems by wearing eyeglasses or contact lenses, doctors can now correct some vision problems with surgery. The surgeon typically uses a laser to cut and reshape the cornea in order to correct nearsightedness or farsightedness. The cornea can then focus light images at the appropriate spot on the retina.

Lesson Assessment

Review

1. **Cause and Effect** Explain how differences in the shape of the eye cause nearsightedness or farsightedness.

2. **Define** What type of task might someone with farsightedness have difficulty completing?

3. **Identify** Which type of energy waves are associated with sight?

4. **Explain** Describe how a part of the eye helps prevent too much light from entering.

Critical Thinking

You have a brother and a sister. Your mother tells you that one of them has a color deficiency. Which one is more likely to have this vision problem?

Writing in Science

Using only your vision, write a description of something you own. Then write a description of it using a sense other than vision.

◀ If you can't tell red from green in the test card on the left, you may have a color deficiency.

Reading Skills and Strategies

• Review text connections, comprehension monitoring, SQ3R, and word-learning strategies.

Lesson 1

Introduction to Earth Science

As YOU Read

What You'll Learn
- The branches that make up earth science

Why It's Important
The study of earth science helps us understand our planet.

Key Terms
- geology
- oceanography
- meteorology
- astronomy

Earth science is a complex subject with many parts. The study of Earth includes its weather, the ground it's made of, the life it supports, its vast waters, and the space system of which it is a part. To study Earth more easily, earth science is divided into specialized areas.

Geology

One of the most obvious forms of earth science is **geology.** Geology is the study of all the materials that make up Earth and the

▲ Fossils can reveal information about ancient life on Earth.

processes that act on them. The information geologists obtain about Earth tells us much about the past, including the life-forms that have lived on our planet. Geologists get this type of information from fossils of organisms preserved in rock.

Geologists also study the processes and structures that form and change the surface of Earth, including earthquakes, landslides, and volcanoes.

Oceanography

Most of Earth's surface is covered with water. The study of **oceanography** focuses on the oceans. Oceanographers learn about the ocean floor and the organisms and ecosystems found there. The study of ocean currents and undersea Earth movements is an important part of learning about Earth. Ocean currents also affect Earth's weather.

Exploring the Ocean Floor

One of the remaining unexplored areas on Earth is the ocean floor. The study of the ocean floor is changing as scientists gain access to new technology that allows them to explore deep beneath the ocean surface. Miniature submarines can be operated by remote control and sent to great depths to gather information from the ocean floor.

You may be familiar with the *Titanic,* a ship that sank on an ocean voyage in 1912. For decades, the ship was lost on the ocean floor because the vessel was too deep for divers and exploration submarines to find. Eventually, small remote-controlled submarines were developed that could search deep underwater, and in 1985, explorers finally found the sunken ship. Remote-controlled submarines have also allowed scientists to discover and observe new forms of life and features on the ocean floor.

Meteorology

Some earth scientists focus on Earth's atmosphere. These scientists are called meteorologists. **Meteorology** is mainly concerned with weather conditions and weather forecasting. You have likely seen meteorologists on television tracking storms or describing and forecasting the weather.

Hurricanes

Hurricanes are tropical storms that develop over water and produce strong winds and rain. These huge storms can be destructive if they move from warm ocean areas onto populated land. Meteorologists cannot stop hurricanes, but they can track storms and warn people when one is approaching.

▲ A hurricane is a storm made up of strong winds that rotate. In the center of the hurricane is the "eye," a calm spot with no winds.

Tornadoes

Tornadoes are storms that form over land. A tornado consists of a tube or cylinder of very strong winds that extend from a storm cloud to the ground. Tornadoes destroy buildings and harm people as the storms move across the land. Tornadoes are especially dangerous because they are unpredictable and difficult to track. Most tornadoes appear and disappear quickly, often without warning.

Astronomy

The study of Earth extends beyond the planet to include the systems to which Earth belongs. This special area of science is called **astronomy.** Astronomers study the universe and Earth's place in it. The forces of the universe and the solar system that act on Earth have a huge impact on life. The movements of Earth and other bodies in space cause day and night, determine Earth years, and give us different seasons.

Telescopes are the main tools astronomers use to gather information about space. Although most people think of telescopes as tools for collecting visual images with light, astronomers also use telescopes to detect radio waves. Radio waves can be collected from deep space and analyzed to make images of the universe.

Lost in the Stars

More than a hundred billion billion stars make up our universe. These stars churn out light and heat energy and exert huge gravitational pull on other objects. Our sun is a star. It provides Earth with the energy we need to live. Earth and the other planets orbit the sun.

Special Branches of Earth Science

Because earth science covers everything on Earth and in the universe, it includes many other scientific disciplines.

Environmental Science

Environmental science is a fairly new area of earth science. Environmental scientists study the interactions between humans and their environment on Earth. This scientific specialty combines the study of Earth's environment with the science of living things and natural resources.

Ecology

The study of systems of living things and their interactions is called ecology. Ecologists work to solve problems related to populations and communities of organisms.

Geochemistry

Many of the rocks around us are millions of years old. However, each rock went through a cycle that produced it. Geochemistry is the study of the chemical processes that involve rocks, soil, and minerals. Geochemists use this information to understand the interactions between Earth's solid matter and the water and atmosphere that surround Earth.

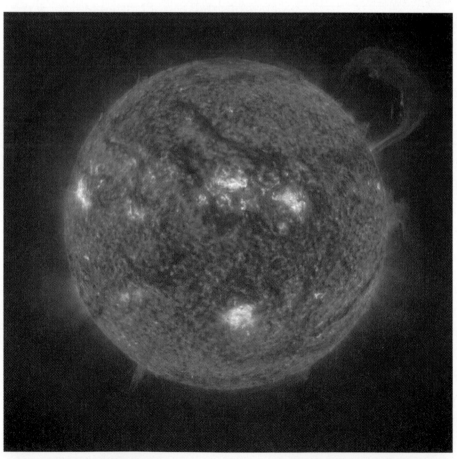

▲ Our sun is the star closest to Earth. Earth orbits the sun and receives energy from it.

Geography and Cartography

The branches of geography and cartography are concerned with Earth's surface. Geography is the study of Earth's features and the people who live on Earth.

Surface features often determine where people settle and form cities and countries. Cartography is the science or art of making maps. Cartographers use geographical information to make maps for many purposes.

▲ Ancient maps were drawn by cartographers who based their work on information then available. This information sometimes included long-held beliefs and the notes of explorers. Cartographers now have access to satellite images and precise measurements.

Lesson Assessment

Review

1. **Cause and Effect** How might information learned from geography affect work done by a cartographer?

2. **Predict** Describe a research project a geologist and a biologist might work on together.

3. What types of information do meteorologists provide?

4. **Identify** List some of the topics that are included in the study of geochemistry.

5. **Define** Which branch of earth science is concerned with the moon?

Critical Thinking

• Give some examples of how technology can play a big role in making advancements in some branches of earth science.

• How do the various branches of earth science help us learn about our planet? Give specific examples.

Writing in Science

• Choose one of the branches of earth science, and write a diary entry from the point of view of a scientist working in that field.

• Compare and contrast the various branches of earth science. How are they different? What similarities do they have?

Unit 14
Science

Reading Skills and Strategies

- Review text connections, comprehension monitoring, SQ3R, multipart words, and word-learning strategies.

Lesson 2 Igneous Rock

As YOU Read

What You'll Learn

- How igneous rocks form

Why It's Important

The study of igneous rocks can tell us much about what is happening beneath Earth's surface.

Key Terms

- intrusive igneous rock
- extrusive igneous rock

Igneous rock forms when molten rock beneath Earth's surface cools into solid form.

Hot Magma to Cool Rock

All igneous rock comes from magma or from lava as it cools. Magma is molten rock that flows under Earth's surface. Lava is magma that reaches the surface and flows above the ground. Usually this happens as magma flows up through Earth's crust and erupts from a volcano. However, often magma will cool underground without reaching the surface. As magma or lava cools, it changes from a liquid to a solid state. The result is igneous rock.

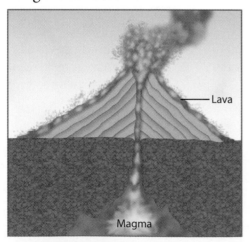

▲ Igneous rock forms as hot liquid magma or lava cools and becomes solid.

Igneous Rocks: Formation

Several things happen to magma when it cools. First, minerals begin to cool and become solid at different rates. This happens because different minerals become solid at different temperatures. As the magma cools, more and more minerals become solid. The second factor affecting the process is that as minerals solidify, they become crystals. These two stages, occuring at various rates, are what make igneous rocks different from one another.

Color

The minerals contained within each igneous rock determine the color of the rock. If the magma contains certain minerals, the resulting rock will be light in color. The magma may, instead, contain other minerals that will cause the rock to be dark in color after it cools.

Texture

The texture of an igneous rock depends on how fast it cools. As magma cools, the minerals inside become solid crystals. If the magma cools slowly, the minerals form

▲ This igneous rock has light and dark layers. The difference is due to the various minerals in the dark- and light-colored parts.

large crystals. If the magma cools quickly, smaller crystals form. The size of the crystals determines the texture of the rock. Rocks with large crystals are coarse-grained, and rocks made of small crystals are fine-grained. If magma cools quickly, no crystals will be formed, and the rock will be smooth in texture.

Intrusive and Extrusive Igneous Rock Formations

An intrusion occurs when molten rock seeps into existing rock formations and cools. When an intrusion occurs beneath Earth's surface, it forms **intrusive igneous rock.** If you look at a cross section of rock layers, you will notice that the intrusive igneous rock cuts across other layers of rock.

If an intrusion forms above the ground, it produces an **extrusive igneous rock.** Typically, this type of rock forms when lava flows from a volcano and cools, producing a rock formation. Usually, extrusive rock cools more quickly than intrusive rock. Therefore, extrusive igneous rock tends to be fine-textured. Intrusive igneous rock is usually coarse because it has cooled slowly underground.

Lesson Assessment

Review

1. **Explain** If all igneous rock comes from magma, why do some igneous rocks look different from others?

2. **Contrast** What is the difference in composition between a dark igneous rock and a light one?

3. **Describe** How do extrusive igneous rocks form?

4. **Relate Cause and Effect** Why do igneous rocks that form from volcanic eruptions typically have smaller crystal structure than rocks that form under Earth's surface?

5. **Define** Why is intrusive igneous rock so named?

Critical Thinking

A team of scientists discovers an igneous rock that is coarse-grained, with large crystal structures, on the surface of a volcano. One of the scientists theorizes that the rock must have formed underground and then been pushed up. Why would the scientist think this? What clues help you answer this question?

Writing in Science

On the Internet, find a photograph of an igneous rock. Write a description of the rock. What color is it? What texture do you think it has? What process do you think it went through to look the way it does?

Reading Skills and Strategies

- Review text connections, comprehension monitoring, SQ3R, and word-learning strategies.

Lesson 3

Sedimentary Rock

As YOU Read

What You'll Learn
- The characteristics of sedimentary rock
- How sedimentary rock is formed

Why It's Important
Sedimentary rocks provide information about the history of Earth.

Key Terms
- strata
- stratification

Sediments are particles that are transported by wind and water and deposited throughout Earth's surface. Sediments are often pushed together and compressed to form sedimentary rock.

The Formation of Sedimentary Rock

Sedimentary rock forms when sediment is deposited in one place and becomes compacted. Sediment can include dust, grains of sand, and rocks of any size that are carried by wind or water. After they're buried, these sediments become stuck together over time. The weight of materials above the sediment presses the particles together into **strata,** or layers. Dissolved minerals flow between the particles and cement them together. Although pressure is involved in the production of sedimentary rock, the pressure is not intense enough to break down the sediment particles.

Generally, there are three types of sedimentary rock: clastic, chemical, and biochemical.

▲ Notice the strata, or layers, of rock lying on top of one another, just as they were deposited.

Clastic Sedimentary Rock

Clastic sedimentary rock is formed from pieces of parent rock that break off and become cemented together. Weathering and erosion cause the pieces to break off. Often the pieces are transported by water before they become cemented together. The pieces making up clastic sedimentary rock can vary in size. Some coarse-grained clastic sedimentary rock consists of large pieces of parent rock.

Chemical Sedimentary Rock

Chemical sedimentary rock is formed when solutions with minerals in them evaporate. As the solution evaporates, the minerals in it become more and more concentrated until the solution is gone and the minerals are stuck together.

Biochemical Sedimentary Rock

Some sedimentary rocks are formed from the remains of once-living organisms. These sedimentary rocks are referred to as biochemical sedimentary rocks. Many of

◀ This natural chalk was formed when the skeletons of microscopic organisms decayed and became packed together over time.

these rocks are made of calcium from marine organisms that have decayed and been pressed together over time on the ocean floor. One example of this type of sedimentary rock is natural chalk. Natural chalk is made of calcite from decayed microorganisms. Coal is another example of a biochemical sedimentary rock made over millions of years from the compressed remains of plants.

Sedimentary Rock Layers

Sedimentary rock is deposited in strata, or layers. This process is called **stratification.** Stratification can tell scientists many things about the environment in the past. For one thing, the stratification generally occurs in order from the bottom to the top. This means scientists can tell which rock layers are older or younger by their positions. Because the rock layers are formed at different times, they look different and are made of different materials. These materials can provide information about the environment at the time the rock layer was formed. Together, these pieces of information can reveal some of the history of an area.

Lesson Assessment

Review

1. **Identify** List the three types of sedimentary rock.

2. **Define** What is stratification?

3. Draw a picture of rock strata. Label the layers from oldest to youngest in age of formation.

4. **Compare and Contrast** How are chemical and biochemical sedimentary rocks alike and different?

5. **Explain** Describe the process by which sedimentary rocks form.

Critical Thinking

- Do you think that breaking apart a sedimentary rock can change the nature of the rock? Explain your answer.

- What information do different types of sedimentary rock give you about the history of Earth?

Writing in Science

- Write a short story about the journey of a sediment that becomes part of a sedimentary rock.

- Create a compare-and-contrast chart that shows the differences and similarities among the three types of sedimentary rock.

Reading Skills and Strategies

• Review text connections, text structure, comprehension monitoring, SQ3R, and word-learning strategies.

Lesson 4 Metamorphic Rock

As YOU Read

What You'll Learn
- How metamorphic rock is formed
- How metamorphic rock is structured

Why It's Important
Understanding how metamorphic rock forms helps scientists understand geological change.

Key Terms
- metamorphosis
- foliated
- nonfoliated

You are probably familiar with the **metamorphosis** of a caterpillar into a butterfly. The word *metamorphosis* means "change." Metamorphic rock is a type of rock that starts out as one kind of rock and changes into another because of heat and pressure.

The Formation of Metamorphic Rock

The process of metamorphosis in rocks is caused by heat or pressure or a combination of both. Metamorphic rock can begin as any type of rock. This rock is usually buried deep within Earth. There it encounters heat from magma. The magma may contact the rock or merely be close enough to radiate heat. The temperatures that are typically needed to form metamorphic rock are much higher than are found on Earth's surface but not high enough to melt the rock. If the heat melts the rock into magma, igneous rock will be formed. Metamorphic rock is formed when the temperature is high enough to change the rock but not entirely melt it.

As parts of Earth's crust move together, intense pressure is produced. This pressure can change existing rock. Often, both heat and pressure are present and contribute to the formation of metamorphic rock.

Contact Metamorphosis

Metamorphic rock can be formed by heat in two ways. The first way is through contact metamorphosis. Contact metamorphosis occurs when extremely hot material, such as molten rock, or magma, comes into contact with the rock and changes it. Often, the heat is great enough that it changes the types of minerals in the rock.

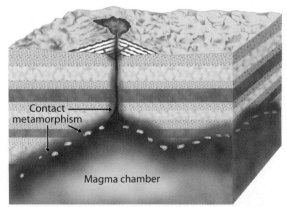

Contact metamorphism

Magma chamber

▲ Contact metamorphosis forms metamorphic rock when hot magma contacts existing rock. The rocks at the very edge of the magma are undergoing contact metamorphosis.

Regional Metamorphosis

Regional metamorphosis occurs when rocks are deep underground. The pressure of the rocks above them builds until that pressure begins to cause metamorphosis. Usually, the increasing pressure produces an increase in temperature that helps form metamorphic rock. The forces that cause regional metamorphosis usually affect a large area of rocks.

Index Minerals

The extreme pressure and heat that form metamorphic rocks sometimes change the minerals inside the rocks. Many minerals have only a small range of temperature and pressure under which they can exist. Information about the minerals in a rock can help scientists determine the conditions that formed the rock. Specific minerals called index minerals serve as a reference to estimate the temperature and depth at which a metamorphic rock formed.

Foliation

The process of metamorphosis often causes the minerals in the changing rock to line up. These minerals align to produce the appearance of bands or layers in the metamorphic rock. Rocks with these bands are called **foliated** metamorphic rocks. Rocks that do not have these bands are called **nonfoliated** metamorphic rocks.

▲ These photographs show a foliated metamorphic rock on the left and a nonfoliated metamorphic rock on the right.

Lesson Assessment

Review

1. **Compare and Contrast** Draw pictures of foliated and nonfoliated metamorphic rocks.

2. **Define** What does the term *metamorphic rock* tell you about the rock's origins?

3. **Describe** Explain how regional metamorphosis forms metamorphic rocks.

4. **Explain** Describe a situation in which a scientist could use an index mineral to find out more about a metamorphic rock.

5. **Relate Cause and Effect** What two factors are responsible for forming metamorphic rocks?

Critical Thinking

• You know that contact metamorphosis causes changes when hot material comes into contact with rock. How will the distance from the hot material affect the metamorphosis? How will the distance affect the resulting metamorphic rocks?

• How do metamorphic rock forms help scientists understand geological change on Earth?

Writing in Science

• Write a poem about the formation of a metamorphic rock.

• Write a letter to a friend describing a metamorphic rock you found. What is the rock's color and texture? What else do you know about the rock?

Reading Skills and Strategies
- Use higher-order thinking skills.
- Review text connections, comprehension monitoring, SQ3R, and word-learning strategies.

Lesson 5 Rocks

As YOU Read

What You'll Learn
- How rocks decompose and re-form through the rock cycle

Why It's Important
The rock cycle is the process by which all rocks are formed and changed.

Key Terms
- rock
- rock cycle

You may never have considered what a **rock** is. A rock is a solid collection of one or more minerals that occur in nature. Similarly, you have probably never thought about where rocks come from. It may seem that all rocks were formed long ago and have never changed, but rocks are changing and forming all the time in a continuous cycle.

Making and Transforming Rocks

The minerals that make up rocks are constantly being assembled, disassembled, and reassembled as old rocks are transformed and new rocks are formed. There are several Earth processes that act on these minerals.

Weathering

Rocks are broken down into their mineral components in a process called weathering. Water, wind, ice, and heat contribute to weathering. Weathering can take many years, even millions of years, to wear away minerals. Even large mountains are eventually leveled because of weathering.

Erosion and Deposition

The fragments that result from weathering are called sediment. After rocks have been reduced to sediment, the sediment is carried away in a process called erosion. There are many agents of erosion. Water and wind can carry sediment, and sediment can also move with ice. Sometimes erosion occurs simply as a result of gravity, as pieces of rock break and fall. The sediments are then deposited in new locations. This process is called deposition.

▲ Wind can serve as a weathering agent. Over the years, wind has eroded sediment from this rock and carried away part of it, leaving an interesting mushroom-shaped formation.

The Rock Cycle

As sediment is broken down and relocated, it becomes building material for new rocks. The process of breaking down rocks into sediment and building new rocks from that sediment is known as the **rock cycle.** The processes of the rock cycle are particular to the three types of rock: sedimentary rock, igneous rock, and metamorphic rock. The ultimate principle of the rock cycle is that rock is never destroyed or created. Instead, rock changes form. In short, each of the three types of rock can change into any one of the other types.

The Endless Cycle

All types of rocks already exist on Earth, so there is no starting point in the rock cycle. Instead, consider each type of rock as a starting point to form any other type of rock.

For example, beginning with sedimentary rock, several paths are possible. If the sedimentary rock is subjected to heat or pressure, it may become metamorphic rock, or if the heat is intense, the rock may melt completely and become magma. A sedimentary rock may break up into loose particles. Metamorphic rock may melt into magma or break down into sediment, which may then be compressed into sedimentary rock. The processes of the rock cycle are weathering, erosion, and deposition; melting; cooling; and heat and pressure.

The Importance of Rocks

When you see a pebble, a stone, or a rock in your path, you may think of it as worthless and kick it away. However, throughout history, rocks have been used to fashion tools, weapons, buildings, monuments, and other structures. The pyramids in Egypt are made of limestone, a sedimentary rock, and the Washington Monument is made of marble, a metamorphic rock transformed from limestone.

Lesson Assessment

Review

1. **Relate Cause and Effect** Explain how minerals and rocks are related.

2. **Define** What is a rock?

3. **Explain** Draw a simple diagram that shows where rocks come from.

4. **Compare and Contrast** Compare and contrast several agents of erosion.

5. **Identify** Which type of rock is formed through the process of cooling?

Critical Thinking

All three types of rock can be formed through the processes of melting, cooling, compression, weathering, and erosion. However, only one type of rock can be formed directly from the other two types. Which type of rock is this?

Writing in Science

Write and illustrate a story that shows one type of rock changing into another type of rock. Include the process in your story.

CARLSBAD CAVERNS

NATIONAL PARK
Merriweather Tours

CARLSBAD CAVERNS

➤ ➤ ➤ Carlsbad Cavern is one of more than three hundred limestone caves that sit below the Chihuahuan Desert and the Guadalupe Mountains of southeastern New Mexico and west Texas. Carlsbad Caverns National Park contains 113 of these caves, as well as 33,000 acres of gorgeous hiking trails, desert ecosystem, bat caves, and more. Call Merriweather Tours today to plan the trip of a lifetime!

CAVERN HISTORY

One of the most extensive cave systems in the world, the caverns were created 250 to 280 million years ago as part of an inland sea's fossil reef. American Indians lived in the mountains above the caves 12,000 to 14,000 years ago, leaving behind pictographs still visible today. In 1930, Congress designated Carlsbad Caverns National Park. New areas in the cavern are still being discovered; the latest was in 1993, when "Chocolate High"—a maze of small passages totaling nearly a mile in combined length—was found.

What to See

Carlsbad Cavern contains some of the most interesting and important geologic structures in the United States, including:

➤ **The Hall of Giants:** The largest chamber, with a floor space of 357,469 square feet.

➤ **The Witch's Finger:** A stalagmite more than twenty feet tall.

➤ **Longfellow's Bathtub:** A rock bridge stretching over subterranean water.

➤ **The Queen's Chamber:** A chamber with millions of breathtaking rock formations.

Fright Night

Every evening from spring to fall, hundreds of Mexican free-tailed bats take to the skies—all at once. Join us for an evening spectacular as the sky becomes black with wings.

Visit our Web site for more information
www.merriweathertours.mgh

DID YOU KNOW?

Did you know that Lechuguilla Cave, located in Carlsbad Caverns National Park, is the deepest cave in the continental United States? Scientists are studying microbes there that may lead to a possible cure for cancer.

Extension Activity

You've learned important skills and strategies in the first fourteen units of this program. Using your own classroom science textbook, find the section you're assigned to read next, and follow the instructions below. Write your responses on notebook paper.

a. **Use** the SQ3R strategy on the textbook section. Be sure to survey, question, read, reflect on, and review the section you're assigned. When you've completed these steps and have taken careful notes, describe what you did.

b. **Find** one example of text structure. Write the page number, title (or subhead), and paragraph on which you found the example so your teacher can find it easily.

c. **Which** of the following text structures best fits the paragraph(s) for this example—Description-or-List, Order-or-Sequence, Cause-and-Effect, or Compare-and-Contrast?

d. **Why** did you choose this text structure? Give an explanation.

e. **Choose** one bold and highlighted word to look up in the dictionary or in an online dictionary. Write the definition you find. Can you find the word in the textbook glossary? If so, write the glossary definition as well. Are these definitions similar? Explain.

f. **Write** a sentence using the word you looked up in the dictionary.

DID YOU KNOW?

Most single-sheet brochures are either bifold (folded into halves) or trifold (folded into thirds). Brochures with multiple pages are most commonly saddle-stitched (stapled on the folded edge) or perfect bound (like a softcover book).

Reading Skills and Strategies
- Use the QHL strategy: questions.
- Use the QHL strategy: how.
- Use the QHL strategy: learn.

Lesson 1

Origins of Native Americans

As YOU Read

What You'll Learn

- Why scientists hold different theories about the origins of early Americans
- Why different cultures developed in the Americas

Why It's Important

Understanding the development of past cultures helps us appreciate the role environment plays in the way people live.

Key Terms

- ice age
- glacier
- archaeologist
- artifact
- marine biologist
- geneticist

People sometimes wonder where Native Americans originated. Where did they come from? Historians and scientists have developed theories about the origins of Native Americans. These theories are based on evidence from the past. This evidence shows that changes in Earth's surface over the years have affected where people live and how they move from place to place.

Beringia

Earth has experienced several periods of extreme cold. These periods are known as **ice ages.** The last ice age began about a hundred thousand years ago. Much of the water on Earth froze and formed **glaciers,** or ice sheets, over the land. The frozen water did not evaporate, form clouds, and fall as rain as it would have in warmer times. As a result, the oceans grew smaller.

During the last ice age, the ocean receded between present-day Siberia and Alaska, and a wide strip of ocean bottom became dry land. This land formed a bridge connecting Asia and North America. Historians call this bridge Beringia because the land now lies under a body of water called the Bering Strait.

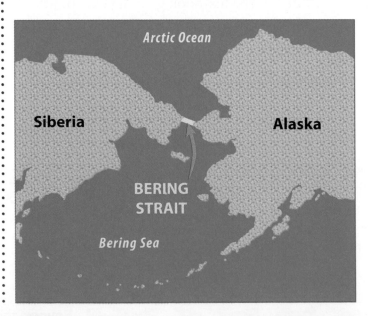

▶ Some historians believe the first Americans walked across a land bridge from Siberia to Alaska.

Conflicting Theories

No one is certain how the first people migrated, or moved, into the Americas. Historians and scientists have several theories. Many believe that people from Siberia walked across Beringia to the Americas; others think the first people in North America arrived by boat from Japan. Both groups agree that the ancestors of Native Americans were Asians. Both groups estimate that these early Asians began arriving between thirty thousand and fifteen thousand years ago.

Arguments and Evidence

Historians in the first group base their theory on discoveries by **archaeologists.** These are scientists who study artifacts to find out about people from the past. **Artifacts** are objects people left behind. Archaeologists trace early human migration by comparing the ages of the earliest artifacts found in one place and the earliest artifacts found in another. They determine the age of artifacts by measuring the radioactive carbon in materials, such as bone and wood, that were once part of living things.

Archaeologists have discovered early bone tools in Siberia near the Bering Strait and also at the tip of South America. The Siberian tools are about thirty thousand years old, and the South American ones are about fifteen thousand years old. These findings suggest that Siberians crossed Beringia, and their descendants moved south over thousands of years until they reached the southernmost part of South America.

Coastal archaeologists and **marine biologists**—scientists who study sea life—developed the second theory. They think that seafaring people from Japan and nearby islands sailed north to Beringia. From there the descendants of the sailors continued along the coast of the Americas, building settlements on the way. As evidence, the scientists point to the remains of early coastal settlements. These remains lie near kelp forests, underwater stretches of dense seaweed. The scientists argue that unlike barren Beringia, the kelp forests along coasts from Japan to southern South America would have provided kelp, fish, shellfish, and sea mammals for food. In addition, kelp reduces wave action. The kelp forests would have made a safe "highway" of calm waters for the voyagers. In contrast, people migrating overland would have faced harsh and constantly changing landscapes—frozen plains, steep mountain ranges, dense forests, and hot deserts.

A third group has recently made discoveries that support the Beringia theory. This group is made up of **geneticists**—scientists who study genes, the material in living things that carries inherited traits. They compared present-day Siberians with Native Americans from North, Central, and South America and uncovered a common gene found in no other groups. This evidence suggests that Native Americans are descended from Siberian peoples.

Ice Age Game

After reaching the Americas, early peoples gathered nuts, roots, and berries to eat, but most of their food came from hunting. They moved from place to place, following animal herds. During the last ice age, many animals in North America were huge. They included giant bison, saber-toothed tigers, woolly mammoths, and mastodons. Mammoths and mastodons looked like shaggy elephants with long tusks. We know this from pictures early people drew on rocks and from the remains of animals that have been discovered.

▶ Mastodons and woolly mammoths were at one time two of the largest animals in North America.

Bands of hunters stalked these large animals. The hunters carried spears with stone points. When a bison or a mammoth was in range, the hunters rushed forward and hurled their spears.

Early Americans depended on large animals for survival in a cold, harsh environment. One mammoth provided meat for many people for a long time. The people used the animal's hide and sinews to make clothing and shelters. They shaped its tusks and bones into tools and weapons.

About fifteen thousand years ago, temperatures began to rise. Glaciers melted and shrank. Oceans rose and expanded, and water submerged Beringia. During this time, the herds of large animals thinned and eventually disappeared. Perhaps they could not adapt to a warmer climate, or they may have been hunted to extinction. People in the Americas had to find other sources of food, shelter, and clothing.

Early American Farmers

Early Americans adapted to the loss of big game by fishing and by hunting small game, such as birds, deer, and squirrels. People also gathered wild berries and grain. However, hunters and gatherers had to work harder for less food than earlier hunters had.

About nine thousand years ago, people in what is now Mexico planted seeds from the wild and raised the first crop. They developed an early form of corn, which provided a dependable source of food. These people no longer moved from place to place to gather wild plants or to hunt animals. They settled in one place and experimented with other crops, such as beans and pumpkins.

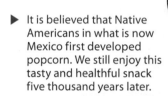

▶ It is believed that Native Americans in what is now Mexico first developed popcorn. We still enjoy this tasty and healthful snack five thousand years later.

Different Cultures

Farming spread northward, and people in what is now the southwest United States also settled in farming villages. Some groups of Native Americans, however, continued to follow game and hunt for food. These groups lived on the Midwestern plains where buffalo (bison) were plentiful. They also lived in the Northeastern forests where deer and birds abounded. Other groups, along coasts, rivers, and lakes, relied on gathering, fishing, and trading to meet their needs. However, farming caused the most changes among early Americans.

People in farming villages harvested crops and stored food for the future. They no longer spent all their time hunting and gathering. As a result, they had time to cultivate other skills. They learned to make bricks and pottery and to weave cloth. Many groups established systems of laws to keep order among their growing population. Over time, farming villages grew into cultures with their own government and customs.

Lesson Assessment

Review

1. **Compute** About how long was the last ice age?

2. **Explain** How did the cold climate cause the oceans to recede during the last ice age?

3. **Identify** What kinds of scientists have contributed information about the migration of early people in the Americas?

4. **Summarize** What evidence supports the theory that the first people in the Americas came across Beringia?

5. **Analyze** How did natural environments affect the cultures developed by early Americans?

Critical Thinking

Some archaeologists claim that Siberians were the first people in the Americas. Are they stating an opinion or a fact? Explain your answer.

Writing in Social Studies

Investigate a highly developed culture of early Native Americans. Then write a report about it.

Reading Skills and Strategies
- Use the QHL strategy: questions.
- Use the QHL strategy: how.
- Use the QHL strategy: learn.

Lesson 2: Unrest in the Colonies

As YOU Read

What You'll Learn
- Why the British passed new restrictions on colonists after the French and Indian War
- How colonists responded to British laws

Why It's Important
This era in history instructs us about our rights as citizens and how to resist when those rights are taken away.

Key Terms
- treaty
- smuggling
- writs of assistance
- boycott

▶ The map shows British and Spanish territory in 1763 after the French and Indian War.

How do you feel when someone says you can't do something you've always done in the past? The American colonists resisted British laws that took away their freedoms and their rights. The British responded with more laws.

After the French and Indian War

The French and Indian War ended with the Treaty of Paris. This **treaty,** or agreement, gave Great Britain control over much of North America—including all the land between the Appalachian Mountains and the Mississippi River. Soon after, the British issued the Proclamation of 1763. This law made it illegal for colonists to settle west of the Appalachians.

The proclamation was passed in part to soothe Native Americans in the West because British companies needed their cooperation to control the profitable fur trade. To enforce the new law and to protect British traders, the British government stationed ten thousand soldiers in North America.

American colonists objected to the proclamation and to the troops. They resented British restrictions on settlement. They also feared the troops would try to limit their other rights.

Paying for the War

The British government had borrowed money to wage the war. George Grenville, the British prime minister, insisted that the colonists help repay the debt. Ideally, the colonists' share would come from taxes on imported goods. However, many merchants avoided taxes on imports by **smuggling,** or bringing goods into the country without reporting to customs officers, who regulated trade. Sometimes customs officers caught the smugglers, but when the smugglers were tried, local juries often freed them.

In 1763, Grenville persuaded Parliament to allow vice-admiralty courts, which had no juries, to try smugglers. One year later, Grenville pushed through the Sugar Act. This law lowered the tax on imported molasses but also allowed customs officers to seize the cargo of suspected smugglers. Then, in 1767, Parliament authorized **writs of assistance,** which permitted customs officers to search any location for smuggled goods.

Taxation without Representation

Merchants in the colonies protested that the new laws violated their rights as English citizens. Vice-admiralty courts violated their right to a trial by jury. The Sugar Act and the writs of assistance took away their freedom from unnecessary searches.

In 1765, Parliament passed the Stamp Act. This law levied taxes on printed materials such as wills, pamphlets, newspapers, and playing cards. Almost every colonist was required to pay the tax.

Objecting to the Stamp Act

Across the colonies, people rallied against the tax. In Virginia, the House of Burgesses declared that only it had the right to tax its citizens. In Boston, a group called the Sons of Liberty held a protest march. Nine colonies sent delegates to New York to the Stamp Act Congress. The congress petitioned Parliament to repeal the tax. In other cities, colonists **boycotted,** or refused to buy, British and European goods.

British merchants lost so much money they demanded Parliament do something. In March 1766, Parliament repealed the Stamp Act. However, it also passed the Declaratory Act. This law asserted Parliament's right to tax and make decisions for the colonies.

◀ Sam Adams, a merchant, brewer, and tax collector in Boston, organized the Sons of Liberty.

Lesson Assessment

Review

1. **Restate** Why did colonial merchants smuggle goods?

2. What new powers did Parliament give customs officers in 1764 and 1767?

3. **Explain** Why did colonists oppose the writs of assistance?

4. **Conclude** Was the colonists' boycott of British goods effective? Explain.

5. **Analyze** Why did colonists object to the Proclamation of 1763?

Critical Thinking

Why might the colonists have protested the Stamp Act more strongly than the writs of assistance?

Writing in Social Studies

Write a petition asking school administrators to repeal a school policy with which you disagree. Persuade other students in your class to sign your petition.

Reading Skills and Strategies

- Use the QHL strategy: questions.
- Use the QHL strategy: how.
- Use the QHL strategy: learn.

Lesson 3

The Road to Revolution

As YOU Read

What You'll Learn

- Who emerged as leaders in the colonies
- How colonists sought independence from Great Britain

Why It's Important

Understanding the origins of American ideals helps us evaluate their usefulness today.

Key Terms

- militia
- arsenal
- petition

▶ Paul Revere, an American patriot, warns Yankee rebels the British are coming.

To end colonial challenges to British authority, Parliament passed laws that took away even more of the colonists' rights. To enforce the laws, Great Britain's King George III sent General Thomas Gage and two thousand troops to Boston, Massachusetts. Where would it all end?

The Colonies Unite

Legislators in Virginia, New York, and Rhode Island suggested that colonists meet to discuss what to do next. In May 1774, delegates from twelve colonies met at the First Continental Congress in Philadelphia. They set up committees to enforce more boycotts of British goods. Meanwhile, colonists formed citizen armies called **militias** and drilled for battle.

General Gage wanted to quash the rebellion before it began. In April 1775, he sent soldiers to seize the **arsenal,** or weapons, of the Massachusetts militia. Militiamen near the towns of Lexington and Concord fought the British and drove them back. Militias in nearby colonies heard the news, rushed to Massachusetts, and surrounded Boston. General Gage and his troops were trapped.

The Second Continental Congress

On May 10, 1775, the Second Continental Congress met to discuss the defense of the colonies. Delegates included America's most respected leaders. John Hancock from Massachusetts was a wealthy merchant who funded the Sons of Liberty. John Adams from Massachusetts was a brilliant Boston lawyer. Pennsylvania's Benjamin Franklin, a publisher, inventor, and legislator, played an important role in the repeal of the Stamp Act. Virginia's George Washington was a wealthy planter with military experience. Patrick Henry spoke eloquently for liberty in the Virginia House of Burgesses, and Thomas Jefferson, another member of the House of Burgesses, wrote persuasively on human rights.

The Congress considered itself the colonies' new government. The members had money printed and established a post office. They also established the Continental Army with George Washington as its commander. As Washington organized his forces, the other delegates drew up a **petition,** or request, to King George. It demanded that the king protect their rights as British citizens. The king rejected the petition and hired thirty thousand German soldiers to fight with British troops in the colonies.

The Declaration of Independence

In June 1776, Virginia delegate Richard Henry Lee proposed that the colonies break political ties with Great Britain. The delegates debated the proposal and appointed a committee to draft a Declaration of Independence. The committee members chose Jefferson to write the draft.

Jefferson drew on writings of other political thinkers. In the introduction to the Declaration, he echoed Englishman John Locke's defense of natural rights.

> "We hold these truths to be self-evident, that all men are created equal, that they are endowed by their Creator with certain unalienable Rights, that among these are Life, Liberty, and the pursuit of Happiness."

Next, Jefferson listed grievances against King George that American Tom Paine had first spelled out in his pamphlet *Common Sense.* Finally, Jefferson ended the Declaration with Americans' resolve to be a free nation.

◀ Benjamin Franklin (left) and John Adams (center) were also on the committee to draft the Declaration of Independence but urged Jefferson (right) to do the actual writing.

Reading Skills and Strategies
- Use the QHL strategy: questions.
- Use the QHL strategy: how.
- Use the QHL strategy: learn.

Lesson 4

A More Perfect Union

As YOU Read

What You'll Learn
- Where the Framers of the Constitution got their ideas
- Why the Constitution was amended

Why It's Important
The Constitution explains how our government works.

Key Terms
- writ of habeas corpus
- preamble
- ratify
- amendment

The fifty-five delegates who met at the Constitutional Convention developed an almost perfect document. However, they could not take full credit for the Constitution because they borrowed most of its best ideas.

British Influence

In 1215, England's King John signed the Magna Carta and thereby agreed to limits on his and his successors' power. According to the Magna Carta, the king could no longer punish people without a jury trial or collect taxes unless a group of nobles called the Grand Council approved.

Later, King Edward I established Parliament to help make laws. Parliament took the place of the Grand Council and assumed control of British finances. In 1689, William and Mary, the joint rulers of England, signed the English Bill of Rights. One condition in this document was that monarchs could not make laws or suspend laws passed by Parliament.

Principles from the Magna Carta are evident throughout the U.S. Constitution. Article I guarantees accused persons access to a **writ of habeas corpus,** which is the right to a trial. Article III assures them the right to a jury trial. Article I also limits the president by giving Congress the power of the purse. Only Congress can collect taxes, coin money, and approve spending. Like the English Bill of Rights, Article I states that the legislature, not the executive, makes laws.

Enlightenment Ideas

The Framers of the Constitution drew from Enlightenment ideas as well as English institutions. The Enlightenment was an era in Europe when great thinkers promoted reason and science. Enlightenment figures who influenced delegates such as James Madison were John Locke of England and Baron de Montesquieu of France.

Locke wrote that all people have natural rights to life, liberty, and property. Locke believed a ruler had a contract with the people to protect their rights. In the **preamble,** or introduction, to the Constitution, the Framers express their idea that the purpose of government is to protect people's rights.

> ......*We The People* of the United States, in Order to form a more perfect Union, establish Justice, insure domestic Tranquility, provide for the common defence, promote the general Welfare, and secure the Blessings of Liberty to ourselves and our Posterity, do ordain and establish this Constitution for the United States of America.

▲ This is the text of the preamble to the Constitution.

Montesquieu stressed that government functions should be divided among independent branches. In this way, no one person or branch could become all powerful. Following Montesquieu's suggestion, the Framers gave separate powers to the executive, legislative, and judicial branches of the government. The executive branch includes the president and all the people who report to the president. The legislative branch is Congress, which includes the Senate and the House of Representatives. The judicial branch is the Supreme Court of nine justices and all other federal courts across the country.

The First Ten Amendments

Nine of the thirteen states had to **ratify,** or approve, the Constitution before it became law. State legislatures held conventions to vote on ratification. Franklin, Madison, and others tried to persuade convention delegates to adopt the new Constitution. Those in favor of adopting the Constitution and a strong centralized government were known as Federalists. They called critics of the Constitution Antifederalists.

Antifederalists believed that the strong central government described in the Constitution would ignore the rights of states and individuals. These critics wanted **amendments,** or additions, to guarantee rights like those in the English Bill of Rights. These rights included the right to petition the government and the right to be free from cruel punishments.

Delaware was the first state to ratify. It did so on December 8, 1787. On June 21, 1788, the ninth state, New Hampshire, ratified the Constitution. Virginia and New York, the two largest states, refused to ratify unless the Constitution was amended to protect the rights of individuals. When promised that a Bill of Rights would be added, Virginia approved the Constitution. By May 1790, all the states had accepted the new plan of government. In 1791, the first ten amendments were added.

Lesson Assessment

Review

1. **Identify** What part of the Constitution guarantees accused persons a trial?

2. **Explain** Why is the preamble to the Constitution important?

3. **Restate** What is another name for the first ten amendments to the U.S. Constitution?

4. **Name** Which Enlightenment writers discussed natural rights and separation of powers?

5. What English documents provided models for the Framers of the Constitution?

Critical Thinking

In which states, do you think, were Antifederalists especially strong? Explain your answer.

Writing in Social Studies

Write a brief speech to delegates at a state convention. Argue for or against ratification in your speech.

Lesson 5

Traveling West

Reading Skills and Strategies

- Use higher-order thinking skills.
- Review text connections, text structure, comprehension monitoring, SQ3R, multipart words, and word-learning strategies.

As YOU Read

What You'll Learn

- How westward movement affected American life
- Why traveling across the United States became easier in the nineteenth century

Why It's Important

Learning about roads and waterways used by the first westward travelers helps us appreciate the importance of modern transportation.

Key Terms

- pioneer
- canal

Although the United States extended from the Atlantic coast to the Mississippi River in 1790, most Americans lived east of the Appalachian Mountains. For centuries, the mountains had discouraged people from moving farther west. However, as the number of Americans increased, eastern lands became crowded. The mountains became a challenge instead of a barrier.

Life of the Early Western Settlers

By 1803, enough **pioneers,** or early settlers, had braved the mountain crossing to populate three new western states—Kentucky, Tennessee, and Ohio. Life in these states was different from life on the Atlantic Coast. Easterners lived in frame houses, but pioneers lived in cabins made of logs. Unlike houses in the East, few log cabins had glass in the windows or planks on the floor. These materials had to come from eastern factories and sawmills. However, shipping goods from the East was difficult because no rivers and few roads ran through the mountains. Both settlers and manufacturers wanted better routes to the West.

Many pioneer families settled along rivers. They used the waterways for transporting goods and people. Going downstream was easy, but the voyage upstream took a great deal of time and effort. Barges hugged the riverbanks as crews used poles to push on the river bottom to move the barges against the current. Another problem with river travel was that most rivers in the eastern United States run north and south while most people and goods needed to go east and west.

Roads West

For settlers who chose to travel overland, the journey was rough. Early roads to the West were surfaced with gravel or split logs. Private companies built the roads and charged tolls to cover the cost of construction. Few pioneers could afford to travel hundreds of miles on these bumpy roads.

Ohioans asked the federal government to build a free road connecting them with the East. In 1806, Congress approved the funds for the National Road but took five years to agree on a route. The section between Maryland and what is now West Virginia opened in 1818, but the road did not reach Ohio until 1833. Seventeen years later, construction ended in southern Illinois. Many years passed before the federal government attempted to build another major road.

Canals Tie East to West

Canals are human-made channels between natural waterways. In the early nineteenth century, canals were much more efficient than roads for hauling goods. Four horses were needed to haul one and a half tons over a good road. Just two horses or mules, walking beside a canal, could pull a hundred tons on a barge. Several short canals existed before the 1820s, but they had little impact on life in western states.

New York City business owners wanted to ship their manufactured goods to Ohio. The Hudson River already linked New York City to Albany. A canal was needed to link Albany with Buffalo at the eastern end of Lake Erie, where barges could sail on to Ohio. With the help of New York Governor DeWitt Clinton, business owners persuaded New York legislators to fund the canal. Construction began in 1817 and ended eight years later.

In 1825, Governor Clinton boarded the *Seneca Chief* and traveled the brand-new, 363-mile canal from Buffalo to Albany. From there, he continued to New York City, where he poured a keg of Lake Erie water into the harbor. The Erie Canal was officially open. It soon became the quickest, cheapest, and busiest route to the West.

Here are the words to a song drivers might have sung to their teams as they walked along the canal.

> *I've got a mule. Her name is Sal.*
> *Fifteen miles on the Erie Canal.*
> *She's a good old worker and a good old pal.*
> *Fifteen miles on the Erie Canal.*
> *We've hauled some barges in our day*
> *Filled with lumber, coal, and hay,*
> *And we know every last inch of the way*
> *From Albany to Buffalo.*

▲ Horses haul a barge along the Erie Canal.

Lesson Assessment

Review

1. **Define** Who were the pioneers?

2. **Contrast** How are canals different from rivers?

3. **Explain** Why is traveling upstream difficult?

4. **Analyze** How did the westward migration bring business and government together?

5. Did the National Road or the Erie Canal have a greater impact on westward settlement? Support your answer with facts from the lesson.

Critical Thinking

Why, do you think, did Governor Clinton pour water from Lake Erie into the harbor at New York City?

Writing in Social Studies

Write two or three journal entries a pioneer might have made during a journey across the Appalachians.

Reading Skills and Strategies
- Use the QHL strategy: questions.
- Use the QHL strategy: how.
- Use the QHL strategy: learn.

Lesson 1

The Real Wild West

As YOU Read

What You'll Learn
- How mining and cattle ranching changed the West
- Why people moved west

Why It's Important
Resource development and population changes still challenge us today.

Key Terms
- longhorn
- open range
- vaquero
- black codes
- Mexicano
- Anglo

Many classic films reenact the legends of the Wild West. The actors play noble braves, dashing cavalry officers, and quick-drawing outlaws living on the Great Plains or in the Rocky Mountains between 1850 and 1900. The real West had a much wider cast of characters and many more tales worth telling.

The Mining Boom

Gold was discovered in the Rocky Mountains near Pikes Peak in 1859. About a hundred thousand prospectors rushed to what is now Colorado to stake claims. Many settled in a mining camp that eventually became the city of Denver.

That same year, miners found gold and silver in western Nevada. The discovery was called the Comstock Lode. A lode is an abundant deposit of valuable metal in layers of rock.

◄ Between 1860 and 1890, gold and silver mining experienced first a boom and then a bust in the West.

Some Comstock miners became millionaires and built elaborate mansions in nearby Virginia City—Nevada's first boomtown. The population of Virginia City exploded from three thousand to thirty thousand in about ten years. By 1876, the residents were enjoying many benefits of big city life, including an opera house, five newspapers, and a stock exchange.

The Mining Bust

Many prospectors failed to strike it rich. They moved on to other gold fields. There always seemed to be a major strike somewhere else—in the Black Hills in Dakota Territory, at Cripple Creek in Colorado, or in the Yukon in Canada.

After a while, individual miners could no longer scratch out livings from surface mines. Large companies moved in with heavy machinery and paid workers to toil underground to extract ore. By the 1890s, even the large companies had abandoned the mines. Recovering what little ore was left cost the companies too much money. The miners who worked for the companies drifted away to find new jobs. However, enough people stayed on to qualify Nevada, Colorado, and South Dakota for statehood.

For Land and Longhorns

The West was rich in land as well as in gold and silver. After the Mexican War, the United States government purchased five hundred thousand square miles of grasslands from Mexico. This land included present-day California, Utah, Nevada, and parts of Wyoming, New Mexico, Arizona, Colorado, and Texas.

While still under Mexican rule, Texas ranchers developed a type of cattle called **longhorns,** a breed especially suited to dry grasslands. However, the major markets for beef were in the East. Ranchers had no way to transport their cattle to eastern markets, and the cattle cost more to raise than they sold for in Texas. Consequently, ranchers let many of their cattle run wild.

By the 1860s, wild longhorns numbered in the millions. Meanwhile, most eastern cattle had been butchered to feed Civil War soldiers. After the war ended, beef was in big demand. Enterprising settlers recognized a golden opportunity. They rounded up longhorns and fattened them on the **open range,** land that belonged to the government.

The first cattle drive took place in 1866. Ranchers drove 260,000 longhorns from southern Texas to Sedalia, a railroad town in Missouri. Freight cars carried the cattle from Sedalia to slaughterhouses in the East. Some of the cattle died on the long journey, but the ranchers still made a huge profit.

Soon, other ranchers were hiring cowhands to drive their cattle north to the railroads. Cowhands found the fastest, least difficult routes and followed them year after year. The routes became well-worn cattle trails, such as the Chisholm Trail that ended in Abilene, Kansas.

Cowhands

Cattle drives needed cowhands. These workers came mainly from the South and the Southwest. Many cowhands were former Confederate soldiers who could no longer make a living in the South. More than one-third of all cowhands were Mexican or African American.

Mexican cowhands, or **vaqueros,** had worked in the Southwest for centuries. Experienced vaqueros taught newcomers how to round up, rope, and brand cattle. Vaqueros were the first to wear the high-heeled boots and wide-brimmed hats that American cowhands are seen wearing in movie westerns. Words that American cowhands still use, such as *corral, lasso,* and *stampede,* came from vaqueros.

Most African American cowhands were born enslaved but gained their freedom during the Civil War. They traveled west in the 1870s, after many Southern states passed **black codes.** These were laws that allowed plantation owners to abuse the freedmen who worked for them. Many freedmen chose to move west rather than stay in the South.

Life on the trail was lonely. Cowhands rode for hours under the hot sun and slept outside in freezing cold. Part of their job was calming restless cattle. Thunder and lightning often caused stampedes, so cowhands would sit up on rainy nights singing to the cattle. The following lines are from a traditional cowhand ballad, "The Old Chisholm Trail":

Come along, boys, and listen to my tale.

I'll tell you of my trouble on the old Chisholm Trail.

Come a ti yi yippee, yippee yea, yippee yea,

Come a ti yi yippee, yippee yea.

▲ Cowhands preferred fast, strong, and tough quarter horses, which were combinations of racing horses and mustangs, the wild horses of Texas.

End of the Trail

As railroads built tracks closer to Texas, the cattle drives became shorter and easier. This helped the cattle business grow. However, other events would bring the cattle boom to an end about twenty years after the first cattle drive.

Land attracted farmers as well as ranchers to the plains, but grazing cattle herds often destroyed farmers' fields. In 1874, an inventor named Joseph Glidden patented barbed wire, and farmers began to use it to fence their land. Sharp barbs, or points of twisted wire, tore into cattle's skin and stopped the animals from trampling crops. Barbed-wire fences closed the open range and rerouted the cattle trails. Then, in the winter of 1886–1887, temperatures dropped, and thousands of cattle froze to death, finishing off many large cattle ranches.

Changes in the West

Booms and busts in the West affected population growth in the region. For example, tens of thousands of people abandoned Virginia City when the mines played out.

Denver, on the other hand, grew from a mining camp to a major city.

By 1867, Denver was the capital of the Colorado Territory, and the city became the state capital in 1877. One reason for its survival was the foresight of its citizens. They built a railroad spur that linked Denver to the transcontinental railroad. By 1890, Denver had a population of 107,000. The railroad also contributed to population surges in Des Moines, Iowa; Omaha, Nebraska; and Portland, Oregon.

The language as well as the population changed in the Southwest. For centuries, southwesterners had been Spanish-speaking people called **Mexicanos.** Between the 1860s and the 1890s, mining, ranching, and farming attracted many **Anglos,** or English-speaking white people, to the Southwest. These Anglos took over Mexicanos' land, and American courts refused to recognize grants made by the Spanish and Mexican governments before the area became part of the United States. With the support of the courts, Anglos also took away the Mexicanos' political power and became the mayors and governors in the region.

Lesson Assessment

Review

1. **List** Where were the major gold and silver strikes?

2. **Explain** Why was the open range a boon to the cattle industry?

3. **Analyze** Discuss the vaqueros' impact on American culture.

4. **Identify** What two events contributed to the end of large cattle ranches?

5. **Summarize** What factors contributed to Denver's growth?

Critical Thinking

- Evaluate the Anglos' treatment of Mexicanos.

- Why did people move west, and what changes happened in the West during the end of the 1800s?

- How did vaqueros influence others in the West?

Writing in Social Studies

Write a brief radio play about miners in Nevada. Include ideas for sound effects to suggest a busy mining camp in the background.

Reading Skills and Strategies

- Use the QHL strategy: questions.
- Use the QHL strategy: how.
- Use the QHL strategy: learn.

Lesson 2

The Birth of Corporate Industry

As You Read

What You'll Learn

- Why industry grew in the United States after the Civil War
- Who benefited from industrial growth

Why It's Important

Corporations have even more power today than they had in the late nineteenth century.

Key Terms

- corporation
- monopoly
- trust

The Industrial Revolution had been under way in the United States since the late eighteenth century. In 1860, however, most people still lived on farms, and city workers were only a small part of the nation's population. After the Civil War, new factors arose that sped industrialization.

Steel and Electricity

One factor that propelled industry forward in the late nineteenth century was cheap steel. In the 1850s, Englishman Henry Bessemer came up with a steelmaking process that required less coal than older processes. American steel mills adopted the Bessemer process and produced high-quality steel more cheaply than before.

Steel output increased dramatically between 1867 and 1900. Factories used the steel to make nails, plows, barbed wire, rails for railroads, and beams for buildings. Steel beams made skyscrapers possible. These tall buildings changed the skylines of big cities. Skyscrapers housed the offices in which people planned, directed, financed, and promoted American industries.

Another factor that fueled industrialization was electrical power. In 1876, American inventor Thomas Alva Edison opened a laboratory in Menlo Park, New Jersey. Workers there developed applications for electricity. Edison's best-known invention was an electric lightbulb safe enough for home use. He also established a central power station to supply electricity to New York City.

▲ Thomas Alva Edison invented the first practical electric lightbulb.

Communication Technology

A third factor contributing to industrial growth was improved communications. In 1868, Christopher Latham Sholes secured a patent for the typewriter, and the Remington Arms Company mass-produced it in the

1870s. (After the Civil War, Remington diversified by making sewing machines as well as typewriters.)

In 1876, Alexander Graham Bell invented the telephone. The telephone helped businesses coordinate wide-flung concerns. It also became the basis for a major new industry—telephone companies. The typewriter and the telephone not only increased business efficiency, they also increased job opportunities. Many people, especially women, became typists and switchboard operators.

From Businesses to Corporations

In the early nineteenth century, most businesses were owned by individuals or partners. With new technology, the cost of doing business soared. Many business owners raised money for modern machinery by selling shares of their companies. An investor who bought shares became a part owner. A business owned by shareholders is called a **corporation.**

Some corporations bought other companies. An example was John D. Rockefeller's Standard Oil Company. The company started with one oil refinery in 1863. Rockefeller bought other refineries to eliminate competitors. Soon Standard Oil controlled the oil-refining industry; in other words, it held a **monopoly.**

Another way Rockefeller eliminated competition was by establishing a **trust.** A trust holds stock in many companies, often in the same industry. By 1880, Rockefeller's trust controlled almost all the oil refineries in the United States. Owners in other industries followed Rockefeller's example, and by 1900, just a few corporations controlled much of the American economy.

Lesson Assessment

Review

1. **Contrast** How did corporations differ from businesses in the early nineteenth century?

2. **Infer** Do you think Rockefeller's monopoly benefited people who needed oil to heat their homes? Explain.

3. **Conclude** Could trusts have existed in the early nineteenth century? Why or why not?

4. **List** What three factors contributed to the growth of industry after the Civil War?

5. **Infer** How, do you suppose, did small businesses fare in the late nineteenth century? Explain your answer.

Critical Thinking

- Give some general characteristics of inventors in the nineteenth century. How have their inventions influenced your daily life?

- Why did industry grow in the United States after the Civil War? How did John D. Rockefeller influence business in the United States?

Writing in Social Studies

- Use the Internet to investigate a corporation today, and write a report comparing it to corporations of the late nineteenth century.

- Write a journal entry from the point of view of an inventor. What invention did you make? How has it helped others?

Reading Skills and Strategies
- Use the QHL strategy: questions.
- Use the QHL strategy: how.
- Use the QHL strategy: learn.

Lesson 3

Women Demand More Rights

As YOU Read

What You'll Learn
- Why women became social reformers
- How women won the vote

Why It's Important
Women still struggle to gain equal rights with men.

Key Terms
- progressive
- prohibition
- suffrage
- suffragette

In 1776, Abigail Adams wrote her husband, John, that women would "not hold ourselves bound by any Laws in which we have no voice." John Adams paid no attention. In the late nineteenth century, women were still demanding civil rights.

Women's Lives outside the Home

Almost one-third of American women between the ages of twenty and twenty-four worked outside the home in the 1890s. Well-educated women found jobs as teachers, nurses, and secretaries. Other women worked as maids, typists, telephone operators, store clerks, and laborers in garment and food-processing factories. About half of these women left their jobs when they married.

Some women were forced to leave their jobs. For example, several states barred married females from teaching. As a result, many well-to-do educated women gave up

paid careers and focused on social reforms. People who campaign for social reforms are called **progressives.**

In 1893, Jane Addams was a recent college graduate looking for a progressive cause to champion. She and her friends decided to establish a settlement house, called Hull House, to help poor families in Chicago. Volunteers at the house supplied recent immigrants with information about settling in the United States. Hull House also had a health clinic, citizenship classes, a nursery, a kindergarten, and after-school clubs. Nurse Lillian Wald established a similar settlement house in New York City.

Kansas wife and mother Carry Amelia Nation was another progressive. She helped poor families by trying to enforce a state law prohibiting the manufacture and sale of alcoholic beverages. She was convinced that alcohol abuse destroyed families because many husbands spent their entire paychecks in saloons.

Nation and her followers marched through Kansas towns such as Medicine Lodge, Wichita, and Topeka protesting liquor "joints" and smashing the joints' windows. Her protests became famous, and she toured the country giving lectures on the need for **prohibition**—the outlawing of the manufacture and sale of alcoholic beverages. In 1919, eight years after Nation died, the Eighteenth Amendment was added to the U.S. Constitution, making nationwide prohibition a reality.

The Suffragettes

Progressive women wanted to use elections to pressure government officials into passing reforms. By 1896, only four states—Wyoming, Utah, Idaho, and Colorado—allowed women to vote. Female progressives began demonstrating for woman **suffrage,** or the right to vote. People called these women **suffragettes.**

Early suffragette leaders included Susan B. Anthony and Elizabeth Cady Stanton. Each served as president of the National American Woman Suffrage Association (NAWSA). This group urged states to grant women the vote. Thanks to NAWSA, women were voting in eleven states by 1914.

▲ Like many progressive activists, suffragettes marched in the streets to gain support for their cause.

Carrie Chapman Catt was NAWSA president when World War I began in Europe. She supported Woodrow Wilson's reelection and offered the services of NAWSA's two million members if the United States entered the war. In return, Wilson told Congress that a woman-suffrage amendment was important to the war effort. In 1920, the Nineteenth Amendment was ratified, giving the vote to women nationwide.

Lesson Assessment

Review

1. **Restate** Define *progressive* in your own words.

2. **Theorize** In 1933, the Twenty-first Amendment repealed the Eighteenth Amendment. Why, do you think, did Americans end Prohibition?

3. **Explain** Why was suffrage important to female progressives?

4. **Describe** List adjectives that apply to Carry Nation, suffragettes, and Carrie Chapman Catt.

Critical Thinking

Here are the words of the Nineteenth Amendment: "The right of citizens of the United States to vote shall not be denied or abridged by the United States or by any state on account of sex." In your own words, state the main idea of the amendment in a simple sentence.

Writing in Social Studies

Use the Internet to investigate the life of Susan B. Anthony or Elizabeth Cady Stanton, and write a brief biography.

Reading Skills and Strategies
- Use the QHL strategy: questions.
- Use the QHL strategy: how.
- Use the QHL strategy: learn.

Lesson 4 — FDR's New Deal

As YOU Read

What You'll Learn
- Why Roosevelt sympathized with struggling Americans
- How the New Deal helped farmers and the jobless

Why It's Important
Some social reforms introduced as part of the New Deal are under attack today.

Key Terms
- optimist
- bank holiday
- fireside chat

Millions of Americans lost their savings, their jobs, and their homes during the Great Depression. President Herbert Hoover refused to act on their behalf, so voters elected a president who promised them a "New Deal." After he took office, Franklin Delano Roosevelt took steps to restore the economy.

The People's President

Roosevelt had grown up in a wealthy family, but he knew what it meant to struggle. At age thirty-nine, he contracted polio and lost the use of his legs. For years, Roosevelt spent hours every day trying to move his toes or to stand up unassisted. Despite his disability, he ran for governor of New York in 1928 and won.

Struggling with polio and at the same time succeeding in politics made Roosevelt a confirmed **optimist.** He came to believe he could overcome huge obstacles. He also became more aware of difficulties others faced. Franklin's wife, Eleanor, told how polio affected Franklin: "Anyone who has gone through great suffering is bound to have a great sympathy and understanding of the problems of mankind."

Restoring Confidence

Roosevelt was elected president in 1932 and put into office in a formal ceremony on March 4, 1933. The day after he was inaugurated, he declared a **bank holiday.** Since 1929, many banks had failed, and depositors had lost their savings. Roosevelt hoped to restore Americans' confidence in the economy by closing banks throughout the country while the government determined which ones were sound enough to reopen.

On March 12, the president gave the first of many **fireside chats**—easy-to-understand talks about government and economic policy. These talks were broadcast over the radio to millions of listeners. In his first chat, Roosevelt assured listeners their savings would be safe in federally licensed banks. On March 13, the banks reopened, and people deposited more money than they withdrew.

▲ More than sixty million Americans listened to Roosevelt's first fireside chat.

Relief, Recovery, and Reform

Roosevelt's New Deal offered relief to the unemployed by organizing and funding work programs. The most popular of these programs was the Civilian Conservation Corps (CCC). The CCC hired young men to plant trees, fight fires, and dig reservoirs for the national forestry service. During its nine years of operation, the CCC employed three million workers.

Another program for the jobless was the Federal Emergency Relief Administration (FERA). This agency gave money to cities and states to use in their relief projects. In this way, FERA provided salaries and jobs for administrators of aid throughout the nation.

In May 1933, Congress set up the Agricultural Adjustment Administration (AAA). The AAA paid farmers to raise less of certain kinds of livestock and to plant less of certain crops. As a result, the supply of these products fell and their prices rose, benefiting farmers.

The Works Progress Administration (WPA) brought jobs and social reform. It paid companies to build and repair dams, schools, highways, waterworks, and sewer systems. A condition for receiving funds was that companies hire African Americans to do some of the work. In this way, the WPA tried to rid the construction industry of racist hiring practices.

Lesson Assessment

Review

1. **Explain** What purpose did the bank holiday serve?

2. **Conclude** Was the first fireside chat effective? Support your answer with facts from the lesson.

3. **Analyze** How might Roosevelt's life experiences have prepared him to be president?

4. **Identify** Which New Deal program helped reduce discrimination in the workplace?

5. **Synthesize** What programs provided employment and produced long-lasting benefits for the nation?

Critical Thinking

- Not everyone approved of the New Deal reforms. What might have been some criticisms of New Deal programs?

- The New Deal programs were sponsored and paid for by the United States government. What problems may have occurred when the government spent taxpayer money to pay workers holding jobs created by the New Deal?

Writing in Social Studies

- Use facts from the lesson to prepare a two-column chart with the headings "New Deal Program" and "Purpose."

- If you were giving a fireside chat about what is currently going on in the United States government, what would you discuss? What message about the condition of the United States government would you want to convey?

Reading Skills and Strategies

- Use higher-order thinking skills.
- Review text connections, comprehension monitoring, SQ3R, QHL, and word-learning strategies.

Lesson 5

The Fifties in the United States

As YOU Read

What You'll Learn

- How the government spent tax dollars in the 1950s
- What the culture of the 1950s was like

Why It's Important

As in the 1950s, the priorities of government today affect American prosperity and values.

Key Terms

- suburb
- conformity

What was life like when your grandparents were young? They lived in a different America, without the Internet or the possibility of global warming. Instead, they had the new medium of television for entertainment, and they worried about Communists and the possibility of nuclear war. (Communists believe government should control the production of all food and goods and there should be no private ownership of property.)

Government Priorities in the Fifties

In 1952, Dwight D. Eisenhower was elected president. Eisenhower referred to his plans for the country as "dynamic conservatism." He wanted government to play an active part in supporting American business. The Eisenhower administration cut spending in many areas by supporting reductions in taxes and in federal funds for public housing. Eisenhower also slashed the budget for the Tennessee Valley Authority—a New Deal agency that brought electricity to rural Americans.

In two areas, however, Eisenhower was an enthusiastic spender. He persuaded Congress to pass the Federal Highway Act. Under this act, a massive federal highway-building project, which became the interstate freeway system, was begun. Eisenhower also wholeheartedly approved the Great Lakes Saint Lawrence Seaway system, which would connect the Great Lakes with the Atlantic Ocean. Both projects encouraged industrial growth. The highway bill was a boon to trucking companies that distributed goods across the nation, and the seaway saved money for the shipping industry.

Population Boom

Between 1950 and 1960, the U.S. population increased by thirty million. The main reason for the surge was a high birthrate. Couples had large families that matched their big expectations for the future.

Many families moved to larger homes in the **suburbs,** the outlying areas around cities. Suburban communities expanded along with the population. Automobile sales increased because suburbanites drove into the city to work. The number of automobiles in the United States more than doubled between 1946 and 1960.

▲ Both cars and people multiplied in the 1950s.

Fifties Culture

Conformity, or acting and thinking alike, was important to many people in the mass culture of the 1950s. In 1950, only one household in ten in the United States owned a television set. By the end of the decade, only one household in ten did *not* own a set. Television helped spread a set of common values and American myths. Popular westerns reinforced standards of right and wrong. Family programs like *Father Knows Best* and *The Adventures of Ozzie and Harriet* showed stereotypes of ideal families, in which the father went to work, the mother stayed home, and the children were well behaved. Many families aspired to these ideals. In addition, television ads implied that having the latest products was part of the American dream.

One disturbing problem in the early fifties was the imagined threat of Communists infiltrating government, the army, and the movie industry. Senator Joseph McCarthy claimed to know of many Communists within these groups. He held Senate hearings, which were televised, to grill and bully his opponents and those he suspected of Communist leanings.

Besides television, another phenomenon of the fifties was Elvis Presley. Presley's hip-gyrating performances disturbed parents, but teens loved this new star who would become the king of rock and roll.

▲ Elvis Presley performs in Miami in 1956.

Lesson Assessment

Review

1. **Restate** Use *suburb* in a sentence that defines its meaning.

2. **Judge** Do you think a culture based on conformity can produce original works of music and art? Give reasons for your opinion.

3. **Infer** What groups benefited and what groups suffered under the Eisenhower administration?

4. Whose interests did the government and the mass culture promote during the decade of the fifties?

Critical Thinking

- Why are the fifties considered a time of conformity?

- Why do you think President Eisenhower reduced some New Deal programs such as the Tennessee Valley Authority while increasing funding for highway programs and other transportation programs? Do you think these decisions helped or hurt Americans as a whole?

Writing in Social Studies

- Watch a video of an episode from a 1950s television series, and write a review.

- If you had been a young adult in the fifties, do you think you would have been a conformist and bought a television set and moved to the suburbs? Why or why not?

In 1848 a man found a gold nugget in California. Soon after, I remember hearing talk about all the gold. I, Phillip Harrison, was one of many who took the California Trail across the United States to find my fortune. On March 12, 1849, I left Council Bluffs, Iowa, with my wife, Caroline, and my two sons. We bought a covered wagon, oxen, and supplies and headed west to Sutter's Fort in California.

I was sure this was a real-life treasure hunt that would end in great wealth. Nearly eight months later, we arrived, but by then the most easily accessible gold was gone, and we'd already made dreadful sacrifices. I made this map so my great-great-great-grandchildren can know what our small family endured on that journey.

Day 1: March 12, 1849
Council Bluffs, Iowa
We excitedly began our trip aboard a wagon bought with most of our savings.

Day 51: May 1, 1849
Scottsbluff, Nebraska
The oxen belonging to travelers before us had eaten much of the trail grass. Our oxen began to starve. One soon died.

Day 109: June 26, 1849
Fort Laramie, Wyoming
I removed our wagon wheels to float across the North Platte River. We lost one of our sons to the waters and buried him at the water's edge.

Day 190: September 15, 1849
Humboldt River, Nevada
Water and food had nearly run out. To survive, we strained mosquito-infested water through handkerchiefs. Caroline contracted cholera.

Day 237: November 1, 1849
Sutter's Fort, California
Ill, grieving, and nearly starved, we reached our destination to find the gold mostly gone. We had no choice but to start our lives again from scratch.

Missouri River
Montana
Yellowstone River
North Dakota
Idaho
Wyoming
South Dakota
North Platte River
Fort Laramie
Scottsbluff
Missouri River
Iowa
Council Bluffs
START
Humboldt River
Sutter's Fort
END
Nevada
Nebraska
Kansas
Missouri
Arizona
Mexico
Oklahoma
Arkansas
Texas
Louisiana

Extension Activity

You've learned important skills and strategies in the first sixteen units of this program. Using your own classroom social studies textbook, find the section you're assigned to read next, and follow the instructions below. Write your responses on notebook paper.

a. **Use** the SQ3R and QHL strategies on the textbook section. Be sure to survey, question, read, reflect on, and review the section you're assigned. Develop a question, and find the answer to that question. When you've completed these steps, have written your question and answer, and have taken careful notes, describe what you did.

b. **Find** one example of text structure. Write the page number, title (or subhead), and paragraph on which you found the example so your teacher can find it easily.

c. **Which** of the following text structures best fits the paragraph(s) for this example—Description-or-List, Order-or-Sequence, Cause-and-Effect, or Compare-and-Contrast?

d. **Why** did you choose this text structure? Give an explanation.

e. **Choose** one bold and highlighted word to look up in the dictionary or in an online dictionary. Write the definition you find. Can you find the word in the textbook glossary? If so, write the glossary definition as well. Are these definitions similar? Explain.

f. **Write** a sentence using the word you looked up in the dictionary.

Reading Skills and Strategies

- Take lecture notes.
- Review text connections, text structure, comprehension monitoring, SQ3R, QHL, and word-learning strategies.

Lesson 1

Nonrenewable Energy Resources

As YOU Read

What You'll Learn

- How humans use nonrenewable energy sources

Why It's Important

Humans depend on nonrenewable energy sources, but these energy sources are in limited supply.

Key Terms

- fossil fuel
- coal
- oil
- natural gas

▶ Coal, oil, and natural gas are sources of nonrenewable energy. Eventually, all will run out.

Humans rely on energy to cook food, heat homes, provide light, power vehicles, and run machinery. The energy we use can be classified as renewable energy or nonrenewable energy, depending on the resources used to generate the energy. Most of the energy we use comes from nonrenewable resources. This means that these resources are not replaced naturally as we use them. This is a problem because eventually they will be completely used up.

Types of Nonrenewable Energy Resources

Most nonrenewable energy comes from **fossil fuels.** Fossil fuels are formed when living things die, decay, and become organic material that can be used for energy. The process of forming fossil fuels usually takes millions of years. The most common examples of fossil fuels are coal, oil, and natural gas.

Coal

Coal is the most common source of electrical energy throughout the world. Coal is a black rock found in the earth that can be burned to release heat energy. Coal is formed over millions of years. Because it takes so long for coal to form, it is considered a nonrenewable resource. In addition to being limited in supply, coal produces a great deal of pollution when it's burned. Coal-burning power plants release large amounts of soot and carbon dioxide into the air. Two advantages of using coal for energy are that coal is relatively inexpensive to obtain and currently there is plenty of it.

How Coal Forms

Coal forms in swampy areas in which leafy plant materials pile up and are buried. As plant layers build up, air does not reach them, so the organic matter does not break down as quickly as dead plants on the surface do. The plant material becomes compressed over time and decomposes at a slow rate until a hard, rocky material remains.

Coal consists mostly of carbon, which releases energy when it's burned. Other materials in coal include sulfur and other minerals. Coal is literally a fossil fuel. You can often see the outlines of the dead plants that formed it in the pieces of rock.

◀ Coal is a fossil fuel. Here you can see the outlines of the fern leaves that decomposed and hardened over millions of years as they became coal.

Coal Mining

Coal is found in large seams under Earth's surface and is obtained by mining. Some coal is mined by digging large holes on the surface to reach the coal deposits beneath. This type of mining is called strip-mining, or surface pit mining. Other coal mines consist of extensive tunnels deep below ground level. In these tunnels, workers dig the coal and haul it out in carts. Coal mining is a dirty, dangerous job.

The process of mining coal can destroy soil and pollute water sources. Care must be taken to preserve the wildlife around the mining area. Mining companies are required to take measures to reclaim, or restore, natural areas after coal mining is completed. They do this by returning the soil to the surface and planting trees and grasses. Reclamation projects are especially important in areas that are strip-mined because strip-mining involves tearing apart so much of the surface. However, it is also important to repair the land used in underground coal mining. If the mines are simply abandoned, the area can become polluted and unsafe. If the mines are not closed properly, part of the land can collapse into the abandoned mine shafts.

► Coal miners use large machines to dig tunnels and harvest coal from deep within Earth.

Oil and Natural Gas

Oil and natural gas are also fossil fuels. Both are formed from the remains of once-living organisms. **Oil,** or petroleum, is a black liquid that is refined into heating fuel for buildings and gasoline for automobiles. Like coal, oil takes millions of years to form. The process of forming an oil deposit begins when billions of microorganisms that live in water die and accumulate on the seafloor. As these organisms become covered, they slowly decompose into liquid oil.

Natural gas is a fossil fuel in a gaseous state. It is formed in a manner similar to oil. The organisms that produce natural gas decompose into a lighter material that becomes a gas instead of a liquid. Natural gas is used to heat buildings and to fuel stoves. Both oil and natural gas produce air pollution when they're burned for energy. However, natural gas is generally considered to be cleaner and to cause less pollution than oil or coal. Both oil and natural gas are limited sources of energy. Like coal, they take millions of years to form. When existing supplies have been used, another form of energy will have to be found.

Removing Oil and Natural Gas from the Ground

Oil and natural gas have one big advantage over coal when it comes to removing them for use. Because oil and natural gas are liquid and gas in state, they can be pumped out of the ground. They do not require mining, as coal does.

Oil and natural gas are usually found in pockets of rock underground. They are obtained by drilling into these pockets. As the drill cuts through the ground, pipe is placed in the hole that's formed. When the drill reaches a pocket of natural gas or oil, pumping equipment is activated, and the material is pumped up the pipe above the ground, where it's captured and stored.

◀ This oil rig obtains oil by drilling a deep well. After the well reaches the oil deposit, pipes are put into the well to pump the oil to the surface.

Pollution

Pollution is a major problem in using most fossil fuels. When fossil fuels such as oil, coal, and natural gas are burned for energy, they release pollution into the air. Here are some of the most common problems caused by the pollution that comes from fossil fuels.

Global Warming

When fossil fuels are burned, they release large amounts of carbon dioxide. Carbon dioxide builds up in the atmosphere and traps heat, causing global temperatures to increase. The possibility of global warming has become a concern, and burning fossil fuels has been recognized as one of its correctable causes.

Acid Rain

Another pollutant that is released when fossil fuels are burned is sulfur dioxide, which is produced mainly by burning coal. Sulfur is released into the air and combines with water vapor in clouds, producing an acid in the water vapor that falls to Earth as what is called acid rain or acid snow. This acidic water harms plants and animals. Fish and animals that live in water are especially hurt as acid levels increase in their habitats. In recent years, government regulations have succeeded in reducing pollutants that cause acid rain.

Lesson Assessment

Review

1. **Relate Cause and Effect** Explain how using fossil fuels can increase the levels of pollution in the environment.

2. **Define** Why are coal, oil, and natural gas referred to as fossil fuels?

3. **Explain** How is coal formed?

4. **Compare and Contrast** Compare and contrast the different types of nonrenewable energy.

5. **Describe** Explain how coal is obtained.

Critical Thinking

What might the future be like if humans continue to rely on fossil fuels for most energy?

Writing in Science

Write a diary entry of a day in the life of a coal miner. Be imaginative, and describe the miner's activities and the environment in which the miner works.

Reading Skills and Strategies

- Take lecture notes.
- Review text connections, text structure, comprehension monitoring, SQ3R, QHL, multipart words, and word-learning strategies.

Lesson 2

Renewable Energy Resources

As YOU Read

What You'll Learn
- How humans use renewable energy sources

Why It's Important
Renewable energy sources are inexhaustible, meaning they can be used forever.

Key Terms
- solar energy
- hydroelectric energy

Humans will eventually use up all fossil fuels on the planet, but other types of energy are available. Forms of renewable energy can be used indefinitely.

An Endless Supply of Energy

There are several renewable energy resources available. Each type of renewable energy has advantages and disadvantages. However, all renewable energy resources have one thing in common: They cannot be exhausted, and thus they provide an endless supply of energy. The most common sources of renewable energy are the sun, the wind, and the water that flows across the surface of Earth.

Solar Energy

Solar energy is the most plentiful form of energy on Earth. Because plants need light from the sun to make food eaten by humans and animals, solar energy maintains most life on Earth. We can also harness the sun's light to generate electrical energy for human needs.

▶ Solar panels capture energy from the sun and transform it into electrical energy.

There are two types of solar energy: passive and active. We use passive solar energy by drawing window coverings to allow sunlight into our rooms instead of turning on electric lights. We use dark-colored shingles on our roofs to absorb the sun's heat instead of using heaters. We can also use solar energy in an active way with the help of solar cells. Solar cells collect light energy from the sun and transform that energy into electrical energy humans can use for various purposes. You've probably used calculators powered by solar cells. Larger panels of solar cells can be mounted on roofs to collect solar energy and send it into buildings for general use.

Although there is an endless supply of solar energy, there are some disadvantages in its use. The biggest disadvantage is that we haven't yet developed technology that captures solar energy efficiently. The solar cells we currently use are expensive to produce and don't do a good job of capturing energy, especially during periods when the sun is not shining brightly. The only way we now have to use solar energy on cloudy days or at night is to store the energy in batteries. This procedure is expensive and inefficient and produces chemical waste in the form of batteries that must be disposed of.

Wind Energy

Wind is another renewable energy resource that can be harnessed for human use. The power of the wind can be transformed into electrical energy by windmills, which turn in the wind and generate electricity. However, wind energy is not dependable. Many places on Earth do not get much wind. Some people think windmills are unattractive and don't want to see them in their neighborhoods.

Water Energy

Just as moving wind can be used to make electrical power, running water can be a source of renewable energy. Energy that comes from moving water is called **hydroelectric energy.** Hydroelectric energy is captured by first building a dam that blocks the flow of a stream or river. Openings water can run through are then built in the dam. As water runs through the openings, it turns wheels in a motor that produces electrical energy. Using hydroelectric power can be damaging to natural environments, however. Large dams can alter the landscape, cause erosion problems, and disrupt the movement of fish and animals.

Lesson Assessment

Review

1. **Define** Explain the concept of renewable energy resources.

2. **Compare and Contrast** Choose two forms of renewable energy, and list the advantages and disadvantages of each.

3. How could solar energy provide power at night?

4. **Explain** In the future, why might solar power become more acceptable as a source of energy?

5. **Relate Cause and Effect** Explain how wind power and hydroelectric power work to generate electricity in similar ways.

Critical Thinking

A newscaster describes renewable energy as a source of energy "that does not harm the environment." Explain why this may not be a completely true statement.

Writing in Science

Write a description of the area you live in. Choose the most suitable form of renewable energy for your area, and explain why it is the best choice.

◄ Hoover Dam generates hydroelectric power by means of water running through chambers in the dam wall. As the water runs through the chambers, electricity is generated.

Renewable Energy Resources **215**

Reading Skills and Strategies

- Take lecture notes.
- Review text connections, text structure, comprehension monitoring, SQ3R, QHL, note taking, and word-learning strategies.

Lesson 3 Landforms

As YOU Read

What You'll Learn

■ Earth's surface is made up of many different landforms.

Why It's Important

Humans use land in various ways, depending on the type of landform.

Key Terms

■ plain

■ plateau

The surface of Earth has many different forms. Three of these are plains, plateaus, and mountains.

Plains

A **plain** is a large flat landform. These flat areas are ideal for farming and building homes and other structures. There are interior plains, which are in the center of a continent, and coastal plains, which are near the ocean.

▶ On the left is an interior plain. On the right is a coastal plain.

Differences between Interior Plains and Coastal Plains

An interior plain is a large flat area located in the middle of a landmass. Interior plains are typically characterized by good soils and a variety of plants and animal wildlife.

A coastal plain is a flat area of land near a coast. Coastal plains are typically separated from the interior of a landmass by other features, such as mountains. A coastal plain extends from the land into the water. Often a coastal plain is wet and swampy because the flat areas can be flooded by rising coastal waters.

Plateaus

A **plateau** is a landform that rises above the land around it. The tops of plateaus are usually flat. The general shape of a plateau is that of a table. For this reason, a plateau is often called a tableland. Some plateaus rise high above their surroundings.

Plateaus are formed when Earth forces push large blocks of rock from within Earth to the surface. Most plateaus are millions of years old.

Mountains

A mountain is a landform that reaches high above surrounding landforms. Mountains vary in height but usually have steep slopes. Many mountains are so high the atmosphere at the top of the mountain is very different from the atmosphere at the base. The top of a mountain may be covered in snow while the atmosphere at the base is mild and pleasant. Mountains form in several ways and are classified by the way they form.

Volcanoes

Many mountains are formed from active volcanoes. As a volcano erupts and lava pushes out the top and cools, the volcano grows larger and higher. After the volcano stops erupting, a mountain remains. Mountains formed in this way may become active volcanoes again.

▶ Mount St. Helens, a mountain in the state of Washington, suddenly erupted in 1980 after more than a century of inactivity. This photo shows the mountain two years after it blew its top.

Folded Mountains, Upwarped Mountains, and Fault-Block Mountains

Other mountains are formed when forces inside Earth push parts of Earth's crust together and push large pieces upward. Folded mountains, such as the Appalachian Mountains, are formed when a piece of Earth's crust is squeezed from both sides and folds upward.

Upwarped mountains are formed when pieces of Earth's crust are pushed upward and slide past and above surrounding crust. The Adirondacks are an example of upwarped mountains.

Fault-block mountains result when one piece of Earth's crust moves upward and an adjacent piece moves downward. The Grand Tetons in Wyoming are an example of fault-block mountains.

Lesson Assessment

Review

1. **Define** List the three main types of landforms.

2. **Describe** Give a description of a plain.

3. **Compare and Contrast** Make a table that compares and contrasts the features of a plateau and a mountain.

4. **Relate Cause and Effect** Explain how forces within Earth work in different ways to form mountains.

Critical Thinking

What makes a plain more suitable than a plateau or a mountain for human habitation?

Writing in Science

Pretend you're an alien on a spacecraft exploring Earth. Describe the landforms you observe.

Reading Skills and Strategies
- Take lecture notes.
- Review text connections, text structure, comprehension monitoring, SQ3R, QHL, note taking, and word-learning strategies.

Lesson 4

Forces inside Earth

As YOU Read

What You'll Learn
- How forces within Earth cause earthquakes

Why It's Important
Earthquakes are a major cause of destruction on Earth.

Key Terms
- earthquake
- fault

Our planet is not just a big ball of dirt. Deep inside Earth, hot liquid material cycles and moves, even reaching the surface at times. These movements act as powerful forces on the material that makes up our planet.

Causes of Earthquakes

Earth may seem like a big chunk of motionless rock, but it's actually a dynamic mixture in constant motion. The materials that make up Earth are always moving, fueled by heat energy deep below the surface. These motions cause activity that is felt on the surface as an **earthquake,** a shaking or movement of the ground.

Formation of Faults

The surface of Earth is not one smoothly continuous material. Instead, it's made of large pieces of rocklike earth called "plates." These plates move toward each other, away from each other, and beside each other. The movement of plates causes and releases tension. When plates move forcefully enough to break, a **fault** is formed. The plates move up, down, or sideways along these faults, or fault lines.

Some faults form on a diagonal. The rock on one side of a fault is called the hanging wall. A hanging wall occurs above the fault and rests or hangs on top of the footwall. You could hang from the top, but no other part of your body would touch the rock. The rock on the other side of the fault is called the footwall. Can you guess why?

Fault

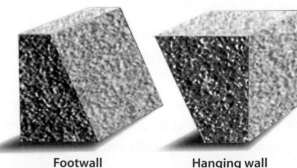

▶ You can see from the drawing that the footwall and the hanging wall once fit together smoothly.

Footwall   **Hanging wall**

Types of Faults

The forces that move plates produce three basic types of faults: normal faults, reverse faults, and strike-slip faults. These faults are characterized by the positions and movements of the plates involved.

Normal and Reverse Faults

When tension pulls rocks apart, a normal fault results. The hanging wall moves *down* in relation to the footwall. A reverse fault is the opposite. Rocks are compressed in a reverse fault. The hanging wall moves *up* in relation to the footwall.

Strike-Slip Fault

In a strike-slip fault, neither part moves up or down. Instead, the two rocks move sideways, scraping against each other. In other words, one side moves and rubs against the other. This movement causes tension on the fault line. As a result, many earthquakes occur on strike-slip faults. You've probably heard of the San Andreas Fault in California. It's a famous strike-slip fault that produces frequent earthquakes in the western United States. The motion of the two rocks sliding past each other causes vibrations in the ground that people experience as earthquakes. Movement is constantly occurring on a strike-slip fault like the San Andreas Fault. That is why earthquakes happen frequently along this fault line.

◀ The photograph shows the San Andreas Fault from the air.

Lesson 5

Reading Skills and Strategies

- Use higher-order thinking skills.
- Review text connections, text structure, comprehension monitoring, SQ3R, QHL, multipart words, and word-learning strategies.

Earthquake Destruction

As YOU Read

What You'll Learn

■ How scientists detect earthquakes and people prepare for them

Why It's Important

Early detection of earthquakes can save lives and reduce damage if preparations are made.

Key Terms

■ seismologist

■ magnitude

■ tsunami

Earthquakes have caused mass destruction throughout human history. One example of the power of earthquakes occurred in Mexico City in 1985. An earthquake destroyed hundreds of buildings and was responsible for the deaths of at least nine thousand people. The extent of the destruction was so great some experts believe the death toll was many thousands higher.

The Science of Earthquakes

Scientists are working to understand earthquakes to avoid disasters like the one in Mexico City. Seismic waves occur during earthquakes, and scientists who study earthquakes are called **seismologists.**

The Richter Scale

You've probably heard earthquakes described in terms of the Richter scale. The Richter scale is a measure of the energy released during an earthquake, the **magnitude** of the earthquake. The scale's values are based on readings of seismic waves. Each whole number on the Richter scale signifies a multiple of ten. An earthquake with a Richter value of 6 ($10 \times 10 \times 10 \times 10 \times 10 \times 10$) is a hundred times more powerful than an earthquake that scores a 4 ($10 \times 10 \times 10 \times 10$). The most powerful earthquakes fall between 7 and 9. Most earthquakes have a value of 3 or less on the Richter scale and are not noticed by humans.

Measuring Intensity

Although the Richter scale provides objective, scientific information about the energy released by an earthquake, a subjective, or personal, evaluation may be more helpful to the ordinary person. This kind of information is known as earthquake intensity. The Mercalli intensity scale that follows describes the type of damage caused by earthquakes of various intensities and the feelings of people living through such earthquakes. Instead of magnitude numbers, this scale describes what a person will feel and what will happen to certain structures during an earthquake of a certain intensity.

Modified Mercalli Intensity Scale

I. Most people don't feel anything.

II. A few people at rest indoors feel something. Hanging objects may swing slightly.

III. People indoors feel vibrations as if a truck were passing.

IV. Many people indoors and a few outdoors feel vibrations as if a heavily loaded truck were passing. Dishes rattle, and walls creak.

V. Most people indoors and outdoors feel vibrations. Buildings tremble. Dishes and glasses break.

VI. Everyone feels vibrations, and many are frightened and run outdoors. Pictures fall from walls.

VII. Everyone is frightened and runs outdoors. Chimneys crack, and windows break. Driving is affected.

VIII. Some people panic. Damage to ordinary buildings is substantial.

IX. There is general panic. The ground cracks. Damage to structures built to withstand earthquakes is considerable. Some underground pipes break.

X. Ground cracks several inches in width appear. Wood structures are destroyed. Landslides occur.

XI. Dams and dikes are severely damaged. Bridges collapse. Rails on railroads buckle. Underground pipelines go out of service.

XII. This is the ultimate catastrophe. Most structures are destroyed. Objects are thrown into the air. Many people die.

Tsunamis

Often the most devastating damage caused by an earthquake does not come from the earthquake itself. Some earthquakes that occur on the ocean floor or near shores release seismic waves that grow into huge ocean waves, called **tsunamis.** A tsunami can travel a long distance before crashing onto land, where it can cause massive destruction. A tsunami can be especially deadly because it is both high and long. Tsunamis can travel far inland, destroying structures and sweeping people away. Because tsunamis are most often formed far out in the ocean, no one is aware of them, so they often strike with little or no warning. Scientists are setting up detection systems in the ocean to provide early warning of tsunamis and allow people time to evacuate.

Lesson Assessment

Review

1. **Explain** How will better techniques for detecting earthquakes help reduce the damage earthquakes cause?

2. **Define** What is meant by the magnitude of an earthquake?

3. **Compare and Contrast** Compare and contrast the information provided by the Richter scale and the Mercalli scale.

4. **Infer** Why would an earthquake be more deadly if it struck a large city instead of a rural area?

5. **Relate Cause and Effect** Explain how earthquakes in the ocean cause tsunamis.

Critical Thinking

Why do seismologists focus on *detecting* earthquakes rather than on *preventing* them?

Writing in Science

In the last lesson, you wrote a description of an earthquake. Now write a poem or a song about an earthquake. Use words like *quake, shake, break* and *rumble, grumble, tumble* to make your verses rhyme.

Reading Skills and Strategies

- Take lecture notes.
- Use Strategy Bookmark: comprehension strategies.
- Use Strategy Bookmark: vocabulary strategies.

Lesson 1

The Atmosphere

As YOU Read

What You'll Learn
- What gases make up Earth's atmosphere

Why It's Important
The atmosphere supports all Earth's living things.

Key Terms
- atmosphere
- troposphere
- stratosphere
- ozone layer

The layer of air that covers Earth's surface is called the **atmosphere.** Earth's atmosphere is made up of many different gases and is essential for maintaining life on Earth.

The Structure of the Atmosphere

Earth's atmosphere is a layer of gases that reach from Earth's surface into outer space. The atmosphere does not actually end at any specific boundary but begins to fade and thin as it gets farther from Earth's surface. Atmospheric space is actually small compared to the size of Earth.

▲ Earth's atmosphere keeps the temperature of our planet in a range that can support life.

Gases That Compose the Atmosphere

Which gas, do you think, makes up the majority of the atmosphere? Many people think oxygen is the most predominant gas because it supports life. Although oxygen is important and plentiful in our atmosphere, it's not the most predominant gas. The gas that makes up the greatest part of Earth's atmosphere is nitrogen. Our atmosphere is made up of approximately 78 percent nitrogen and 21 percent oxygen. The remaining 1 percent of the atmosphere is made up of argon, carbon dioxide, and other trace gases.

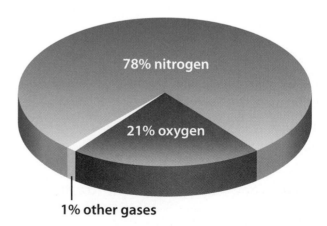

78% nitrogen

21% oxygen

1% other gases

▲ Most of the gas in Earth's atmosphere is nitrogen. Oxygen is also plentiful.

Other Substances in the Atmosphere

Although we think of the atmosphere as being made up solely of gases, it also contains some solids and liquids. The atmosphere is filled with solid particles of dust, pollen, and other materials, although the solids are generally too small to be seen. You are probably familiar with the liquids present in our atmosphere—the clouds in the sky. Clouds are made of tiny drops of water suspended in the air.

Layers of the Atmosphere

The atmosphere can be divided into layers based on composition and density. In general, the lower layers are denser and contain most of the air that supports life. Farther from Earth, the layers of atmosphere become thinner and contain less of the kind of air capable of supporting life.

The Troposphere

The atmospheric layer that supports life and is closest to Earth's surface is the **troposphere.** Most of the gas that makes up the atmosphere is found in the troposphere. The gases in this layer are responsible for supporting life. The troposphere contains almost all Earth's water vapor. That is why clouds and weather are found there.

The Stratosphere

The **stratosphere** is found just above the troposphere and contains almost all the remaining gases in the atmosphere. The stratosphere is also where the **ozone layer** is located. The ozone layer is a concentration of a gas called ozone. Ozone filters harmful radiation from the sun and prevents the radiation from striking Earth's surface. You may have heard concerns about a "hole" in Earth's ozone layer. This hole is caused by pollutants that destroy ozone. Since scientists discovered the hole in the ozone layer, people have been working to reduce the pollution that causes the hole.

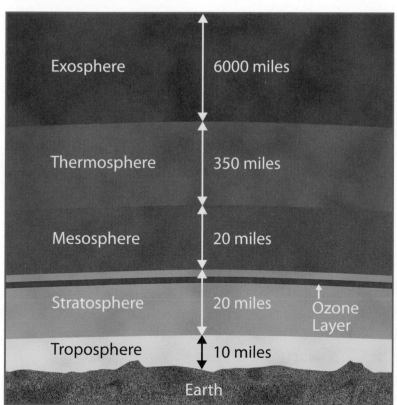

Exosphere — 6000 miles

Thermosphere — 350 miles

Mesosphere — 20 miles

Stratosphere — 20 miles — Ozone Layer

Troposphere — 10 miles

Earth

◄ In the atmosphere, the passage from one layer to the next is gradual, and the heights given in the diagram are approximate.

The Upper Atmosphere

Above the stratosphere, the next three layers of the atmosphere are the mesosphere, the thermosphere, and the exosphere. These layers contain very little air and become thinner farther from Earth. The area occupied by the exosphere is generally considered the boundary where the atmosphere ends and outer space begins. Space shuttles orbit Earth in the thermosphere.

Air Pressure

Many people are surprised to learn that air has weight and mass. If you think about it, you already know this is true. When you blow up a balloon, you are packing it with air. The air builds up and pushes against the walls of the balloon, expanding it. If you put too much air in the balloon, the material cannot hold against the pressure, and the balloon bursts.

Air pressure varies depending how far from Earth's surface you are. In locations close to Earth, gravity pulls the air downward, and the air is dense. Higher up, the air is thinner and less dense. You have probably experienced differences in air pressure if you have flown in an airplane or traveled in the mountains. As you move upward, the air pressure around you lessens. Finally, the difference between the air density inside your ears and the air density around you is so great that the air in your ears rushes out, making a popping noise and relieving the pressure.

The Ozone Layer

Humans have a love-hate relationship with ozone. On the one hand, ozone is a pollutant that damages our lungs. It is given off by automobiles and can accumulate in cities and be unhealthful for all living things. On the other hand, natural ozone in the atmosphere keeps us alive. If it weren't for the ozone layer within the stratosphere, ultraviolet radiation from the sun would destroy all life on Earth. The concentration of ozone absorbs most of this radiation and makes Earth a habitable place. Recently, scientists have discovered that the ozone layer is disappearing, and many believe humans are to blame.

The Hole in the Ozone Layer

Scientists have determined that there is a hole in the ozone layer. Actually, what is happening is that the amount of ozone in the ozone layer is decreasing in the Antarctic region of the stratosphere. This decrease in ozone produces spots in which the ozone content is thin, thus allowing more radiation through to Earth's surface. This depletion of ozone has been traced to chemicals called chlorofluorocarbons, or CFCs. These chemicals were used in air conditioners, foam packaging, and aerosol-spray products. The CFCs were released into the atmosphere, where they broke apart ozone particles, destroying ozone. If CFC production continued to destroy ozone, it was feared the amounts of radiation reaching Earth would continue to increase, leading to increases in cancer and skin damage. The use of CFCs was banned in response to this problem. However, CFC molecules last a long time, and it will be many years before the ozone layer can recover.

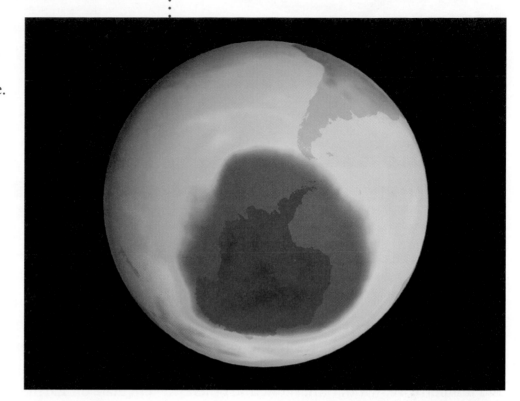

▲ The amount of ozone found above Antarctica is much less than the amount found around the rest of Earth. The small amount of ozone results in a "hole" in the ozone layer, shown here in dark blue.

Lesson Assessment

Review

1. **Identify** In which level of the atmosphere do humans live?

2. **List** List the layers of Earth's atmosphere in order from closest to Earth to farthest away.

3. **Explain** What other substances and states of matter exist in the atmosphere besides gases?

4. **Identify Cause and Effect** Explain how human activity caused the ozone layer to deteriorate.

5. **Describe** Explain how air pressure varies according to elevation on Earth's surface.

Critical Thinking

- Describe what might happen if humans do not take action to preserve the ozone layer. Will anything happen if humans do not take action?

- Nitrogen makes up the majority of the air we breathe. How might life on Earth be different if oxygen made up the majority of the air we breathe? Would people be healthier? Would people live a lot longer than they currently do?

Writing in Science

- Using the Internet, find and list some products from the past that contained CFCs. Tell how these products have been changed to make them more environmentally friendly.

- Using the Internet, find a model of Earth's atmosphere and see if you can locate all the layers. Write about the thickness of each layer and how important each layer is to the overall health of Earth.

Reading Skills and Strategies

- Take lecture notes.
- Use Strategy Bookmark: comprehension strategies.
- Use Strategy Bookmark: vocabulary strategies.

Lesson 2 Weather

As YOU Read

What You'll Learn
- The elements and activities that combine to cause weather

Why It's Important
Weather affects almost everything people do.

Key Terms
- weather
- precipitation

One of the first things most people do each day is to check the weather forecast. **Weather** is the term we use to describe the conditions in the atmosphere around us. Weather affects almost everything we do, and temperature, wind, rain, snow, and other weather conditions we encounter are an important part of our environment.

▲ People deal with weather every day.

The Source of Weather

If you were asked to think of good weather, you would most likely imagine a sunny day. However, the sun is responsible for all weather, even rain and wind, because weather is caused by energy, and all energy comes from the sun. The solar radiation we receive causes temperatures, but radiation also causes wind and weather patterns that circulate on Earth.

Air Temperature

The sun is one of the most important factors in determining temperature on Earth. It is the source of all our heat. Earth's temperatures vary only about as much as is comfortable for humans and animals to live. That means in winter it is cold, but not too cold for most of us, and in summer it gets hot, but the range of temperatures is narrow enough that we can live on most of Earth's surface. Temperature is the measurement of heat energy in the air around us. Energy from the sun strikes Earth, and that energy is transferred to air molecules. When air molecules have a lot of energy, they move fast, and temperatures are high. When air molecules have less energy, they move more slowly, and temperatures are lower.

Wind

Wind is caused by moving air molecules. Air molecules move from areas of high pressure to areas of low pressure. This activity is typically related to temperature. When air molecules are heated, they move more quickly and expand. Warm air is not very dense because the air molecules are spread out. The molecules in cold air move slowly and are packed together in a higher density. Because air molecules move from high-pressure to low-pressure areas, air in cold areas (high pressure) will move to warmer areas (lower pressure). This causes

wind. You can see from the diagram how wind develops.

Humidity

Humidity is a measure of the amount of moisture in the air. Humidity increases as liquid water is heated by the sun and changes into gas vapor. This gas vapor rises and mixes with the air.

Clouds

You know that clouds bring rain, but you might not know exactly what clouds are. Clouds are not water vapor; they are tiny drops of liquid suspended in air. Clouds form as water on Earth's surface is heated and becomes gas. As the gas rises, it begins to cool. Some of the cooling water vapor turns into liquid in the air as the molecules contact dust and other particles.

When the liquid droplets in clouds combine and become too big and heavy to float, they fall to the ground as **precipitation.** Precipitation may occur as rain, snow, sleet, or hail.

▲ The warm air over land produces a low-pressure zone. The colder, high-pressure air over the water then rushes toward the low-pressure zone, producing a breeze.

Lesson Assessment

Review

1. **Define** Explain the concept of weather.

2. **Compare and Contrast** Compare and contrast the density and speed of air particles in a warm location and air particles in a colder location.

3. Describe how a cloud forms.

4. **Explain** What factors cause wind?

5. **Relate Cause and Effect** Explain how the sun is connected to all weather that occurs on Earth.

Critical Thinking

- Describe the weather in your location at this very moment. Which type of precipitation is most likely to occur under the conditions you describe?

- Describe what happens when clouds become too big. What are some of the things that could be produced by clouds that become too big?

Writing in Science

Weather affects us more than we think it does. It affects how we travel, it affects how we exercise, and it may even affect our moods. Write a short story about a time weather played a large role in your life.

Reading Skills and Strategies

- Take lecture notes.
- Use Strategy Bookmark: comprehension strategies.
- Use Strategy Bookmark: vocabulary strategies.

Lesson 3 Weather Patterns

As YOU Read

What You'll Learn
- How weather acts and moves in distinct patterns

Why It's Important
Recognizing weather patterns makes it possible to predict weather.

Key Terms
- front
- tornado

Predicting Weather Changes

A weather forecast predicts changes in weather conditions. Weather conditions can be predicted because changes in the weather occur in patterns. By studying these patterns and collecting data, it's possible to track weather and predict it to a certain extent.

Air Movement

An air mass is a large volume of air that develops over Earth. Air masses have characteristics based on the environment in which they develop. Air masses move in relation to one another. They are an important part of weather patterns because as an air mass moves from one location to another, the weather in those locations changes.

Pressure Systems

You have learned that wind is caused by air moving from high-pressure areas into low-pressure areas. Weather forecasters keep track of pressure systems to predict how air fronts will move. When air pressure is low,

rain and thunderstorms can occur. When air pressure is high, the weather is usually fair.

▲ This weather map shows areas with high and low pressure. The high-pressure areas are marked with an *H*, and the low-pressure areas are marked with an *L*.

Air Fronts

A **front** occurs when air masses with different densities meet. The front is the boundary between the two masses. Fronts are illustrated on weather maps by curved lines. A cold front, in which a mass of cold air is moving into a warmer area, is shown as a blue line with triangles. A warm front, in which a mass of warm air is moving into a colder area, is shown as a red line with semicircles. You can tell the direction the front is moving by noting the side of the line on which the triangles or semicircles are located. A stationary front occurs when a cold front and a warm front meet, but neither advances.

Severe Weather

There are many types of severe weather. The conditions brought on by severe weather put people and property in danger.

Thunderstorms are made up of wind and heavy rain. Often lightning is present.

If temperatures in the clouds are low, icy hail can be part of a thunderstorm. Wind, lightning, and hail can endanger humans and damage property. Thunderstorms can also release large amounts of rain that can cause flooding.

When weather conditions are especially severe, tornadoes or hurricanes can form. A **tornado** is an extremely powerful column of wind that runs from a cloud toward the ground and moves across the ground. Tornadoes are unpredictable and can be destructive and even deadly.

Hurricanes are storms that form over warm ocean water and grow large and strong. A swirling mass of air and water rotates around a small calm area in the center, called the eye. Hurricanes are especially dangerous when they move onto land. You can see a photograph of a hurricane over water on page 171.

◄ A tornado is an extreme weather condition that can be dangerous to humans and destructive to property.

Lesson Assessment

Review

1. **Define** What occurs to form a front?

2. **Describe** Give an example of how air masses move based on temperature or pressure or both.

3. **Compare and Contrast** Compare and contrast the dangers posed by tornadoes and hurricanes.

4. **Explain** Tell how to interpret the different fronts shown on a weather map.

Critical Thinking

- Explain the differences between a mass of cold air and a mass of warm air. How dense could each mass get? How fast could each mass move?

- What are some of the things that are most likely to occur during a thunderstorm? How many of them are dangerous to humans?

Writing in Science

Severe weather can leave a lasting impression on people. Have you ever witnessed severe weather firsthand? Write a short poem describing the emotional impact of the severe weather you witnessed.

Reading Skills and Strategies

- Take lecture notes.
- Use Strategy Bookmark: comprehension strategies.
- Use Strategy Bookmark: vocabulary strategies.

Lesson 4 Climate

As YOU Read

What You'll Learn
- How various factors affect the climate of a location

Why It's Important
The climate of a location determines much of the activity and way of life there.

Key Terms
- climate
- tropics

People often confuse the terms *weather* and *climate*. **Climate** refers to the general weather conditions in an area over a long period of time. For example, you know that the temperatures and weather conditions in an area change with the seasons. You probably also know that climates vary. This is the reason many people who live in the northern United States travel south for the winter. The climate in the southern United States is generally warmer than the climate in the northern part of the country.

Latitude and Its Effects

In the United States, the climate in the north is different from the climate in the south. Latitude is the distance of a location from the equator, either north or south. Areas near the equator, between the Tropic of Cancer and the Tropic of Capricorn, are known as the **tropics.** The tropics have the warmest climate because these areas receive heat and light energy, in the form of solar radiation, more directly than the rest of Earth's surface.

As you move away from the equator, the climate becomes cooler. The areas north of the Arctic Circle and south of the Antarctic

Circle are called polar zones and are the coldest on Earth's surface. The North Pole is at the very top of the globe, and the South Pole is at the bottom.

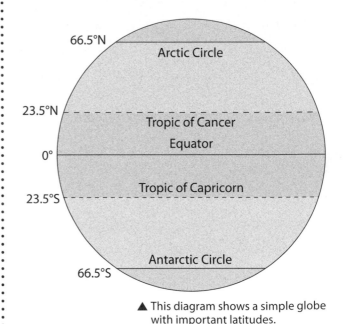

66.5°N — Arctic Circle

23.5°N — Tropic of Cancer

Equator

0°

Tropic of Capricorn

23.5°S

Antarctic Circle

66.5°S

▲ This diagram shows a simple globe with important latitudes.

Land and Water

Another factor that affects climate is the amount of water and land at a location. The reason water and land affect climate is that land and water heat and cool at different rates. Specifically, water takes longer to heat and cool than land does under the same circumstances because water absorbs more energy before it changes temperature. Therefore, locations on or near large bodies of water change temperature more slowly than locations with no water nearby. Thus, locations near water experience milder winters and cooler summers than other locations at the same latitude.

Other Climate Factors

Other factors can affect the climate of a location. All these factors combine to make the climate of a specific area.

▲ Because of the difference in elevation, the summit of this mountain is much colder than the land at the base.

Elevation

The elevation of an area can have a dramatic effect on climate. Elevation is the height above sea level. Generally, in locations that are high above sea level, the climate is cold. You can see examples of this change in climate in mountains. Although the base of a mountain may be warm, with trees and grasses, the summit is often covered in ice and snow.

Urban Areas

People can affect climate through their activities. When people cut down forests and build large cities, they can increase the average temperatures of a location. Trees, shrubs, and grasses absorb heat and lower temperatures. Concrete and asphalt get hot and increase the surrounding temperature. Pollution from cars and factories also increases temperature.

Lesson Assessment

Review

1. **Define** Explain the difference between climate and weather.

2. **Relate Cause and Effect** Explain why areas near Earth's equator are generally hot while locations near the poles are cold.

3. **Compare and Contrast** Tell how the climates between two locations at the same latitude might be different if one location is near a large body of water.

4. **Explain** Why is there often snow on the tops of mountains, even though the mountains are located in warm climates?

Critical Thinking

- Discuss some ways humans might reduce the negative effects large cities have on climate.

- Discuss how global warming might change climates in different parts of the world. Would places near the equator feel the effects of global warming to a larger degree than people who live between the equator and the north pole?

Writing in Science

How many places have you visited? List some places you have visited. How did these places differ in terms of climate? How did they differ in terms of elevation? Describe the climate and elevation of each place. Did the climate and the elevation of the different places appear to correlate? If so, give reasons to explain why.

Reading Skills and Strategies

- Use higher-order thinking skills.
- Review text connections, comprehension monitoring, SQ3R, QHL, note taking, Strategy Bookmark, and word-learning strategies.

Lesson 5 — Air Pollution

As YOU Read

What You'll Learn

- Ways air can be polluted

Why It's Important

The quality of our air has an impact on human health.

Key Terms

- photochemical smog
- acid rain

Clean air is important to all living things. Humans must have clean air to breathe. Plants and animals also depend on clean air for survival. Most people think of air pollution as thick, dark, smoky clouds pouring from a smokestack on top of a factory. However, there are many different types of air pollution and many different sources that produce air pollution.

Smog

One of the most common forms of air pollution in cities is smog. The word *smog* is a combination of *smoke* and *fog*. Smog is a health hazard that can cause breathing problems for older people, children, and anyone with asthma or other health problems.

Photochemical Smog

Photochemical smog is a particular type of smog that is produced when chemicals in the air react with sunlight to form a dangerous gas. The chemicals that combine with sunlight to form photochemical smog come from industrial factories.

Factors That Affect Smog

Environmental factors can reduce smog or make it worse. For example, many cities with severe smog problems sit in deep valleys that don't get much wind. Without wind to blow away the smog, it builds up. The same situation occurs in cities surrounded by mountain ranges that restrict the movement of air in and out of the city.

Temperature can sometimes make a smog problem worse as well. Although normally the air near the surface is warmer than the air higher up, warm air can sometimes become trapped above cool surface air. When this happens, smog near the surface cannot escape.

▲ Los Angeles, California, lies in dense smog.

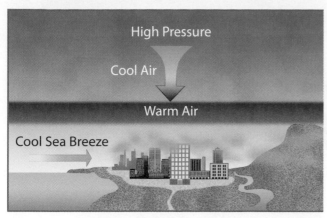

▲ You can see from this diagram why smog hangs over Los Angeles in the photograph on the opposite page. The mountains to the east of the city and the band of warm air above the city trap polluted air.

Acid Rain

Acid rain is a form of air pollution caused by industrial activity. Acid rain is produced when sulfur from burning coal is released into the air. The sulfur combines with moisture in the air and then falls as rain. This rain has a high level of acid. The acid rain is harmful to plants and animals. It can also destroy stone and other structures.

The Ozone Layer

Ozone is a gas that can harm humans. However, ozone is also important in protecting humans and other life on Earth from harmful solar radiation. There is a large amount of ozone found at a high level in the atmosphere. This is called the ozone layer. The ozone in the atmosphere absorbs most of the dangerous ultraviolet radiation from the sun.

However, chemicals called chlorofluorocarbons, or CFCs, destroy ozone in the atmosphere. Most of the CFCs have accumulated in the atmosphere above Antarctica. This accumulation has resulted in an area in which the ozone levels are thinner than in other areas. This thin area of ozone is commonly referred to as a "hole" in the ozone layer. Most CFCs come from air conditioners, foam products, and aerosol sprays. Humans have worked to eliminate CFCs from products in order to restore the ozone layer.

Lesson Assessment

Review

1. **Explain** How does air pollution affect humans?

2. **Define** Where does the term *smog* come from?

3. **Contrast** Contrast the effect of smog on people who live in a windy, elevated city with the effect of smog on people who live in a city in a valley surrounded by mountains.

4. **Infer** How will banning CFCs in products help restore the ozone layer?

5. **Relate Cause and Effect** Explain how acid rain forms and how it damages the environment.

Critical Thinking

• Many factories once dealt with air pollution by making their smokestacks very tall so the pollution was released far from the ground. Why, do you think, might this not be an effective way to deal with the pollution the smokestacks send into the air?

• Describe CFCs. From where do most CFCs arise? Are humans the main reason so much CFC is in the air? What have humans been doing to help reduce the amount of CFC in the air?

Writing in Science

Although smog is harmful to humans, many people have commented that smog often results in beautiful sunsets. Find a photograph of a smoggy sunset, and compare it to a sunset without smog. Write your findings. Conclude by writing whether you believe smoggy sunsets are more beautiful than sunsets without the presence of smog.

Reading Skills and Strategies

• Review text connections, text structure, comprehension monitoring, SQ3R, QHL, note taking, and word-learning strategies.

Lesson 1

Ocean Water: The Key to Life

As YOU Read

What You'll Learn

■ What Earth's oceans are made of and how they were formed

Why It's Important

Oceans are an essential part of life on Earth.

Key Terms

■ basin
■ ion
■ salinity
■ desalination

Most of Earth's surface is covered with water, and the majority of this water makes up the oceans. In fact, more than 97 percent of Earth's water is contained in our oceans. We think of oceans as vast unlivable areas, but Earth's oceans are actually packed with life. The oceans are a vital part of what makes Earth a habitable planet.

▶ Most of Earth's surface is covered with ocean water.

Facts about Earth's Oceans

Traditionally, we say that Earth has five oceans: the Atlantic, the Pacific, the Indian, the Arctic, and the Southern. However, these distinctions are mainly geographic. Because all Earth's oceans are connected, we can consider the planet as having one large ocean body that covers approximately 71 percent of the surface. The global ocean is a place where life is abundant. Large populations of plants and tiny organisms live in ocean waters. These small organisms serve as food for larger fish and for animals. In turn, these larger fish and animals serve as food for humans. Ocean waters are deep—often reaching a depth of ten thousand feet. This means there is more living space in an area of ocean than in the same-size area on land because, in the ocean, organisms can live at many depths.

Oceans provide another major resource for humans. Large quantities of minerals and energy resources are obtained from oceans. Many of the drilling wells humans use to obtain oil and natural gas are located in the ocean. These wells are situated on platforms on the surface and bore into the ocean floor to extract fuels.

The water in the ocean is rich in minerals. These minerals supply many organisms, including humans, with nutrition. If you have swum in the ocean, you may have noticed that ocean water is salty. Humans can remove the salt from ocean water and use it as table salt to flavor food.

◄ Many of Earth's oil reserves are located beneath the ocean floor. This oil rig is stationed on the surface to drill and extract oil from below.

The Formation of Oceans

Earth's oceans formed long ago over millions of years. Soon after the planet formed, most of the water was in the form of water vapor. This water vapor was a part of the gases that were blasted into the atmosphere by the many active volcanoes that covered Earth's surface. After a long time, the water vapor built up in the atmosphere, and Earth cooled. As temperatures dropped, the water vapor condensed, and water fell to the surface as rain. The rains collected in low areas, called **basins,** and formed oceans over time.

Water on Earth is the main key to supporting life here. Earth is the only planet in our solar system known to have surface water. However, exploration of Mars has indicated that water may be present there in the form of ice. The possible presence of water leads many scientists to believe that life may exist on Mars or may have existed there in the past.

Ocean Composition

You probably think of oceans as water. Although oceans are primarily water, they also contain solids and gases.

Oxygen, carbon dioxide, and nitrogen gases are found in large quantities throughout ocean waters. Oxygen is important in supporting ocean life. Most organisms that live in the ocean need oxygen to survive. Carbon dioxide is needed by ocean plant life and other photosynthetic organisms to capture sunlight and produce food energy. Nitrogen gases are also important to many microscopic forms of ocean life, such as bacteria.

Besides sodium, there are many minerals that are either suspended or dissolved in ocean water. We commonly call sodium salt, but *salt* refers to a variety of ions that are dissolved in water. An **ion** is a type of charged atom or a substance made of charged atoms. A charge helps an atom combine with water and dissolve. Salts, or ions, are originally part of rocks. The ions are released into water when the water dissolves part of the rock over time.

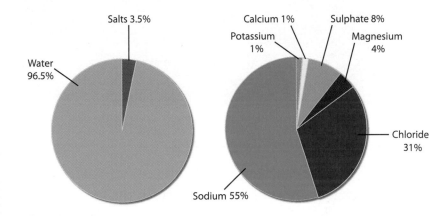

▶ The pie chart on the left shows that almost 97 percent of the ocean is water. The other 3.5 percent is salts. The second pie chart breaks down the salts that make up that 3.5 percent.

Salinity

You know that ocean water contains a variety of salt ions dissolved in the water. The **salinity** of the water is the amount, or concentration, of salts in the water. Almost all ocean water is approximately 3.5 percent dissolved salts. The salinity of ocean water makes it unsuitable for humans and other animals to drink.

The salinity of Earth's oceans has remained constant over millions of years. Although minerals and salts are constantly being added to the ocean as rocks dissolve, minerals and salts are also constantly being removed. Most commonly, salts and minerals are removed when they become too concentrated. At high concentrations, salts become solid and fall into the sediment of the ocean floor or are deposited along the shore. Salts and minerals are also removed from the water by living organisms that use the salts and minerals for nutrition.

The Desalination Process

Ocean water makes up about 97 percent of the water on Earth. Because this water contains salts and minerals, it is unsuitable for drinking by humans. However, new technology is allowing humans to make ocean water drinkable. The process of removing salts from ocean water to make freshwater is called **desalination.** Desalination occurs naturally when seawater dries in the sun, leaving minerals behind. We can mimic this process in a desalination plant to produce drinking water. One process works by heating seawater in a tank until it evaporates. The minerals are left in a solid state, and the water vapor rises as a gas. The gas is collected and cooled in another tank. As the water vapor cools, it becomes liquid again. Because the minerals are no longer present, the collected water is fresh and can be used by humans.

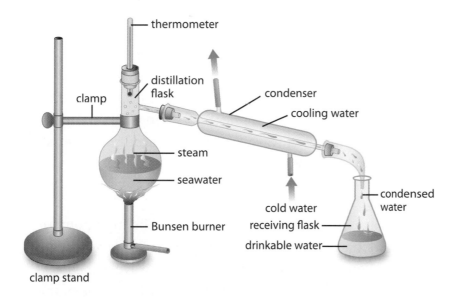

Scientists are working on other ways to desalinate water. They have developed filters that will collect the minerals and allow the water to pass through. Desalination can also be achieved by freezing water slowly. As the water freezes, the ice that forms is pure water, leaving the salt and minerals concentrated in the remaining liquid. The ice is then removed and thawed in a freshwater tank. The resulting water can be consumed by humans and other organisms.

Lesson Assessment

Review

1. **Identify** What types of things make up ocean water?

2. **Define** What is salinity?

3. **Explain** How did Earth's oceans form?

4. **Identify Cause and Effect** How are minerals constantly being added to and removed from the oceans?

5. **Describe** Explain the process of desalination.

Critical Thinking

In what locations might desalination be a vital method for obtaining water?

Writing in Science

Write a passage that describes an experience you have had with the ocean. If you have never visited the ocean, write the impressions you've received from pictures and films.

◀ This diagram illustrates one method of desalination.

Reading Skills and Strategies

• Review text connections, text structure, comprehension monitoring, SQ3R, QHL, note taking, multipart words, and word-learning strategies.

Lesson 2
Ocean Waves and Tides

One of the things people love about the ocean is the presence of waves. Surfers enjoy riding the waves on boards, and everyone loves playing in the water among the crashing waves. Some people confuse waves and tides when they describe the two. While waves move regularly during short time periods, tides are a slow rise and fall of water levels, and these rises and falls occur over time during a day.

Waves

Waves are the movement of energy in water. In the ocean, waves appear as the rise and fall of water as it strikes the shore. You know waves can be different from one another in size and appearance. Some waves are higher and stronger than others. The various characteristics of waves are based on the characteristics of the energy they're carrying.

Measuring Waves

Waves have high points and low points. The high point of a wave is called the **crest,** and the low point of a wave is called the **trough.** You can measure the length of a wave, called a wavelength, from the middle of one crest to the middle of the next crest or from the middle of one trough to the middle of the next trough. A wave's height is the distance from the trough to the crest.

▶ Can you define *crest, trough, wavelength,* and *wave height* based on this drawing?

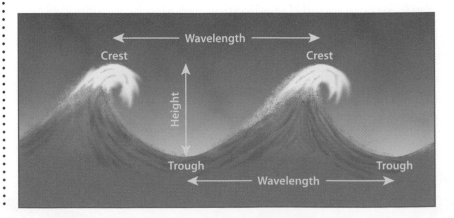

The amplitude of a wave is half the distance of the wave height. Amplitude is related to the amount of energy carried by the wave. A wave with high amplitude carries more energy than a wave with low amplitude. You may have experienced this if you've been in the ocean and noticed that larger waves have more force.

How Waves Form

Wave energy comes from the wind. As winds blow over the surface of the ocean, they transfer energy to the water. The transfer of energy causes the water to move, and a wave forms if enough energy is available. The size of the wave depends on the strength of the wind and the amount of energy that's transferred. As the strength of the wind increases, the amount of energy transferred becomes greater, and larger waves are produced.

Tides

The level of all water in the ocean rises and falls during the day. You can see this if you observe several places on the beach that water reaches at different times of the day. The rise and fall of sea level on the shore is called a tide. Maximum sea level is called high tide, and minimum sea level is called low tide.

How Tides Form

Unlike waves, tides are not caused by wind energy. Instead, tides are caused by the gravitational pull between the moon, Earth, and the sun. As the moon orbits Earth, it exerts a pull on the ocean water nearest it. This gravitational pull produces a bulge on the part of Earth facing the moon and on the opposite side of Earth at the same time. The pull of the moon on Earth produces a gravitational force on the opposite side that works against the force of motion. Both the side of Earth facing the moon and the side of Earth opposite the moon experience high tides as the water bulges outward. The locations between the high tides experience low tide as the water levels sink.

◄ Which photograph shows high tide? Which one shows low tide?

Unit 19
Science

Reading Skills and Strategies

• Review text connections, text structure, comprehension monitoring, SQ3R, QHL, note taking, and word-learning strategies.

Lesson 3
The Seafloor

As YOU Read

What You'll Learn

■ The features of the ocean floor

Why It's Important

The seafloor contains many valuable resources needed by humans.

Key Terms

■ mid-ocean ridge
■ trench

People rarely consider the ocean floor. Because most of Earth's surface is covered with ocean water, the seafloor is the largest surface feature on Earth. Deep beneath thousands of feet of water, the ocean floor takes many different forms and changes in several ways.

Ocean Basins

The ocean basins are the lowest areas on Earth. These basins filled with water millions of years ago and formed Earth's oceans. Although you might think of basins as smooth-bottomed depressions, this is not at all true. The ocean basins have a vast array of features, and the elevation of the seafloor varies dramatically from place to place.

Ocean basins begin where the land extends from the shore into the ocean. This land is called the continental shelf, and after stretching shallowly into the ocean, the continental shelf suddenly drops like a cliff deep toward the ocean floor. This sudden drop is called the continental slope. Although deep valleys and steep mountains can be found on the seafloor, there are also large stretches of flat areas called abyssal plains. The abyssal plains are formed by vast amounts of sediment settling on the ocean floor.

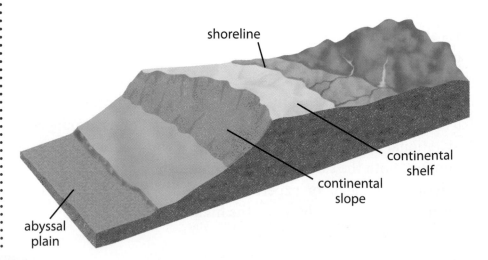

shoreline

continental shelf

continental slope

abyssal plain

▶ This diagram gives a picture of the seafloor as it descends from the shore to the ocean depths.

Mid-ocean Ridges

A **mid-ocean ridge** is a place on the ocean floor where two ocean floor plates are moving away from each other. This is where new seafloor is formed. As the plates move away from each other, hot liquid magma pours up onto the ocean floor and cools. As this material cools and becomes solid, it forms a new part of the ocean floor.

Trenches

A ridge is a place where two pieces of ocean floor are moving away from each other. A place where two pieces of ocean floor are moving toward each other is called a **trench.** At a trench, the two plates come together with great force. The result is that one piece of ocean floor is forced under the other piece in a process called subduction. The subduction activity at a trench produces deep areas surrounded by steep underwater mountains. Trenches are the deepest parts of the ocean. Volcanoes and earthquakes often occur in trench areas.

Resources from the Seafloor

The ocean floor is a source of many resources humans need. However, the depth of the seafloor and the conditions on the ocean surface can make retrieving these resources difficult. Some of the most valuable resources obtained from the seafloor are oil and natural gas. A wealth of minerals and valuable metals is also found on the seafloor. These materials accumulate over time as streams and rivers carry sediments to the ocean.

Lesson Assessment

Review

1. **Compare and Contrast** How does the area of seafloor compare to the area of land on Earth's surface?

2. **Describe** Describe the transition from land to ocean floor as you move from the shore outward into the ocean.

3. **Define** What occurs at a mid-ocean ridge?

4. **Explain** Describe the process that produces new ocean floor.

5. **Relate Cause and Effect** Explain what happens at a subduction zone.

Critical Thinking

Why are so many minerals and other natural resources found in large deposits on the ocean floor?

Writing in Science

Pretend you're exploring the ocean floor in a submarine. Write a narrative that describes what you see.

◄ As ocean plates move toward each other, one of the plates is pushed under the other to produce a subduction zone, thus forming a deep ocean trench.

Reading Skills and Strategies

• Review text connections, text structure, comprehension monitoring, SQ3R, QHL, note taking, and word-learning strategies.

Lesson 4

Ocean Life

As YOU Read

What You'll Learn

■ The variety of life-forms in Earth's oceans

Why It's Important

The health of land environments and the health of ocean environments are interdependent.

Key Terms

■ photosynthesis
■ chemosynthesis

A quick look at the ocean and a forest or a grassland might lead you to believe that land is filled with life but ocean waters are empty. On the contrary, the oceans are filled with resources that allow life to flourish. In addition, because ocean waters can be very deep, there is much more room for organisms to live in a section of the ocean than there is in a similarly sized section of land. The two areas are not isolated from each other either, for the well-being of land-dwelling organisms is linked to the health of ocean environments.

Obtaining Food

On land, plants use sunlight to make food. Other organisms eat plants, and still more organisms eat other organisms. Similar systems of organisms live in the ocean. Just as on land, the cycle begins with the organisms that make food from sunlight.

Photosynthesis

On land, plants produce energy from sunlight. For this reason, they are called producers. Ocean life also depends on producers to harness solar energy to make usable energy in the form of food. This process is called **photosynthesis.** The ocean contains not only plants but also algae. Algae include a variety of organisms. Some algae are microscopic; others are large and look like plants.

Producers are an important part of any environment. All the food energy used in the ocean environment, or any environment, comes first from producers. If there were no producers in an environment, all organisms would eventually die.

Chemosynthesis

Not all producers use photosynthesis to make food. Many ocean organisms live so deep beneath the surface of the water that sunlight does not reach them. Bacteria in these dark environments are producers that use **chemosynthesis** to produce food. The process of chemosynthesis uses sulfur or nitrogen chemical compounds instead of sunlight to make available energy for other organisms in the form of food.

Life-forms of the Ocean

There are many types of life in the ocean. Their sizes and shapes vary, and their ways of living differ depending on the needs of each organism and its environment.

Plankton

Plankton, a diverse group of organisms, are one of the most common producers found in the ocean. Some plankton are so small you need a microscope to see them, but other plankton, such as jellyfish, are fairly large. The one thing all plankton have in common is that they drift freely in the water and obtain food passively. Most plankton are photosynthetic producers, and plankton serve as a food source for many ocean organisms.

Nekton

Organisms that actively swim in the ocean are called nekton. Nekton include a wide variety of organisms, such as fish, turtles, whales, and other swimming animals. These organisms actively seek and obtain food by moving around in their environment.

Bottom Dwellers

Bottom-dwelling organisms live on the seafloor and include crabs, worms, sponges, and bottom-feeding fish. Although most bottom-dwelling organisms live in the dark at great depths, some bottom dwellers live in shallow locations on the seafloor.

Lesson Assessment

Review

1. **Define** What occurs in the process of photosynthesis?

2. **Relate Cause and Effect** How is energy from the sun transferred from a producer to other organisms?

3. **Compare and Contrast** What is the difference between plankton and nekton?

4. **Describe** How does the process of chemosynthesis work?

5. Describe some of the different environments in the ocean, and explain how organisms adapt to these differences.

Critical Thinking

What would happen if all the producers in the ocean disappeared?

Writing in Science

Describe some of the ways humans depend on ocean organisms.

◀ Plankton come in many shapes and sizes. You're seeing these plankton through a microscope.

Water Pollution

Reading Skills and Strategies

- Use higher-order thinking skills.
- Review text connections, text structure, comprehension monitoring, SQ3R, QHL, note taking, Strategy Bookmark, multipart words, and word-learning strategies.

As YOU Read

What You'll Learn

- How water pollution affects humans and the environment

Why It's Important

Clean water is essential for supporting all life on Earth.

Key Terms

- point source pollution
- nonpoint source pollution

Water is the most important resource on Earth. All living things need water to survive. Water is an especially precious resource because it can become polluted so easily. If even a small amount of some kinds of pollution finds its way into a reservoir, it can ruin a large quantity of clean water. If water becomes polluted, it can be unusable or dangerous to organisms that drink it or live in it.

▶ Water is essential to all life.

Sources of Water Pollution

Water pollution can be classified in two ways, depending on the source of the pollution. **Point source pollution** is pollution that enters the water from a single identifiable source. An example of point source pollution is pollution released by a pipe into a stream. **Nonpoint source pollution** is any pollution that comes from a source that can't be identified or that comes from a large general source. An example of nonpoint source pollution is polluted water that runs off mountains and feeds into a nearby lake. Most of the pollution in the United States is nonpoint source pollution.

Sediment

Many people might not consider dirt and rocks to be pollution. However, if too much sediment material is added to freshwater, the water becomes cloudy and unusable. Sediment is produced when water wears away small pieces of rock and mineral and carries them along. Sediment can choke organisms or irritate the skin or eyes of animals that live in the water. Sediment can also block light, making it difficult for plants to capture energy and make food. Sediment is the most common form of water pollution.

Chemicals

Chemicals are another source of water pollution. Although some chemicals are dumped directly into water as waste, many chemicals find their way into water indirectly. Humans use pesticides and fertilizers on crops and lawns. These chemicals are not completely absorbed by plants. The remaining chemicals either run off into lakes and streams or are washed underground where they can infiltrate wells and other water supplies.

◀ The chemicals sprayed on these crops can eventually run off into water and pollute it.

Sewage

Human waste can also be a cause of dangerous water pollution. In some places, water from toilets and drains is dumped into lakes and streams. This water often contains deadly organisms or household products that can poison humans and other organisms. Most human sewage in the developed world is now directed to sewage treatment plants, where it is made safe.

Other Forms of Water Pollution

Some forms of pollution are released from products buried in the ground. Heavy metals from discarded paint and electronic products, such as cell phones and computers, can leach into water from landfills or garbage dumps. Other metals can get into water as a result of mining. These metals can be harmful to humans and animals.

You may not realize that heat can be a form of water pollution, but many factories and power plants release very hot water or waste products into lakes. The extreme change in temperature can suddenly kill large numbers of fish and other organisms. This is one of the most preventable forms of water pollution, for mercly retaining the water until it cools will remove the threat.

Lesson Assessment

Review

1. **Explain** How does water pollution affect humans?

2. **Define** What kinds of chemicals often cause water pollution?

3. **Compare and Contrast** What is the difference between point source pollution and nonpoint source pollution?

4. **Infer** Why, do you think, did it become necessary to develop and build large sewage treatment plants?

5. **Relate Cause and Effect** How can a coal mine cause water pollution?

Critical Thinking

What types of organisms do you think would be most affected by sediment water pollution? What organisms do you think would be least affected?

Writing in Science

Write a list of adjectives that describe clean water. Then write a list of adjectives that describe polluted water.

Reading Skills and Strategies

• Review text connections, text structure, comprehension monitoring, SQ3R, QHL, note taking, Strategy Bookmark, and word-learning strategies.

Lesson 1 Earth

As YOU Read

What You'll Learn

■ What Earth is made of and how it moves in our solar system

Why It's Important

Earth movements cause us to experience seasons and night and day.

Key Terms

■ rotation

■ revolution

■ solstice

■ equinox

Throughout most of history, people didn't ask many questions about the planet they called home. For thousands of years, they thought Earth was flat because that's how it appeared to them. They assumed the sun, the moon, and the stars all moved around Earth because they observed these movements every day. However, as people developed better technology and adopted scientific ways of thinking, they learned more about Earth. They learned their earlier thoughts about the shape of Earth were wrong.

Properties of Earth

Earth's shape, its movements, and its other properties are responsible for some characteristics of life on this planet.

Shape

As already mentioned, for thousands of years, people assumed Earth was flat. However, many early scientists, such as some of the ancient Greeks, theorized that Earth was a sphere. A sphere is a round, three-dimensional shape, like a ball. There were many observations that led to this belief. First, anyone could observe that other bodies in the sky, such as the sun and the moon, were round. Second, people could see that the shadow cast by Earth on the moon during eclipses was round. Finally, people observed that ships sailing away from land toward the horizon did not suddenly disappear. Instead, observers could first see the whole ship and later just the masts and sails poking above the horizon, and at last the ship would appear to sink gradually out of sight. These observations suggested that the ships were heading down a slope, such as the surface of a sphere.

Technology confirms that Earth's shape is a sphere. Not only do we now have the means to measure the size and shape of Earth, but we also have photographs of Earth taken by satellites from space.

◀ This photograph of Earth taken from space shows its spherical shape.

Rotation

Earth does not stand still. It is in constant motion and moves in many different ways. One of the main forms of motion is **rotation.** Rotation is the spinning motion Earth makes. Earth spins around an imaginary line, called an axis, that runs between the north pole and the south pole. Earth makes one full rotation every twenty-four hours. As Earth rotates, every location on its surface faces the sun during half that period, or twelve hours, and faces away from the sun during the other twelve hours. This rotation causes us to experience day and night. Earth's rotation also causes humans to see objects "move" in space. From Earth's surface, it appears as if the sun, the moon, other planets, and the stars move across the sky. In reality, it is Earth's rotation that makes it seem the other bodies are moving.

Magnetic Field

Have you ever used a compass to find direction? The needle in a compass points toward the north pole. The compass needle is magnetized and is attracted to the magnetic field that surrounds Earth. Earth has a magnetic axis that runs between the north pole and the south pole. The magnetic axis is not the same as Earth's rotational axis, and they are not aligned with each other. The magnetic axis acts like a giant bar magnet inside Earth.

Scientists are not sure what causes Earth's magnetic field, but most think it may be caused by liquid metal in Earth's core. The rotation of Earth would cause the liquid metal to move, producing a magnetic field. Another interesting thing about Earth's magnetic field is that it changes from time to time. The positions of the magnetic poles move slowly over time, and the poles have even reversed at points throughout history.

Earth's Orbit

Another movement Earth makes is an orbit around the sun. This movement is called **revolution.** The path of the orbit is elliptical in shape. A revolution is considered complete when Earth has gone around the sun and returned to its starting position in the orbit. It takes approximately 365 days to complete a revolution, and this movement is what marks the passing of a year on Earth.

Changing Seasons

The movement of Earth is responsible for the change of seasons we experience. How does this happen? Recall that Earth rotates on an axis. In the diagram of Earth spinning on its axis, you will notice the axis is tilted. Because of this tilt, at any given time, either the northern half or the southern half of the planet is receiving more direct sunlight time than the other half. For example, in the month of July, the northern half of Earth is tilted toward the sun and receives more direct sunlight. This causes the northern half, or hemisphere, to experience summer, while the southern hemisphere has winter. The opposite occurs in January. In that month, the southern hemisphere is tilted toward the sun and experiences summer, while the northern hemisphere is tilted away and has winter weather.

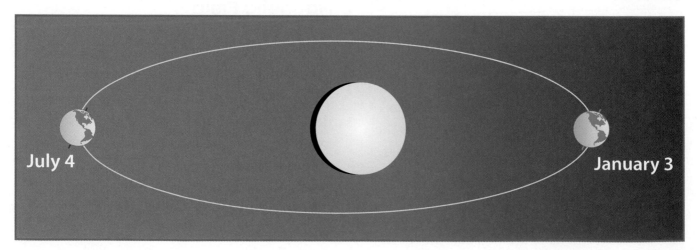

July 4

January 3

▲ The path of Earth's orbit around the sun takes the shape of an ellipse.

Solstices and Equinoxes

Some people mistakenly believe that summer and winter are caused by Earth's distance from the sun. As you now know, this is not true. Summer and winter are instead caused by the tilted Earth receiving sunlight more directly or less directly. As Earth revolves around the sun, the distance between locations on Earth's surface and the sun varies. A **solstice** occurs when the sun is farthest from either the northern or the southern hemisphere. In the northern hemisphere, the summer solstice occurs in June when the sun is farthest from the southern hemisphere and closest to the northern hemisphere. This results in longer days for the northern hemisphere and shorter days for the southern hemisphere. The exact opposite occurs during the winter solstice. On that day, the sun is closest to the southern hemisphere, which experiences the longest day of the year. At the same time, the northern hemisphere experiences the shortest day. The winter solstice occurs in December.

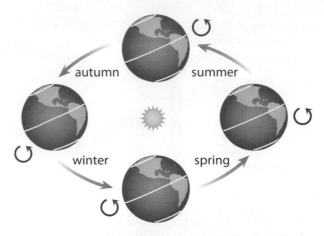

▲ Earth rotates on a tilted axis. As Earth moves around the sun, either the northern or the southern half is tilted toward the sun, experiencing summer. The other half is tilted away from the sun and experiences winter.

An **equinox** occurs when the sun is directly above the equator and is equally distant from both the northern and the southern hemispheres. At this point, neither hemisphere is tilted toward or away from the sun. During an equinox, the length of a day is equal all over Earth. One equinox occurs in March, and the other equinox occurs in September.

Lesson Assessment

Review

1. **Identify** What is the shape of the planet Earth?

2. **Define** What movement makes up one day on Earth?

3. **Cause and Effect** How does the movement of Earth cause humans to experience a change in seasons?

4. **Compare and Contrast** Explain the difference between rotation and revolution.

5. **Describe** In what position is Earth during an equinox?

Critical Thinking

- How might changes of day and night be different if Earth were another shape?

- How might changes of season be different if Earth's orbit around the sun took longer than 365 days?

- What do scientists believe causes Earth to have a magnetic field? Why do you think the magnetic field changes and even reverses over time?

Writing in Science

Write a description of seasonal changes from the viewpoint of a park ranger. Then write a description of the same changes from the viewpoint of a scientist studying Earth's movements.

Reading Skills and Strategies

- Review text connections, text structure, comprehension monitoring, SQ3R, QHL, note taking, Strategy Bookmark, multipart words, and word-learning strategies.

Lesson 2
The Inner Planets

As YOU Read

What You'll Learn
- The characteristics of the inner planets of our solar system

Why It's Important
People have long been interested in the planets nearest Earth and most similar to it.

Key Terms
- Mercury
- Venus

The planets in our solar system are categorized according to their distance from the sun. Earth belongs to the group of planets called the inner planets, which orbit closest to the sun. The inner planets are smaller and warmer than the rest of the planets. In addition, the inner planets are composed of solid, rocklike materials.

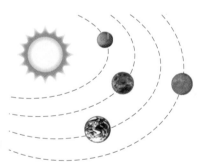

▶ The diagram shows the sun and the inner planets. Can you name each planet? Read on.

Mercury

Mercury is the planet closest to the sun. It is also the smallest of the inner planets. Temperatures on Mercury's surface are extreme compared to those on Earth because Mercury has no atmosphere to regulate temperature. Daytime temperatures reach 425°C, while nighttime temperatures can drop to −170°C. Because Mercury is so close to the sun, it takes only eighty-eight days to complete its orbit. Mercury is also close to

Earth, and you can often see it in the night or early morning sky. Mercury has been observed for much of human history and was named for the god Mercury by the Romans.

Venus

The planet **Venus** is the second planet from the sun and the one that is most similar to Earth. Not only is Venus about the same size and mass as Earth, it also has an atmosphere. The surface of Venus is not visible from Earth because of the thick gases that swirl around the planet. Scientists used to believe that Venus was a likely candidate for supporting life because of its atmosphere and location. However, we now know that the atmosphere on Venus produces a greenhouse effect that causes surface temperatures of 450°C to 475°C. Many robotic space probes have penetrated Venus's atmosphere and mapped its surface. The probes show that

▲ The thick gases of Venus's atmosphere swirl constantly across the planet's surface, making the planet intensely hot.

the surface of Venus has some very large volcanoes and few craters.

Because Venus is so close to Earth in the solar system, it is easily visible from our own planet. As a matter of fact, except for the moon, Venus is the brightest natural object in our night sky.

Earth

Earth is the third planet from the sun. The supply of water on its surface makes it an ideal environment for supporting life. Earth's distance from the sun along with Earth's atmosphere keeps temperatures in an appropriate range for humans and other organisms to survive.

Mars

Like Venus, Mars has long caused speculation that it might be a good candidate for supporting life. Mars is close to Earth,

and scientists have been able to see its surface for much of recent history. Mars, like Earth, has polar ice caps. Space probes have revealed such surface features as valleys and channels. These surface features seem to indicate that water may have been present on Mars's surface at some point in the past. This supposition has led some scientists to wonder whether Mars could have supported life at one time.

You can see Mars in the sky from Earth's surface. Mars appears red because its surface is covered with red soil. Mars has a very thin atmosphere and is very cold, with surface temperatures ranging from −125°C to 35°C.

◀ Mars is often called the red planet. Can you tell why?

Lesson Assessment

Review

1. **Define** Name the inner planets. What characteristics do the inner planets have in common?

2. **Compare and Contrast** Compare and contrast Earth and Mars.

3. Why did scientists once believe that Venus might be capable of supporting life? What characteristics did scientists discover that make the planet an unlikely place for life as we know it?

4. **Relate Cause and Effect** Temperature ranges on the surface of Mercury are much more extreme than the temperature ranges of the other inner planets. Why is this so?

5. **Explain** Why is Mars called the red planet?

Critical Thinking

• What characteristics make a planet habitable for humans? What causes Earth to have these characteristics?

• Many scientists believe Mars may have supported life at one time. Why do they think that? Is it currently possible for Mars to support life? Why or why not?

• The greenhouse effect is believed to be occurring on Earth. Could the greenhouse effect on Earth turn Earth's atmosphere into that of Venus? Why or why not?

Writing in Science

Look in your local newspaper or on an astronomy Web site to learn which planets are visible in your area at this time. Then try to find them in the night or morning sky. Record your efforts and observations for a few weeks to see if you can track the orbits of the planets. Write your findings in a short report.

Lesson 3

The Outer Planets

As YOU Read

What You'll Learn
■ The characteristics of the outer planets in our solar system

Why It's Important
Modern technology is making it possible for people to explore the outer planets.

Key Terms
■ Jupiter
■ Saturn

The outer planets in our solar system are the planets farthest from the sun. These planets are bigger than the inner planets. Unlike the inner planets, not all the outer planets are made of rocky material. Instead, they are composed of thick gas. For this reason, the outer planets are often referred to as "gas giants."

Jupiter

Jupiter is the largest planet in our solar system. The planet Jupiter contains more than twice the mass of all the other planets in the solar system combined. More than sixty moons orbit Jupiter. The planet is made up mostly of hydrogen and helium gases that swirl around the surface as parts of huge, continuous storms. Beneath the gas, Jupiter is likely made up of liquids and solids. The largest storm on Jupiter's surface is known as the Great Red Spot. This storm has existed for at least four hundred years and is larger than Earth.

Several spacecraft have explored Jupiter and sent back photographs. *Voyager 1* took photos of Jupiter as it sped by in 1979. The most extensive study of Jupiter was done by the spacecraft *Galileo* from 1995 to 2003.

▲ Here the outer planets are shown in their relative sizes and in order from the sun. Can you name them?

Galileo orbited Jupiter for almost eight years, collecting data. The spacecraft even took photographs as a comet crashed into Jupiter. *Galileo* released a probe into Jupiter's atmosphere. The probe took photographs and collected data as it parachuted toward the planet before disintegrating in the intense atmospheric pressure. As *Galileo's* service ended, the spacecraft was deliberately plunged into Jupiter's atmosphere, where it, too, disintegrated.

Saturn

The second-largest planet in the solar system is **Saturn.** Saturn is similar in composition to Jupiter in that the planet consists mostly of hydrogen and helium gases. Beneath the gas layers, Saturn is likely composed of liquid and perhaps rock. Saturn is somewhat smaller than Jupiter, but Saturn is easily recognizable because of the rings that surround it. The rings are made of ice crystals and rock and dust particles that orbit the planet and reflect sunlight. At least sixty moons orbit Saturn, including Titan, the only moon in the solar system with its own thick atmosphere.

Uranus

The seventh planet from the sun, Uranus, appears bluish green in color. The color is due to the atmosphere of methane that surrounds the planet. Underneath the gaseous atmosphere, Uranus may contain water. Like Saturn, Uranus also has rings. However, the rings are very light in color compared to those of Saturn and are not easily visible. Uranus is a large planet, approximately four times the size of Earth. The planet is different from all other planets in the solar system in one way: It rotates on a sideways axis. While all other planets rotate on an axis that is nearly perpendicular to their orbital path, Uranus rotates on an axis that is nearly in line with its orbital path.

Neptune

Neptune is similar in composition to Uranus but is somewhat smaller. It has a bluish green color as well because of its thick methane atmosphere. Neptune's gaseous surface is filled with constant storms, and several very light-colored rings surround Neptune.

Lesson Assessment

Review

1. **Compare and Contrast** List the differences and similarities between Saturn and Jupiter.

2. **Describe** What are Saturn's rings made of?

3. **Define** What characteristics are common among the outer planets?

4. **Explain** Why do Uranus and Neptune look similar?

Critical Thinking

- Why does life on the outer planets seem unlikely?

- If Earth's axis rotated in the same way as Uranus's, how would that change the seasons? How would that change daytime and nighttime?

Writing in Science

Imagine you're in a spacecraft exploring Jupiter or Saturn. Write a description of your journey. What would you observe? What would you want to see?

Lesson 4 Stars

Reading Skills and Strategies

- Review text connections, text structure, comprehension monitoring, SQ3R, QHL, note taking, Strategy Bookmark, and word-learning strategies.

As YOU Read

What You'll Learn
- Characteristics of stars

Why It's Important
Stars, especially our sun, provide solar energy for the universe.

Key Terms
- constellation
- light-year

The stars you see in the sky at night are not like planets. They are massive balls of plasma that release a constant supply of heat and light energy. Our sun is a star.

Constellations

Since early civilization, people have studied the stars and tracked their positions and movements. Early peoples found patterns resembling animals, humans, and objects in the way the stars are arranged. These patterns are called **constellations,** and they were named for the things they resemble. The constellations have remained the same over hundreds and even thousands of years. People often use the constellations as a guide for finding specific stars. For example, the Big Dipper and the Little Dipper are easy to find in the sky, and the North Star, or Polaris, is located in the handle of the Little Dipper. Finding the North Star has always been useful to travelers because the North Star is positioned above the North Pole. Ship captains throughout history have used the North Star to guide their vessels.

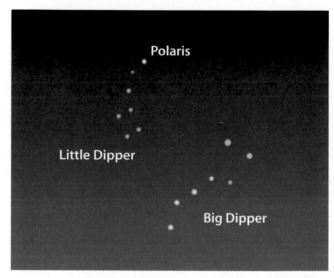

▲ Look for these constellations in the night sky. The North Star, also called Polaris, is at the end of the handle of the Little Dipper.

Magnitude

The magnitude of a star is the measure of its brightness, and the brightness of a star is the result of the amount of light it gives off. However, the brightness we perceive also depends on the distance of the star from Earth. The closer a star is to Earth, the brighter it appears to us. Scientists refer to the amount of light a star gives off as its absolute magnitude. They refer to the brightness of a star seen from Earth as apparent magnitude. A bright star with a high absolute magnitude may be harder to see than a star of lower absolute magnitude that is closer to Earth. The closer star then has a higher apparent magnitude.

Distance in Space

Stars may appear to be approximately the same distance from Earth as Mars and Venus, but in reality, the stars are much, much farther away. The distance between stars is so great it can't be measured with the same units we use to measure other distances. Scientists measure distances in space in **light-years.** A light-year is the distance light travels in one year. Because light travels at the speed of 300,000 kilometers each second, you can understand that a light-year is a very long distance. One light-year is approximately 9.5 trillion kilometers.

Determining Star Properties

Stars have other properties, besides magnitude, that can be determined by observing them. For example, the color of a star is an indicator of its temperature. The hottest stars are blue-white. Cooler stars are orange or red. Our sun is a medium-hot star, as indicated by its yellow color.

Scientists can examine the light energy each star emits in order to determine what the star is made of. The light from the star is passed through an instrument called a spectroscope, which breaks the light into its separate colors. The resulting patterns vary, depending on the substances present in the atmosphere of the star. The reason for this is that light waves are absorbed at different spectra by different substances in the atmosphere as the waves pass through it.

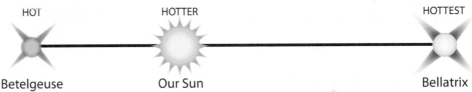

HOT — Betelgeuse   HOTTER — Our Sun   HOTTEST — Bellatrix

▲ All stars are hot, but some are hotter than others, and some are gradually cooling. Red stars, like Betelgeuse, are hot. Our sun, a yellow star, is hotter. Blue stars, like Bellatrix, are hottest of all.

Lesson Assessment

Review

1. **Define** What is a light-year?

2. **Relate Cause and Effect** Explain how distance affects the brightness of stars as seen from Earth.

3. **Compare and Contrast** What is the difference between apparent and absolute magnitude?

4. What does the color of a star indicate?

Critical Thinking

You are looking at constellations with a friend. Your friend points out two stars side by side in a constellation and says they are right next to each other. Why might this not be the case?

Writing in Science

Spend a few minutes looking at the stars. Try to find patterns among the stars you see. Describe some of the patterns you find.

Reading Skills and Strategies

- Use higher-order thinking skills.
- Review text connections, comprehension monitoring, SQ3R, QHL, note taking, Strategy Bookmark, and word-learning strategies.

Lesson 5 — The Sun

As YOU Read

What You'll Learn
- The properties of our sun

Why It's Important
The sun is the source of most energy on Earth and the reason life is possible on our planet.

Key Terms
- photosphere
- chromosphere

Energy from the Sun

The sun is not only the center of our solar system, it is the source of almost all energy on Earth and the primary reason life exists. The energy we receive from the sun is in the form of heat and light. Energy is produced within the sun by nuclear fusion. In the fusion process, hydrogen atoms are fused through intense pressure to become helium gas. This process occurs in the sun's core, the innermost layer of the sun. The energy that is produced moves through the next layer, the radiation zone, and into the third layer, the convection zone, where gases circulate. The final, outermost layer is the sun's atmosphere. Energy passes through the atmosphere and moves outward from the sun, and Earth receives some of this energy in the form of light and heat. The heat helps regulate temperatures on Earth, and light energy is captured by plants and used to produce food for all organisms.

Atmosphere

Because the sun is a ball of gas, it's difficult to determine where its surface begins and ends. The outer edge of the sun is called the atmosphere and has several layers. The inside layer is called the **photosphere.** The photosphere is the most visible part of the outer edge of the sun, so it's often referred to as the "surface" of the sun. Outside the photosphere is the **chromosphere,** which extends outward approximately two thousand kilometers from the photosphere. The chromosphere is the part of the sun that can be seen during a solar eclipse. The layer outside the chromosphere is the corona, which extends outward approximately ten thousand kilometers. The corona is the outermost layer in the atmosphere of the sun, the place where solar energy disperses into space.

Surface Features

From Earth, many features are visible on the surface of the sun. One of the earliest phenomena observed on the sun was the presence of sunspots. Sunspots are dark, cooler areas that flow along the surface as the sun rotates. Sunspots appear and disappear regularly as part of the cycle of solar activity.

Other noticeable features of the sun's surface are solar flares and prominences.

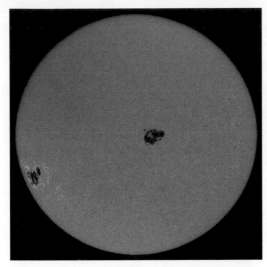

▲ Sunspots may be as large as fifty thousand miles in diameter.

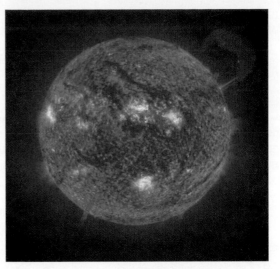

▲ A solar flare blasts off from the surface of the sun.

Solar flares and prominences are often linked to increased sunspot occurrences. Prominences occur when large columns of gas extend from the sun's surface. Solar flares occur when pockets of gas near a sunspot erupt and shoot outward from the surface. In addition, electrically charged pockets of gas are sometimes ejected from the surface of the sun. These ejections often enter Earth's atmosphere and interfere with radio transmissions.

The Sun as a Star

Compared to other stars in the universe, our sun is average in most respects. It is medium-sized and has an average magnitude. Our sun is not a young star, but neither is it very old. Compared to other stars, the sun is very close to Earth. It takes about eight minutes for light to reach Earth from the sun. It takes more than four years for light from the next-closest star, Proxima Centauri, to reach our planet. Light from many of the stars you see in the night sky takes millions of years to reach Earth.

Lesson Assessment

Review

1. **Explain** How is energy produced inside the sun?

2. **Define** Which layer of the sun includes the chromosphere and the photosphere?

3. **Compare and Contrast** How does the sun compare to other stars in terms of size, age, and magnitude?

4. **Relate Cause and Effect** Describe the path energy follows from nuclear fusion in the sun's core to you in the form of food.

Critical Thinking

- You are observing a star through a telescope at an observatory. The scientist who works there tells you the star you are looking at may no longer exist. How can that be possible?

- If the sun had an above average magnitude, what would happen to Earth? What might happen to Mars?

Writing in Science

- Find a poem about stars or the sun. Write a review of the poem, or explain its meaning.

- Find a poem about stars or the sun, and write a poem similar to it while adding your own flavor to it.

Beyond the Book

One day in 1937, Ed Holling was walking along the beach on Captiva Island, Florida, when he happened upon an abandoned shack. A year later, the Shrimp Bucket was born. It quickly became the place to devour shrimp prepared every way imaginable. After more than seventy years of business, we hope you still enjoy Ed's seaside deck, tiki torches, and mouthwatering menu!

We catch our own shrimp daily! We own our own shrimping boats here in Captiva and also in Louisiana. Every shrimp we serve has been caught the night before or early each morning!

Though we're known for our award-winning shrimp dishes, we've also won fame for our key lime pie, our cheesy garlic crab bread, and our unparalleled location and view!

Nibbles

Crab-Stuffed Mushrooms $4.99
Tender mushrooms loaded with our famous crab-and-jack-cheese mixture.

NEW! Seaside Sampler $8.99
A basket of fried clams, shrimp, and scallops. Served with a zesty tartar dipping sauce.

Shrimp Chowder $4.50
Not your typical chowder! Filled with luscious chunks of shrimp and potatoes, this thick soup bubbles with cheese and veggies.

Shrimp Fondue $9.75
Perfect for the entire table. Chunks of shrimp, zucchini, crusty bread, and mushrooms are speared and ready for death by cheese.

* Spicy! (Grab your water.)

Bucket Bests

Lemon Shrimp $11.99
Succulent shrimp marinated in lemon and a blend of the Shrimp Bucket's special seafood spices.

Coconut Shrimp $12.99
An enormous mound of crispety-crunchety-coconutty shrimp. Served with three dipping sauces.

* Blue Crab Chimichanga $13.99
Chunks of fresh blue crab tossed with tomato, chopped jalapeno peppers, and cheese. Wrapped in a large tortilla.

NEW! Grouper with Lobster Cream Sauce $17.99
A flaky grouper fillet doused in a light lobster cream sauce. Sprinkled with roasted red peppers and served on a bed of rice.

Extension Activity

You've learned important skills and strategies in the first twenty units of this program. Using your own classroom science textbook, find the section you're assigned to read next, and follow the instructions below. Write your responses on notebook paper.

a. **Use** the SQ3R and QHL strategies on the textbook section. Be sure to survey, question, read, reflect on, and review the section you're assigned. Develop a question, and find the answer to that question. When you've completed these steps, have written your question and answer, and have taken careful notes, describe what you did.

b. **Find** one example of text structure. Write the page number, title (or subhead), and paragraph on which you found the example so your teacher can find it easily.

c. **Which** of the following text structures best fits the paragraph(s) for this example—Description-or-List, Order-or-Sequence, Cause-and-Effect, or Compare-and-Contrast?

d. **Why** did you choose this text structure? Give an explanation.

e. **Choose** one bold and highlighted word to look up in the dictionary or in an online dictionary. Write the definition you find. Can you find the word in the textbook glossary? If so, write the glossary definition as well. Are these definitions similar? Explain.

f. **Write** a sentence using the word you looked up in the dictionary.

Glossary

A

abiotic factor
A nonliving part of an ecosystem, such as water, light, air, and soil. (p. 83)

acceleration
The rate at which an object's speed or direction changes. (p. 137)

acid rain
A harmful form of air pollution caused by industrial activity; produced when sulfur from burning coal combines with moisture in the air and then falls as rain. (p. 233)

adaptation
A special trait, such as a beaver's tail or a gibbon's long arms, that helps an animal survive in different habitats. (p. 80)

algae
Organisms that have chloroplasts and cell walls like plants. (p. 64)

align
To line up. (p. 179)

amendment
An addition. (p. 193)

amphibian
An animal, such as a frog, that lives on land and in water. (p. 76)

analog signal
A changing electric current that carries information. (p. 156)

ancient history
The second period of history, from 3500 B.C. to A.D. 500. (p. 32)

Anglo
An English-speaking white person. (p. 199)

archaea
Kingdom including bacteria having unique cell structures without a nucleus and containing chemicals different from typical bacteria and able to live in extreme environments. (p. 61)

archaeologist
A scientist who studies objects to find out about people from the past. (p. 185)

arsenal
Weapons. (p. 190)

artifact
A tool, a piece of pottery, a coin, or a weapon dug up from ancient settlements; an object people left behind.
(pp. 35, 185)

astronomy
The study of the systems to which Earth belongs, including our solar system and the universe. (p. 171)

atmosphere
The layer of air covering Earth's surface. (p. 222)

atom
The smallest particle of an element that has all the properties of the element. (p. 98)

autotroph
An organism that can make its own food. (p. 21)

B

bacteria
Simple, one-celled organisms that can produce many new generations in a short time, such as *E. coli*. (pp. 61, 62)

balanced force
A force that combines with other forces to produce a net force of zero; there is no change in motion. (p. 139)

bank holiday
Government closure of all banks. (p. 204)

basin
A low area where rain collects and forms an ocean over time. (p. 235)

Glossary

binomial nomenclature
The naming system scientists use to give each organism a name. (p. 22)

biome
A large area with a common climate and similar types of plants and animals. (p. 88)

biotic factor
A living part of an ecosystem, such as a plant or an animal. (p. 83)

black codes
Laws passed in the South that allowed plantation owners to abuse the freedmen who worked for them. (p. 198)

boycott
To refuse to buy certain products. (pp. 127, 189)

C

cacao
A seed from which cocoa and chocolate are made. (p. 125)

calligraphy
Beautiful writing. (p. 120)

campesino
A rural person who owns no land and works on a large farm. (p. 116)

canal
An artificial waterway; a human-made channel between natural waterways. (pp. 112, 195)

canopy
A covering formed by tall trees in tropical rain forests; it blocks the sun so few plants can grow on the forest floor. (p. 111)

capitalist
A person who owns or finances business. (p. 53)

carrier
An electric current or a radio wave that sends signals. (p. 156)

cartilage
A strong, flexible tissue inside animals such as sharks. (p. 75)

caste
A social group associated with certain occupations. (p. 130)

cell The smallest part of living things. (pp. 18, 24)

cell theory
An explanation of the link between cells and living things. (p. 25)

centripetal acceleration
The rate at which speed or direction changes as an object moves in a circular path. (p. 137)

chemosynthesis
The process by which producers without access to sunlight use sulfur or nitrogen chemical compounds to produce food. (p. 242)

chloroplast
The part of a plant that makes food. (p. 26)

chromosphere
The layer of the sun's atmosphere outside the photosphere; the part of the sun that can be seen during a solar eclipse. (p. 256)

circuit board
A sheet of green insulating material with many small parts used for processing information in electronic devices. (p. 154)

civil war
A war between citizens of the same country. (p. 41)

classic
An ancient Greek or Roman writing. (p. 45)

classification
The process of grouping things that are similar; putting things into categories of the same type. (p. 22)

Glossary

classify
To put together things that are alike. (p. 7)

climate
The weather patterns and temperature ranges of a large area; general weather conditions in an area over a long period of time. (pp. 88, 230)

coal
A black rock found in the earth that can be burned to release heat energy. (p. 210)

commune
A government-owned farm. (p. 126)

communist
A person who believes government should control the production of all food and goods and there should be no private ownership of property. (p. 206)

community
All the living things in an area. (p. 91)

competition
The fight for resources that occurs among organisms. (p. 92)

compound
A substance formed when specific atoms of different elements bond together in specific proportions. (p. 98)

condensation
The process by which gas particles change to liquid particles; as a gas cools, the energy in the particles decreases, and the particles move more slowly and are drawn together to form a liquid. (p. 105)

conduction
The contact between a charged object and an uncharged object. (p. 147)

conformity
Acting and thinking alike. (p. 207)

constellation
A pattern in the stars that early peoples thought resembled an animal or a person. (p. 254)

construction
The act or process of building something. (p. 194)

consumer
An organism that cannot produce its own food; it must eat other organisms to live. (p. 86)

cooperation
An interaction, such as hunting, avoiding predators, or caring for young, that benefits all the organisms involved. (p. 93)

coral
A rock-hard material formed by the skeletons of tiny sea animals. (p. 109)

corporation
A business owned by shareholders. (p. 201)

crest
The high point of a wave. (p. 238)

cuneiform   The first system of writing. (p. 36)

D

dalit
A person at the very bottom of society in a caste system. (p. 130)

data
Notes and measurements you collect when you make observations. (p. 11)

decibel
The measurement for loudness of sound. (p. 165)

deciduous
Describing trees that drop their leaves during cold, dry weather. (p. 89)

decomposer
An organism that does not make its own food; a decomposer breaks down materials from dead or decaying organisms to make chemicals other organisms can use. (p. 63)

Glossary

deficiency
Lack of ability. (p. 169)

deforestation
The process of destroying trees over a large area. (p. 118)

democracy
A type of government in which citizens rule themselves. (p. 38)

desalination
The process of removing salts from ocean water to make freshwater. (p. 237)

diatom
A one-celled alga that lives in salt water, freshwater, or soil and has hard cell walls made of silica. (p. 65)

dictator
A ruler who has total control of a government. (pp. 41, 115)

digital signal
A signal that carries information in a sequence of 1s and 0s. (p. 156)

diode
A device that controls the flow of electrons between n-type semiconductors and p-type semiconductors. (p. 155)

direct democracy
A government in which every citizen can discuss and vote on laws. (p. 39)

discrimination
Unfair treatment of a person or group of people, such as women receiving less money and fewer benefits than men who do the same work. (p. 129)

divine right
The belief that God gave rulers unlimited power. (p. 50)

domain
Largest classification of organisms; includes Eukarya, Bacteria, and Archaea; a very small

area within a substance where the magnetic fields in the atoms line up. (pp. 58, 151)

Doppler effect
Changes in sound waves as a sound moves toward or away from a listener. (p. 165)

E

earthquake
A shaking or movement of the ground. (p. 218)

echinoderm
An invertebrate sea animal, such as a sand dollar or a starfish, with a hard, spiny covering or skin and a central opening that takes in food. (pp. 71, 72)

ecology
The study of the relationships between living things and their environment. (p. 82)

ecosystem
All the living and nonliving things in an area. (p. 82)

ectothermic
Describing a body temperature that rises and falls as the temperature in the environment rises and falls; unable to regulate body temperature; cold-blooded. (p. 77)

electric discharge
A loss of charges. (p. 148)

electric field
The area around a charged object where it exerts its electrical force. (p. 146)

electrical force
The force a charged object exerts on another charged object. (p. 146)

electric motor
A motor that can convert electrical energy into mechanical energy. (p. 153)

electromagnet
An iron bar with a coil of wire wrapped around it. (p. 153)

Glossary

electromagnetic wave
The form in which light travels, so named because it is made up of both electric and magnetic fields. (p. 166)

electromagnetism
The action between magnetism and electricity. (p. 152)

electron
A negatively charged (–) particle inside an atom. (p. 102)

element
A pure substance that contains only one type of matter. (p. 98)

elevation
Height above sea level. (p. 231)

empire
A group of countries or regions under the control of one nation. (p. 55)

endangered species
A group of organisms that is small and is in danger of having no more living members. (p. 106)

endoskeleton
The bony skeleton on the inside of a vertebrate's body that makes a wide range of movements possible. (p. 74)

endothermic
Describing a body temperature that stays the same as the temperature in the environment rises and falls; able to regulate body temperature; warm-blooded. (p. 78)

engineer
A person who uses science and technology to find ways to improve people's lives. (pp. 12, 45)

Enlightenment
An intellectual movement in the seventeenth and eighteenth centuries in Europe that changed the way some people viewed science and philosophy. (p. 50)

equinox
The point at which the sun is directly above the equator, making the length of day and night equal in all parts of the world. (p. 249)

escarpment
A tall, steep slope or cliff. (p. 110)

ethnic group
People who share a common culture including history, language, religion, and/or traditions. (p. 124)

euglena
An organism that can get energy in more than one way, through sunlight or by absorbing nutrients from other sources. (p. 65)

evaporate
To change into vapor. (p. 100)

evaporation
The process by which a liquid becomes a gas; the energy in liquid particles increases as the temperature increases, and the particles move faster and faster until they escape the surface of the liquid and become gas particles. (p. 105)

experiment
A test that tries something new or sees if an idea is correct. (p. 11)

export
To ship to another country. (p. 114)

extinct
No longer existing. (p. 106)

extrusive igneous rock
Molten rock that has cooled inside existing rock above ground. (p. 175)

F

farsightedness
A condition that occurs when the shape of the eye is too short; a person who is farsighted has trouble seeing things that are close but can easily see images that are farther away. (p. 169)

Glossary

fault
A break formed when plates on Earth's surface move forcefully; the plates move up, down, or sideways along the fault, or fault line. (p. 218)

Federalist
A person in favor of adopting the Constitution and a strong centralized government. (p. 193)

fellaheen
Egyptians who work as farmers and live in villages. (p. 122)

feudalism
A social and governing system in which landowning nobles protected the people in exchange for services such as fighting or farming. (p. 42)

fief
A land grant that nobles gave to knights in return for a pledge of loyalty and military support. (p. 42)

fireside chat
An easy-to-understand talk, given by Franklin Roosevelt, about government and economic policy. (p. 204)

flagella
Tail-like structures that some organisms use to move around. (p. 65)

foliated
Describing rocks with the appearance of bands or layers caused by minerals in the changing rock lining up. (p. 179)

food chain
A model that shows the path of energy as nutrients move from one organism to another. (p. 86)

food web
Several overlapping food chains. (p. 87)

force
A push or pull that acts on an object. (pp. 138, 144)

fossil
A trace of bones, plants, or animals preserved in rock. (p. 35)

fossil fuel
Organic material formed over millions of years from dead or decaying things that can be used for energy. (p. 210)

free enterprise
A system that allows individuals to start businesses and earn profits. (p. 127)

freezing point
The temperature at which a liquid becomes a solid. (p. 105)

friction
A force that opposes the motion of objects. (pp. 140, 145)

front
The boundary between two air masses with different densities. (p. 228)

fungi
One-celled or multicellular organisms, such as molds, mushrooms, and yeast. (p. 60)

G

gas
A state of matter composed mainly of empty space; the particles in gases have so much room to move around that they are never still, resulting in no definite shape or volume. (p. 101)

geneticist
A scientist who studies genes or the material that carries inherited traits. (p. 186)

genus
A group of organisms from different species; the first part of an organism's name. (p. 22)

geocentric
The theory that the sun and the planets move around Earth. (p. 48)

Glossary

geology
An earth science involving the study of all materials that make up Earth and the processes that act on them. (p. 170)

gestation
The time an offspring develops within a mother's body. (p. 81)

glacier
Frozen water that forms an ice sheet over the land. (p. 184)

gravitational force
The pull of gravity. (p. 142)

gravity
The force that pulls everything toward Earth; a force that attracts objects to each other. (pp. 95, 142)

guideline
A rule to follow. (p. 14)

H

hanging wall
The rock on one side of a fault that rests or hangs on top of the footwall or the other side. (p. 218)

heliocentric
The theory that the planets move around the sun. (p. 48)

heterotroph
An organism that cannot make its own food. (p. 21)

hieroglyphics
Ancient Egyptian picture writings. (p. 123)

history
The study of humans in the past. (p. 32)

homeostasis
The ability to maintain stable internal conditions within cells. (p. 21)

host cell
A living cell that helps a virus multiply. (p. 29)

humanism
The belief in human abilities and actions. (p. 45)

hydroelectric energy
Energy that comes from moving water. (p. 215)

hydroelectric power
Electricity generated by rushing water. (p. 110)

hyphae
Strands of fungi cells that release chemicals that break down materials from the soil or from an organism. (p. 66)

hypothesis
A prediction of what you expect to happen. (p. 11)

I

ice age
A period of extreme cold when most of Earth's water freezes. (p. 184)

imperialism
The policy of building empires. (p. 55)

impurity
A small amount of a substance, such as an element or a compound, that changes the conductivity of a semiconductor when added to it. (p. 155)

inaugurate
To put into office in a formal ceremony. (p. 204)

incubation
The process of sitting on eggs to keep them warm so they will hatch. (p. 79)

induction
The process of charges rearranging in an uncharged object without actually touching a charged object. (p. 147)

Glossary

industrialization
The process of building factories and businesses. (p. 55)

inertia
A force that makes objects resist a change in motion; an object at rest will resist being moved, and a moving object will resist a change in speed or direction. (p. 145)

infer
To observe something and then explain what was observed. (p. 8)

inner ear
The part of the ear that changes vibrations from sound waves into electrical signals that travel to the brain. (p. 163)

intense
Very high. (p. 181)

intrusive igneous rock
Molten rock that has cooled inside existing rock beneath Earth's surface. (p. 175)

invertebrate
An animal, such as a worm, that has no backbone. (p. 70)

investigation
A way of exploring scientific questions. (p. 14)

ion
A type of charged atom or a substance made of charged atoms. (p. 236)

irrigation
Bringing water to fields to grow crops. (p. 36)

isotope
An atom with the same number of protons but a different number of neutrons. (p. 103)

isthmus
A narrow strip of land that has water on either side and connects two larger regions. (p. 108)

J

Jupiter
The largest planet; has more than sixty moons. (p. 252)

K

kinetic friction
A force that occurs between moving surfaces. (p. 141)

kingdom
A group of organisms, into which domains are divided, consisting of Animalia, Plantae, Fungi, Protista, Bacteria, and Archaea. (p. 59)

L

larva
An organism that has not yet developed into its adult form. (p. 73)

law of universal gravitation
A law developed by Sir Isaac Newton that states that all objects are attracted to each other by the force of gravity; the amount of gravitational force between objects depends on the masses of the objects and the distance between them. (p. 143)

light-year
A unit for measuring the distance light travels in one year; the distance light travels in one year; the unit scientists use to measure distance in space. (pp. 167, 255)

liquid
A state of matter that has a definite volume but not a definite shape because there is space between its particles that allows them to move around; liquids flow and take the shape of the container that holds them. (p. 101)

Glossary

literacy rate
The percentage of people fifteen years and older who can read. (p. 131)

lock
A section of a canal that adjusts water levels to raise and lower ships. (p. 113)

longhorn
A breed of cattle especially suited to dry grasslands. (p. 197)

longitudinal wave
A wave that contains particles that move back and forth in the same direction as the wave. (p. 161)

loudness
The amount of energy a sound wave carries. (p. 165)

lysosome
The part of a cell that breaks large particles into small ones. (p. 26)

M

magnetic field
An invisible area around a magnet, where magnetic force acts. (p. 150)

magnetic force
The force magnets exert on each other. (p. 150)

magnetic pole
The end of a magnet. (p. 150)

magnitude
A measure of the energy released during an earthquake, as shown on the Richter scale. (p. 220)

mammal
A warm-blooded animal, such as a beaver, an ape, a whale, or a human, that has hair and produces milk to feed its young. (p. 80)

marine biologist
A scientist who studies sea life. (p. 185)

mass
The amount of matter that makes up a substance. (p. 95)

matter
Anything that takes up space. (p. 94)

medium
A substance, such as air, water, or rocks, through which an energy wave moves. (p. 159)

melting point
The temperature at which a solid begins to melt. (p. 104)

Mercury The planet closest to the sun; the smallest planet; has no atmosphere to regulate temperature. (p. 250)

metamorphosis
A change in the development of a living thing; change. (pp. 76, 178)

meteorology
A science that is mainly concerned with weather conditions and weather forecasting. (p. 171)

methodically
Carefully and thoroughly. (p. 49)

Mexicano
A Spanish-speaking person from Mexico. (p. 199)

microscope
An instrument that makes very small objects appear larger so they can be studied. (p. 24)

Middle Ages
The third period of history from A.D. 500 to 1500. (pp. 32, 33)

middle ear
The part of the ear that is made up of three bones that receive sound waves and begin to vibrate. (p. 163)

mid-ocean ridge
A place on the ocean floor where two ocean floor plates are moving away from each other. (p. 241)

Glossary

migrate
To move from one place to another to find food, water, warmer weather, or other resources. (p. 78)

militia
A citizen army. (p. 190)

mineral
A substance, such as tin or salt, formed naturally in rocks and in the earth. (p. 83)

mitochondria
The part of a cell that converts food energy to energy a cell can use. (p. 26)

mixture
A form of matter in which two or more substances are combined in no particular proportions; the components retain their own properties and can be separated physically. (p. 98)

model
An illustration, a chart, a map, or a three-dimensional structure; something that helps a scientist understand a complex process. (p. 9)

modern history
The fourth period of history from A.D. 1500 to the present. (pp. 32, 33)

monopoly
A single company in control of an industry. (p. 201)

monotheism
Belief in one God. (p. 120)

mosque
A Muslim place of prayer. (p. 120)

motion
An object's change in position. (pp. 134, 144)

N

nationalist
A person who feels a strong loyalty to his or her nation. (p. 54)

nation-state
A self-governing country. (p. 54)

natural gas
A fossil fuel in a gaseous state. (p. 212)

natural right
The right to life, liberty, and property. (p. 51)

nearsightedness
A condition that occurs when the shape of the eye is too long; a person who is nearsighted can see things that are close but cannot make out things far away. (p. 169)

net force
The combination of forces acting on an object. (p. 138)

neutron
A neutral particle inside an atom. (p. 102)

newton
A unit of force that measures weight. (p. 96)

niche
The position an organism fills in its habitat. (p. 91)

nomad
A person who wanders. (p. 124)

nonfoliated
Describing rocks that do not have bands or layers. (p. 179)

nonpoint source pollution
Pollution that comes from a source that cannot be identified or from a large general source, such as runoff from nearby mountains. (p. 244)

nucleus
The part of a cell that controls its functions. (p. 26)

numerical
Relating to numbers, such as 0 or 1. (p. 156)

Glossary

O

observe
To use your five senses to make observations. (p. 7)

oceanography
An earth science involving the study of Earth's oceans. (p. 170)

oil
A black liquid formed from decomposed microorganisms; it is used as an energy source for heating buildings and making gasoline for automobiles. (p. 212)

oligarchy
A government in which a few people rule. (p. 38)

one-crop economy
A condition in which a country relies on only one crop for most of its income. (p. 115)

open range
Land that belongs to the government. (p. 197)

optimist
Someone who believes he or she can overcome huge obstacles. (p. 204)

organism
A living thing. (p. 18)

outer ear
The part of the ear that is shaped like a cone or funnel; it collects sound waves and directs them into the ear. (p. 163)

ozone
A highly reactive gas made of oxygen. (pp. 223, 233)

ozone layer
A concentration of a gas called ozone, which filters harmful radiation from the sun and prevents the radiation from striking Earth's surface. (p. 223)

P

patron
Someone who supports another person while he or she studies, paints, or writes. (p. 45)

perspective
A technique, developed by Renaissance artists, that makes a painting look three-dimensional. (p. 45)

petition
A request. (p. 191)

phloem
The part of a plant that transports food produced in the leaves down to other parts of the plant. (p. 69)

photochemical smog
A type of smog produced when chemicals in the air react with sunlight to form dangerous gas. (p. 232)

photosphere
The inside layer of the sun's atmosphere; the most visible part of the outer edge of the sun. (p. 256)

photosynthesis
The process by which plants use the energy in sunlight to produce sugars; the process by which green plants absorb carbon dioxide and give off oxygen and water vapor; the process by which producers harness solar energy to make usable energy in the form of food. (pp. 69, 119, 242)

pidgin
A language that combines English words with the grammar of another language. (p. 125)

pioneer
An early settler. (p. 194)

pitch The highness or lowness of a sound. (p. 164)

placenta
An organ inside a mother that transports

Glossary

nutrients and oxygen to offspring and carries waste from the offspring to the mother's body. (p. 81)

plain
A large flat landform ideal for farming and living. (p. 216)

plankton
Small plant and animal life-forms that drift freely in bodies of water. (p. 243)

plateau
A vast flat-topped highland; a landform that rises above the land around it. (pp. 109, 216)

point source pollution
Pollution that enters water from a single identifiable source, such as a pipe releasing pollution into a stream. (p. 244)

pollution
The act of making something unclean or impure. (p. 13)

population
All individual organisms of a species in a particular area. (p. 90)

preamble
An introduction. (p. 193)

precipitation
Rain, snow, sleet, or hail that forms when the liquid droplets in clouds combine and become too big and heavy to float in the air and thus fall to the ground. (p. 227)

predator
An animal that catches other animals and eats them. (p. 92)

predict
To use experience to guess what will happen next. (p. 8)

prehistory
The time before people developed writing; the first period of history. (p. 32)

prey
An animal that is eaten by another animal. (p. 92)

primary source
A record written by someone who actually witnessed or took part in the events. (p. 33)

producer
An organism that uses energy from the sun to make its own food; it provides food for other organisms and releases oxygen into the environment. (pp. 62, 86)

progressive
A person who campaigns for social reforms. (p. 202)

prohibition
The outlawing of the manufacture and sale of alcoholic beverages. (p. 203)

prokaryote
An organism made of cells without a nucleus, such as those in the Bacteria and Archaea domains. (p. 58)

prosthesis
An artificial body part. (p. 12)

protista
A kingdom including one-celled and multicellular organisms such as amoebas, algae, and seaweed. (p. 60)

proton
A positively charged (+) particle inside an atom. (p. 102)

protozoa
One-celled organisms in the Protista kingdom that get energy by eating other organisms. (p. 65)

Glossary

Q

quota
A limited number or quantity that is officially allowed. (p. 131)

R

radiation
Energy that moves as an electromagnetic wave. (p. 166)

ratify
To approve. (p. 193)

rebellion
A violent action by a large group of people to change a country's government. (p. 113)

reference point
An object that moves or stays in one place and by which the motion of another object can be detected. (p. 134)

Renaissance
A French word meaning "rebirth." (p. 45)

representative democracy
A government in which citizens elect officials to propose and vote on laws. (p. 39)

reproduction
The process by which living things produce more of their own species, such as spore production in a fungus. (p. 66)

reptile
An animal that lays eggs on land and has thick, dry, scaly skin that protects it from moisture loss and predators. (p. 77)

republic
A government in which the rulers are chosen by citizens (also known as a representative democracy). (pp. 39, 40)

revolution   The movement Earth makes as it orbits the sun. (p. 248)

rock
A solid collection of one or more minerals that occur in nature. (p. 180)

rock cycle
The process of breaking down rocks into sediment and building new rocks from that sediment. (p. 181)

rotation
The spinning motion of Earth around its axis. (p. 247)

S

salinity
The amount of salts in water. (p. 236)

Saturn
The second largest planet; similar in composition to Jupiter. (p. 253)

scale
A small, thin plate that overlaps others of the same kind and covers bony fish. (p. 75)

science
The study of the natural world and the knowledge gained through that study. (p. 6)

scientific inquiry
The process scientists use to study the natural world. (p. 10)

scientific law
A rule applied to the natural world. (p. 17)

Scientific Revolution
A period of time from 1540 to 1700 during which the search for scientific truths overturned many old ideas. (p. 48)

scientific theory
An explanation of behavior based on many observations and experiments. (p. 16)

secondary source
A writing that summarizes or reports information from primary sources. (p. 33)

Glossary

seismologist
A scientist who studies earthquakes. (p. 220)

semiconductor
An element or compound that conducts electric current better than an insulator but not as well as a conductor. (p. 155)

serf
A peasant who works from sunup to sundown, cannot own property, and has limited freedom. (p. 43)

sessile
Attached to one place permanently. (p. 72)

sharia
Islamic law. (p. 121)

signal
Anything that sends information, such as a sound, a number, a letter, or a movement. (p. 156)

slash-and-burn
A method of clearing land by cutting down and burning trees. (p. 118)

smuggle
To bring goods into a country without permission. (p. 189)

solar energy
The most plentiful form of energy on Earth; it can be used passively by using sunlight instead of electric light or actively by using solar cells to collect energy from the sun. (p. 214)

solenoid
A coil of wire looped many times to increase magnetic power. (p. 152)

solid
A state of matter that has a definite shape and volume because its particles are packed closely together, allowing no space for the particles to move around. (p. 100)

solstice
The point at which the sun is farthest from either the northern hemisphere or the southern hemisphere. (p. 249)

sound wave
A longitudinal wave that carries sound. (p. 162)

species
The smallest level of classification of living things that share traits and can reproduce. (pp. 22, 90)

spectroscope
An instrument that breaks light into separate colors. (p. 255)

speed
The distance traveled divided by the time that elapses. (p. 134)

sponge
An animal that gets food by filtering it from the water it lives in. (p. 72)

spore
A reproductive cell a fungus produces in order to grow a new fungus. (p. 66)

squatter
A person who builds on land without permission and has little access to clean water or electricity. (p. 117)

state of matter
The form in which matter exists, including liquid, solid, and gas. (p. 100)

static electricity
Electric charges that are not moving. (p. 148)

static friction
A force that balances the force applied to a surface so that an object does not move. (p. 141)

stationary
Not moving. (p. 138)

stimulus
Something that changes the subjects' surroundings and causes them to react. (p. 19)

strata
Layers. (p. 176)

Glossary

stratification
The process by which sedimentary rock is deposited in layers. (p. 177)

stratosphere
The layer of the atmosphere above the troposphere; it contains the ozone layer. (p. 223)

subjective
Based on personal opinions and feelings. (p. 220)

subsidy
Money paid by a government to help an industry or a business. (pp. 116, 128)

substance
A solid, liquid, or gas. (p. 104)

suburb
An outlying area around a city. (p. 206)

subway
An underground railway system. (p. 117)

suffrage
The right to vote. (p. 203)

suffragette
A female who tried to change the law so women could vote. (p. 203)

T

technology
Any way people change the world to meet their needs. (p. 12)

temperate
Describing a forest biome that has mild temperatures. (p. 89)

tertiary
Third-level. (p. 86)

theory
An explanation based on observation and common sense. (p. 48)

tornado
A powerful column of wind that runs from a cloud toward the ground and moves across the surface of the ground. (p. 229)

transverse wave
A wave in which the energy moves in a horizontal direction, at right angles to the up-and-down motion of the particles that make up the wave. (p. 160)

treaty
An agreement. (p. 188)

trench
A place where two pieces of ocean floor are moving toward each other. (p. 241)

tributary
A river or a stream that flows into a larger river. (p. 110)

triumvirate
A government of which three people have equal power. (p. 40)

tropics
An area near the equator that has a very warm climate. (p. 230)

troposphere
The inner layer of the atmosphere within which nearly all weather conditions occur. (p. 223)

trough
The low point of a wave. (p. 238)

trust
An organization set up to hold stock in many companies, often in the same industry. (p. 201)

tsunami
A huge ocean wave caused by earthquakes that occur on the ocean floor or near shores. (p. 221)

U

unbalanced
Not balanced, because of more push or pull in one direction than in another direction. (p. 144)

Glossary

unbalanced force
A force that combines with other forces to produce a net force greater than zero; this causes an object to start moving, stop moving, change speeds, or change direction. (p. 139)

underemployed
Describing persons who do not make enough money to meet basic needs. (p. 114)

V

vaccine
Something given to help protect you from catching a virus. (p. 28)

vaquero
A Mexican cowhand. (p. 198)

variable
A part of an experiment that can change. (p. 11)

vascular system
A network of long, tube-shaped cells through which plants move materials. (p. 68)

vassal
A person who serves a lord of higher rank. (p. 42)

velocity
An object's speed as well as the direction it travels. (p. 135)

Venus
The planet second closest to the sun; most similar to Earth in size and mass. (p. 250)

vertebrate
An animal, such as a dog, that has a backbone. (p. 74)

virus
A nonliving particle of hereditary material covered with a layer of protein. (p. 28)

visible spectrum
The range of light your eyes can detect. (p. 168)

volume
The amount of space an object occupies. (p. 96)

W

water displacement
A method used to find the volume of an object; put the object in water and find the difference between the volume of the water alone and the volume of the water and the object together. (p. 97)

wave
The transfer of any type of energy. (p. 158)

weather
Conditions in the atmosphere around us, including temperature, wind, rain, and snow. (p. 226)

weight
The downward pull of gravity on an object; a measure of the gravitational force exerted on an object by a larger object, such as a planet. (pp. 95, 143)

writ of habeas corpus
The right to a trial. (p. 192)

writs of assistance
Permits for customs officers to search any location for smuggled goods. (p. 189)

X

xylem
The tissue that carries water and nutrients up from the roots of a plant. (p. 69)

Index of Key Terms

Index of Key Terms

F

farsightedness, 169
fault, 218
fellaheen, 122
feudalism, 42
fief, 42
fireside chat, 204
foliated, 179
food chain, 86
food web, 87
force, 138, 144
fossil, 35
fossil fuel, 210
free enterprise, 127
freezing point, 105
friction, 140, 145
front, 228
fungi, 60

G

gas, 101
geneticist, 186
genus, 22
geocentric, 48
geology, 170
gestation, 81
glacier, 184
gravitational force, 142
gravity, 95, 142
guideline, 14

H

heliocentric, 48
heterotroph, 21
hieroglyphics, 123
history, 32

homeostasis, 21
host cell, 29
humanism, 45
hydroelectric energy, 215
hydroelectric power, 110
hyphae, 66
hypothesis, 11

I

ice age, 184
imperialism, 55
incubation, 79
induction, 147
inertia, 145
infer, 8
inner ear, 163
intrusive igneous rock, 175
invertebrate, 70
investigation, 14
ion, 236
isotope, 103
isthmus, 108

J

Jupiter, 252

K

kinetic friction, 141
kingdom, 59

L

larva, 73
law of universal gravitation, 143
light-year, 167, 255
liquid, 101
literacy rate, 131

lock, 113
longhorn, 197
longitudinal wave, 161
loudness, 165
lysosome, 26

M

magnetic field, 150
magnetic force, 150
magnetic pole, 150
magnitude, 220
mammal, 80
marine biologist, 185
mass, 95
matter, 94
medium, 159
melting point, 104
Mercury, 250
metamorphosis, 76, 178
meteorology, 171
Mexicano, 199
microscope, 24
middle ear, 163
mid-ocean ridge, 241
migrate, 78
militia, 190
mitochondria, 26
mixture, 98
model, 9
monopoly, 201
monotheism, 120
mosque, 120
motion, 134, 144

N

nationalist, 54
nation-state, 54

Index of Key Terms

Index

Index of Key Terms

Photo Credits